I Remember Jazz

Other Books by Al Rose

New Orleans Jazz: A Family Album
Storyville, New Orleans
Eubie Blake: A Biography
Born in New Orleans: Two Centuries of Notables

Al Rose

I Remember Jazz

Six Decades Among the Great Jazzmen

Louisiana State University Press

Baton Rouge and London

Copyright © 1987 by Louisiana State University Press
Manufactured in the United States of America

Designer: Laura Roubique
Typeface: Electra
Typesetter: G & S Typesetters, Inc.
Printer: Thomson-Shore, Inc.
Binder: John Dekker & Sons

10 9 8 7 6 5 4 3 2 1

Library of Congress Cataloging in Publication Data

Rose, Al.
    I remember jazz.

    Includes index.
    1. Jazz music.   2. Jazz musicians.   I. Title.
ML3506.R68   1986   785.42'0092'2 [B]   86-15307
ISBN 0-8071-1315-8

*This book is affectionately dedicated to my good friends
Allan and Sandra Jaffe, proprietors of Preservation Hall,
who somehow keep the music alive.*

Contents

Preface ix

A Note on Vernacular xi

Jelly Roll Morton 1

John Casimir 6

Frankie Newton 10

Jack "Papa" Laine 13

Bill Russell 16

Mezz Mezzrow 17

Bobby Hackett 19

Alphonse Picou 20

Irving Fazola 23

Oran "Hot Lips" Page 25

Tony Parenti 41

Dan Burley 46

Allan Jaffe 50

Louis Prima 52

Adrian Rollini 54

Stephane Grappelle 57

George Cvetkovich 58

Sidney Bechet 60

Tom Brown 63

George Girard 65

James P. Johnson 68

Chris Burke 70

Eddie Condon 72

Bunny Berigan 73

Alvin Alcorn 75

Muggsy Spanier 77

Wild Bill Davison 79

Joe Mares 95

Harry Truman 98

Jack Teagarden 101

Eubie Blake 103

The Original Dixieland Jazz
  Band 106

Armand J. Piron 109

The Candy Man 111

Bunk Johnson 113

Edmond Souchon 117

Pee Wee Spitlera 120

Morten Gunnar Larsen 122

Danny Barker 122

George Baquet 126

Louis Armstrong 127

Knocky Parker 130

Johnny Wiggs 133

Jean Christophe Averty 150

Eddie Miller 152

Raymond Burke 154

Spencer Williams 157

Pierre Atlan 159

Claude Luter 163

W. C. Handy 165

David Thomas Roberts 167

Chink Martin 170

Walter Bowe 172

"Buglin' Sam" Dekemel 174

Harry Shields 176

Johnny St. Cyr 178

Sharkey Bonano 180

Armand Hug 183

Earl "Fatha" Hines 185

Gene Krupa 202

The Exterminators: Pete Fountain
  and Al Hirt 204

Dizzy Gillespie 206

Miff Mole 208

Clarence Williams 211

The Dixieland Rhythm
  Kings 214

The Brunies 216

Paul Barbarin 218

Neighborhoods 220

Lagniappe 222

Afterword 244

  Index 247

Illustrations

Following pages 25

                 79

                133

                187

Preface

Sure I remember jazz. I remember more than sixty years of it—from the time I was a kid standing on a French Quarter banquette in New Orleans listening to the breathtaking band that played for dancing on the second floor of the Fern Cafe No. 2 to the ones I tried futilely to put together in the 1980s, combing the lists to find seven good men and true who could, one more time, quicken this fading pulse. Of course, I'm talking about genuine, unhyphenated jazz—not modern, not progressive, not fusion, New Wave, blues, or swing. Just jazz. Only jazz is jazz.

I have worked with jazzmen through concerts, recording sessions, radio, television, movies, and promotions. I have roistered with them on planes, trains, buses, boats, and taxis here and abroad. I have gotten bombed with them in low-class dives and classy saloons in New York, Rangoon, the Louisiana bayous, Dallas, and Singapore. I've filled out their social security applications, bailed them out of jail, stood up for them at weddings, carried their caskets, and run interference for them through mobs of rabid fans. I have introduced them on the nation's most prestigious stages, from Carnegie Hall to the Hollywood Bowl. I have written about them, composed songs they played and sang, gotten visas extended for the foreign ones, patched up domestic difficulties, broken up fights, tried to protect them from the worst of the exploiters.

But, best of all, I've *listened* to them. I've listened not only to their hopes and aspirations, their tales of woe, their philosophical observations, their complaints and exultations. I've listened to the sound of their music, which is really all that ever matters—either to me or to them.

Time has demonstrated that the public, the people who have delighted in these sounds, collected the records, gone to the festivals, want more than the music. They long to know more about the men and the lives that created their music. To meet that demand, the recent past has presented an impressive library of historical and biographical works relating to the people who made the music. There have been some autobiographies, too, which generally prove to be the least reliable information sources.

I put this book together because every time I attend a jazz function—whether as a host, a speaker, a panelist, a master of ceremonies, or merely a ticket holder—people constantly ask me to share my recollections about my six decades of involvement with the musicians.

Of course, the transient nature of the lives of jazz people rarely permits long-lasting, close personal relationships, though I've had my share of those, too. So what I have to tell isn't always incisive or analytical. I have undertaken to tell just one or two things about each of the many musicians I've had dealings with. These vignettes haven't been published before, though some folks might have heard me relate some of them at private or public functions, or even, from time to time, on the radio.

This book is only as autobiographical as it needs to be. After all, I'm telling about the musicians, not about Al Rose, but I do have to tell a couple of relevant things about him in order to make sense of the stories.

I was born in New Orleans in 1916. The first band I remember was the pit orchestra in my grandfather's Dauphine Theater. I remember several musicians who played in it—jazzmen like Martin Abraham, Tony Parenti, Wilbur Dinkel. I was four years old. During the same early years, I remember bands parading in the streets. I didn't then know the name of my favorite one, but I later discovered it had been led by Buddy Petit.

I never made—or tried to make—a nickel out of jazz. Directly or indirectly, the musicians got every cent their performances brought in when they worked under my auspices. Concerts, record sessions, all belonged to them. I have been fortunate enough to have unrelated skills that kept me and my family reasonably prosperous so that my jazz activity stayed free of commercial restraints. My greatest satisfaction has been in the production of what I like to think were among the best jazz records ever made and in seeing the books I wrote in print, knowing how they're appreciated by the world's jazz fans.

I've made sure, here, to include no secondhand tales. There's no hearsay in these pages. It's made up of nothing but things that took place between the world's greatest jazzmen and me. I hope you like it.

A Note on Vernacular

The reader with a reasonably close-hand relationship to the world of jazz may find that the way I've quoted the musicians doesn't ring altogether true. That's because I have deleted most of the obscenities—in the interest of brevity rather than prudery. Had I included every scatalogical utterance of the New Orleans musicians alone, this book would have been many pages longer. I have translated those otherwise speechless jazzmen for whom profanity seems to be the mother tongue, seeking to preserve their meaning rather than the total effect of their informal speech.

A Lonnie Johnson, reading somebody the "dirty dozens," has the effect of suggesting an entirely new art form, and ordinary conversation with any Brunies was a dizzying descent into the lowliest gutters. If we were awarding medals of distinction for the most colorful and original use of obnoxious language, we'd have been hard put to choose among Wingy Mannone, Louis Prima, and Danny Alvin, the Chicago drummer. Wild Bill Davison would have to qualify for at least an honorable mention. Of course, there were a few from whom I never heard an indecent word. Eubie Blake might occasionally have said *damn* behind his hand. Bud Freeman, Bobby Hackett, Knocky Parker, and Doc Evans all had sufficiently sophisticated vocabularies to allow them to express themselves concisely without the use of obscenity. Most of the musicians eschewed swearing in front of the ladies, but our blue ribbon winners were ahead of their times in accepting women as equals, at least insofar as language went.

One other thing. Lots of jazzmen, I suppose because they rarely associated with ordinary people, always had a certain jargon, which was intelligible only to other jazzmen, usually in the same area. Therefore, I refrained from writing a Dan Burley comment that included such phrases as "a deuce of treys on the backbeat" or "the Apple's trash pile," simply because I didn't want to have to stop and translate. In the thirties, I'd have had to do an extended glossary about xii • A Note on Vernacular

terms like *icky, longhair, collegiate hot,* just as the forties hot men had the word *square* all to themselves for a fleeting period. If I had reported it all really faithfully, this book would probably have cost you an extra five.

I Remember Jazz

Jelly Roll Morton

Try to forget for a moment that he was a musician who had a pro-
found effect on American culture, that he was a pimp and a pool
hustler who was racist in his attitudes. Just for now, forget his con-
viction that blacks were inherently inferior beings. What kind of man
was he under all this? Perhaps the following incidents will add to an
eventual full-length portrait of this extraordinary individual.

I was backstage at the Pearl Theater in Philadelphia talking with
the proprietor, Sam Steifel, about vaudeville bookings in his theaters.
It was a day in the early spring of 1938, slightly past noon. Jelly Roll
Morton walked purposefully by on his way to what passed for a men's
room in that decaying structure. I had never laid eyes on him before.
I'm not sure I'd even seen his picture. If I had I hadn't noticed it. But
I knew I was looking at a star. He had the bearing and the manner—
and certainly the clothes.

"Good evenin'," he said as he passed. I knew right then he was
New Orleans; only Orleanians say "Good evenin'" at lunch time.

Sam didn't introduce us. He said, "That's Jelly Roll Morton. You
ever hear him play?"

"Only on records," I answered.

"You think he's pretty good?" Steifel pursued.

"Yeah," I said, absently. In fact, up to that moment I hadn't paid
too much attention to his playing, though I owned lots of his records.
From my twenty-two-year-old vantage point, Jelly was merely an historical figure who, by musical standards, must surely have been artis-
tically surpassed in skill and concepts by stars of *my* generation. After
all, change and progress are inevitable, aren't they?

As it turned out, despite the knowledge I had gained in my full
score and two, I still had a lot to learn about listening to and appre-
ciating music. Sam invited me to stay around and watch the show. He
said he'd like to know what I thought about it.

I stayed and watched Jelly Roll leading a band of mediocre musicians. I never asked who they were, but I assumed that if I didn't know them they were nobody. I wasn't impressed with Jelly Roll's piano playing, but I told Steifel the show was great and that I especially enjoyed the comedy of Eddie Anderson, who was on the threshold of fame as Jack Benny's Rochester. I don't think I commented about the band.

That night I had agreed to meet with Reese Dupree, an elderly fellow who was the composer of record of the "Dupree Blues" and "Short'nin' Bread." We were to meet in the Showboat Room of the Douglass Hotel, the leading black hostelry in town. Reese was always promoting something. This time he had an Ellington concert on his mind, and he wanted me to be his partner in sponsoring this venture.

Now I was dressed, according to my normal practice in those years, in the high fashion of the day. And I must impose for a moment on the reader's patience by describing the details of my sartorial elegance, because it's relevant to the story.

There was a tailor in Philadelphia who sometimes used photographs of me in his window in the fond belief, or so he said, that my irresistible appearance would attract customers into his shop. The legend above the photo identified me as "Impresario Al Rose. Suit by Mike the Tailor." By agreement, I got forty percent off the price of any suit I ordered.

One day Mike said to me, "Al, I've got a real impressive piece of imported English goods. It's a remnant, but I might have enough for a three-piece suit. You wanna see?"

In those days that was a lure I couldn't resist.

The "goods" turned out to be a polychromatic, green-striped worsted, truly beautiful. Mike had no trouble selling it to me. The suit was finished two weeks later on the day of my appointment with Reese Dupree.

"Look," Mike had suggested (a good tailor knows how to flatter his clients), "I don't have to tell *you* what looks good, but I'd like you to consider a pink shirt with this, with a white detached collar and a dubonnet tie, handkerchief, and buttonhole. Can you *see* it?"

I could see it. Cordovan shoes, too.

So when I joined Reese in the Douglass, that's what I was wearing. I couldn't help being aware of the contrast I made with Dupree, whose suits always looked like mattress covers. I was ever so conscious of such matters in 1938.

We had just begun to talk when I noticed a flurry of activity in the entrance. Two noisy, light brown ladies, both grossly overpainted, came in; they were followed by none other than Jelly Roll Morton. He and Reese saw each other and exchanged waves as Jelly escorted his two friends to a table, then returned to have a word with Dupree. I was impressed with the elegance of Jelly's attire—very much impressed, indeed. Polychromatic, green-striped suit, pink shirt with detached white collar, dubonnet tie, buttonhole, and handkerchief—and even a pair of cordovan shoes. Obviously there had been more than a single suit in Mike's remnant. Jelly Roll appeared equally impressed with my attire.

He shook hands with Reese, who then introduced us. Jelly and I had both begun to laugh, and Dupree became uncomfortable, fearing that our joke might have been on him. Reese was not one to notice how people dressed. In a moment, Jelly got up to join his party; as he said goodbye he leaned over and said quietly in my ear, "Next time you see Mike the Tailor, you tell him I'm gonna kick his ass."

That's how I met Jelly Roll Morton. I was delighted with his sparkling good humor and his easy manner. He seemed much younger than his fifty-three years. He related to those around him in the sort of old, universal show-business style I had already encountered in other successful jazzmen.

I saw him again, briefly, at the Rhythm Club in Harlem. Eubie Blake had taken me there expressly to demonstrate his own mastery of the cue stick. The way it worked out, I never did get to see Eubie shoot pool, but I had the opportunity to watch with fascination as Fletcher Henderson demolished Jelly Roll on the green felt and walked away with a large handful of Jelly's cash in his fist.

Jelly stopped where we were sitting and said, "Smack is the luckiest goddamn hustler I ever saw. Now he thinks he can beat me!" He paused to see if we understood how ridiculous that idea was. "'Course, everybody gets lucky sometime."

As Jelly walked away, Eubie said, "Smack [Henderson] beats *everybody*. Jelly never wins from him."

• • •

In 1939 I was a delegate to the KEEP AMERICA OUT OF WAR convention in Washington, D.C. My hotel room had in it a flyer announcing:

THE JUNGLE CLUB

JELLY ROLL MORTON (IN PERSON)

AT THE PIANO

The flyer gave an address on U Street. I think it was a Tuesday night when I paid a cab driver and found myself standing on this unattractive street making a decision about whether it was worth going up the narrow staircase of the dingy building to the Jungle Club on the second floor. Even though it was about ten o'clock, I heard no sounds of music. I was about to turn and leave just as Jelly Roll joined me in the doorway.

"I remember you," he said. "You're Eubie Blake's friend. It's pretty early for things to start around here. Come on up and I'll show you the place."

He had his keys out as we went up the stairs. He opened the door to display the poorly executed African jungle decor. With an all-encompassing sweep of his hand to indicate the grandeur of what I was seeing, he announced, "All genuine bamboo."

In 1939, the cheapest furniture you could find was "genuine bamboo." It was the hallmark of poverty—certainly nothing to boast about. But Jelly seemed oblivious to all that.

"A dollar cover charge," he informed me. "The first drink is free. After that, it's sixty cents a shot."

"Cover charge?" I inquired. "You've got a show?"

"I'm the show," he assured me. "Jelly Roll Morton in Person."

I gave him a dollar, and he asked what I was drinking. I asked for Laird's Applejack, which he didn't have, then settled for Canadian Club and soda. He settled himself down on his piano stool. The piano was an antique upright that had obviously had a lot of work done on it. We were still alone. I was the only customer. That scene would be duplicated on many succeeding nights.

"Whaddya wanna hear?" he asked. I wish I had that night to re-live, knowing what I know now.

"Whatever *you* feel like playing," I said. "I never make requests."

By now he knew that I, too, was a native of New Orleans. "How 'bout somethin' from home!" he announced. "The Milneburg Joys."

The intricacies of his performance absorbed my attention. The harmonies, the counterpoint, the completely syncopated rhythms—they were a game to him, a kind of tonal jigsaw puzzle he took delight in solving. Still, you sensed that he didn't really feel any challenge. He could just nod his head and make the whole thing fall into place, as though he himself had, in fact, *invented* music. He'd say, "Looka this!" and shower a cascade of chords that somehow all managed to make musical sense.

When he finished, I said, "Tell me about that number. I see you're on the copyright with the guys from the New Orleans Rhythm Kings crowd. Tell me who really wrote 'Milneburg Joys.'"

"I'll tell ya, Al," he explained, "I didn't really put nothin' to that but the introduction—this part," and he played it. "But, of course," he continued, "the rest don't amount to nothin'."

Suddenly I understood that this characteristic appraisal wasn't the braggadocio for which he was noted. When you really examine the piece and listen, it's obvious that the introduction is significant. The rest is just plain old blues.

The precise instant when I realized that Jelly Roll wasn't just all talk—an aging musician who had failed to "keep up with the times"—was the same instant that I really knew how to listen to jazz. He was, in fact, creating music more astonishing and ingenious than anything I'd ever been aware of before. Right then I knew that my piano favorites of the moment—Meade Lux Lewis, Albert Ammons, Bob Zurke, or Pete Johnson—couldn't have begun to execute, much less think of, the amazing passages Jelly Roll appeared to handle so effortlessly.

By this time, Jelly and I were casual friends and I found that I just couldn't stay away from his place when he was playing. One day I was walking in the general direction of the Jungle Club, not planning to go there, when I encountered Jelly heading in the same direction.

"This is my bookkeepin' day," he explained cheerfully. "I got bookkeepin'. After all, I had six more customers besides you this week." As we passed a Salvation Army retail outlet, he said, "Lemme stop in here a minute, Al. I need to buy a piano."

I followed him in and watched as he examined half-a-dozen battered instruments that had all played their last choruses. He hailed the attendant.

"How much you want for this one?" he asked, indicating his selection.

"Five bucks," the man told him without hesitation.

Jelly gave him the money and called to a derelict type who was going through the motions of sweeping the place. "Wanna make a quarter?" Jelly asked him. In those Depression days that was an offer not to be ignored. The man assented with genuine eagerness. Jelly took a nail file out of his pocket.

"Watch what I do," he instructed, as he carefully pried the ivory facing off one of the keys. "You use this nail file and take the tops off all those keys."

In a very short time the job was done. Jelly stuffed them all into his overcoat pockets, flipped a quarter to his aide, and told the manager, "I got what I want. You can keep the piano."

As we walked down toward U Street, I couldn't contain my curiosity. "What was that all about?" I asked.

"Public relations," he explained patiently. "I'm gonna sign my name on 'em and give 'em away to my fans for souvenirs." So far I couldn't say I'd actually seen anybody that looked like a fan besides me.

"How about a few for me?" I solicited shamelessly.

"Yeah," he agreed. That night when I came into the club he gave me a handful of keys, carefully autographed. I still have six left, but sad to relate, the signatures have faded away. There's not a trace of ink to be found on any of them.

Just a few nights later, I said to him, "I've got to go to the capitol tomorrow. Can I drop you anywhere?"

"Yeah!" he said brightly. "I've got a gig in the Library of Congress."

So bright and early the next day, I picked him up in a taxi and delivered him to Alan Lomax.

John Casimir

In my own pretensions to civilization I have always scoffed at the practice of or belief in voodoo. Hard as it is to believe, though, thousands of Orleanians accepted it matter-of-factly as I was growing up, and unfortunately many lives were destroyed or impoverished because of this stupid superstition. It seems incomprehensible that there are still those among us who give credence to the alleged special powers of certain charms, potions, and powers. But some people are convinced that they themselves have such powers.

It's always seemed to me that musicians, and especially New Orleans musicians, are more susceptible to believing in the assertions of those who claim good and evil mystical talents. They're as gullible a lot as you'll ever find. There are exceptions, of course, but the exceptions aren't common.

Marie Laveau, the voodoo queen who died in 1903, left thousands of followers insisting that she had been making the city her domain since the mid-eighteenth century. Two of her nephews were jazzmen whom I knew well. Banjoist Raymond Glapion was one; and the other was Alcide (Slow Drag) Pavageau, the renowned bass player in the bands led by George Lewis and Bunk Johnson. Drag was always convinced there were spirits walking beside him. Fortunately, he believed they were good spirits.

The phonograph record entitled *Marie Laveau* was made by Oscar (Papa) Celestin and his orchestra in 1954. Discriminating listeners can make out the dulcet tones of Al Rose harmonizing in the background choral singing. It's a kind of shaky, but not tentative, baritone.

This vignette is about a man who occasionally claimed kinship to the notorious voodoo queen, although the relationship was never clearly defined. John Casimir was the leader and E-flat clarinetist of the Young Tuxedo Brass Band during the fifties. This parade unit was a New Orleans institution dating back to 1911 and is still performing in 1985 as this is written.

Casimir, it is fair to say, was irreproachable in his personal and professional life. He was not the sort one would imagine doing harm to anyone. Nevertheless, he inspired great fear among New Orleans blacks, especially among his musical colleagues. The superstitious were convinced that he had been "born with a caul" and that he had a special ability to determine at a glance whether an ailing person would live or die.

I became aware of Casimir's unique status in the community when I heard one musician say to another, "Poor Steve ain't doin' too good. Casimir passed by his house and left the quarters."

I asked what that meant and they enlightened me. "John Casimir," one of them said, "you see, he got the *power*. If a man be sick, why the man's wife might ask John to pass by his house and look at him. John, he can't make nobody better, but he can tell is the man gon' be all right. If he gon' die, then Casimir leaves two quarters on the mantelpiece fo' the lady who gon' be the widow. Dem quarters is fo' his wife to close his eyes with."

"Do *you* believe," I asked him, "that Casimir can really tell?"

"Sure I believe it! You bettah believe it! It always like he say. He say the man gon' die, he die!"

Several months later, I followed the Young Tuxedo Brass Band through uptown streets during a funeral. Many Orleanians followed brass bands at funerals just to enjoy the exhilarating music. At the end, as the members of the band went their own ways, Casimir seemed to have been left without a ride home. Whoever he'd been expecting hadn't shown up.

"Hey, John!" I called. "You need a ride?"

He came over and got in the car.

"You really wailed out there today," I said. "As hot as that sun was, I'm surprised that you all could play that long."

"That's what we on this earth to do," he assured me. "Some of us is just meant to play music where the people need it."

We had both known the deceased and we spoke of him for a moment. Then John said, "He done last three days. Seven days back I left the quarters by his wife, and then fo' days back he die."

"Do you really believe," I asked him, "that you can see when a person's going to die?" We looked each other directly in the eye, he with a characteristically baleful, other-world look. I thought for a moment he was getting ready to announce my own doom. He inclined his head. I was so fascinated I had pulled the car to a stop at curbside.

"Yes," he acknowledged. "I got the sight. Somebody gon' die, I can look at him and see the death there."

"What does it look like?" I pursued.

"It don't look like nothin'," he insisted. "It's somethin' you jus' see. It ain't like everybody can see it. You got to have the sight."

I wanted to know more. "Do you have any charm or gris-gris? Do you have to say anything to the spirits? Do you talk to the person who's sick? Do you touch him?"

He shook his head through all my questions. "You got the idea wrong," he explained patiently. "I don't need to do nothin'. I jus' come in and look at the cat an' I know! I can't help knowin'. I got the sight."

"Everybody around here believes you've got the sight," I agreed. "Do you ever worry that if a sick man sees you in his house it might scare him to death?"

"Most of the time," he replied, "I don't say the man gon' die—an' he don't. I don't make nobody die. I jus' be lookin' in so folks can get ready do they need to."

I dropped him at his house, and he invited me in for a drink. I had a Coca Cola and he opened a beer for himself. I noted the crucifix over his bed.

"You know," he told me, "there's a world a whole lot of people don't know nothin' about. White folks don't know nothin' about it an' maybe most colored don't know. But you from here. Born an' raised in New Awlins an' you got to know nobody from here never died fo' true. We say they dead an' we puts 'em in the grave—but they ain't dead. They walkin' aroun', they talkin' jus' like you an' me. They don't do no harm. You jus' don't never see them no mo'.

"When I see somebody gettin' ready to die, I kin begin to see through him, see? He jus' begins to disappear, see? He jus' look like you kin see the wall behind of him. When I kin see the wallpaper, you know what I mean?"

"John," I asked, "when your own time comes do you think you'll be able to tell?"

Casimir shook his head.

"No. I ain't gonna know, because sometime before a person like me die, the sight leave him an' go to somebody else. The first time I knowed somebody was gon' die it was my grandma. She had the sight but she didn't know she was goin'. Only I knew she was goin' and that was the first time.

"I always feel dyin' all aroun' me. Sometimes it's far away an' sometimes it's real close. Today it's pretty quiet out there. I don't feel nobody close-by gettin' ready to leave us."

Casimir died on January 3, 1963, seven years after this conversation took place. The funeral was a big one. His band and the Eureka Brass Band were both part of it. I talked that day with Thomas Jefferson, a trumpet player who was a mainstay of the Young Tuxedo Brass Band. I already knew that Jefferson's head was involved in the peculiarly New Orleans occult. He had already told me of the dreaded "gown men" who haunted the trees along Esplanade Avenue and dropped from the branches on unwary passersby, enveloping victims in their flowing attire and carrying them off mysteriously for dissection in the medical schools.

"Tell me, Thomas," I asked him, "do you know if anyone left any quarters at Casimir's house?"

He looked nervous.

"I don't know, man," he admitted, "but I know one thing. That power, the sight he had, passed on to somebody. Before too long, we'll know who it is. That sight don't ever disappear from this place. You wait an' see. Somebody's gon' be able to tell. One time I thought Willie Pajaud had the sight, but jus' before he died—he had a heart attack in his bathroom—he called out to his wife an' he said, 'This is it, Honey!' Now if Willie had the sight it would have left him before that and got into somebody else. So Willie didn't have the sight. John Casimir, he had the sight."

There seems to be something endemic among Orleanians that makes it easy for them to place credence in such legends as this. I don't know how I ever kept from being bogged down in that morass of superstition. New Orleans musicians are not only superstitious, they're also patient. To them it's just a matter of time until someone comes forward with the sight. At any rate, I suppose I'll find out one day who's carrying the quarters.

Frankie Newton

Not too many jazz fans remember Frankie Newton. He was an excit-ing and inventive trumpet player, the one that Bessie Smith collectors hear on her final recording that included "Gimme a Pigfoot" and "You've Been a Good Old Wagon." Frankie lived in Greenwich Vil-lage. Like so many jazzmen, he drank more than was good for him. Also like so many jazzmen, he had all kinds of friends, including the popular painter Beauford Delaney, and authors William Saroyan and Henry Miller.

A middle-aged black, Delaney had a notorious preference for boys over girls; but in the permissive ambience of the Village of the forties, his straight friends overlooked his amorous vagaries in consideration of his exceptional talent, his boundless cordiality, quick wit, and undeni-able wisdom. He was reluctant to sell his work to just anybody, and this idiosyncrasy made it necessary for him to reside and paint on the fourth floor of an abandoned warehouse on Greene Street. He didn't really live in dire poverty, because his more economically stable friends, and a few who were daring and ingenious, saw that he was somehow provided with the necessities of life. A mercenary gun-runner for the Israeli Stern Gang in what was Palestine not only stole a refrigerator from a nearby apartment for him, he then tapped the city's powerline to bring unauthorized electricity into the studio. A telephone was installed the same way. Owners of the building had no idea it was occupied. Friends brought Beauford a pot-bellied stove, which we managed to vent illegally through the roof, and we never went up to visit without carrying a bag of coal, a bottle or two of wine, or maybe a Blind Lemon Jefferson phonograph record that Beauford would play until it wore out. So his studio was a kind of social center that was immortalized in Henry Miller's book *The Air Conditioned Nightmare*, in a chapter entitled "The Amazing and Invariable Beauford Delaney." As often as not, if I were looking for Frankie Newton during the day and didn't find him in the bar across from his apartment, the next place I'd look would be Beauford's studio.

One day in the early forties some of us were sitting around at Beauford's on folding chairs and pillows. Saroyan and Miller were there, as was a young male model named Dante whom we all assumed was Beauford's special friend. Beauford, as usual, was painting and talking at the same time. We suddenly heard footsteps running up the stairs. Most people didn't *run* up those four long flights. In burst Canada Lee, without knocking. Canada Lee, once known as a middleweight pugilist, had by then established himself in New York theater circles and, in fact, distinguished himself in Shakespearean roles, especially with his critically triumphant performance as Iago (in whiteface) in *Othello*. His breathlessness riveted our attention as he announced, "Frankie's place is on fire!"

We all jumped up and ran for the door, fearful that our friend was in danger of injury or worse. We ran the couple of blocks, saw the blaze, and watched the firemen at work. Much to our relief, though, we saw Frankie Newton standing behind the rope barrier watching the blaze.

"My God!" Saroyan shouted. "Are we glad to see you're not hurt!"

"I might as well have burned to death," Frankie moaned. "My horn, my buzz mute, all my clothes are in there—and I got a job tomorrow night. If I can't make the job, I got no food, no money, nothin'." Then as an afterthought, "I got no place to sleep, either."

"How much does a decent horn cost?" I asked, being practical.

"Maybe seventy bucks. Five for a mouthpiece. I guess I can get a mute for three, four dollars."

On the spot, I took up a collection. Twenty from me to start it, twenty from Henry. Saroyan was only carrying fifteen. Beauford had two, Beauford's brother, also a painter, put up ten, and young Dante chipped in the ten he had.

"Tomorrow," I announced, "we'll go up to Teddy's and get Frankie what he needs." (Teddy Napoleon, Phil's brother, was a pretty good drummer, but his main occupation was running a music store near Madison Square Garden.)

Then we all went to Connie's Cafe for one of her matchless West Indian dinners, which she let us put on the cuff in those precredit card days. Connie knew a genuine emergency when she saw one. Frankie wasn't entirely sober yet, not at all interested in food, but he had another drink, which at that particular moment he might well have needed. That night he slept on Beauford's floor.

Next morning—noon, anyway—after I'd had a chance to go to the bank and get a check cashed, Frankie and I went uptown on the subway. The advertising cards carried these large messages for Bell-Ans, a popular indigestion pill of the day. The previous day's events had gotten to Frankie, and he felt the need of such a quasimedical measure right then. So we got off the subway, found a drug store, and then settled down in a Nedick's orange drink stand to give him a chance to ingest his remedy.

Teddy Napoleon had already read in the papers about Frankie's misfortune and gave him an unprecedented deal on the things he needed. People from everywhere volunteered aid. Tyree Glenn, the trombone-xylophone player, had an extra tuxedo to lend. (There were few jazzmen as big as Frankie.) We took the "A" train to Tyree's place to pick it up.

As we went back downtown to the Village, Frankie said, "Thanks, Shaz. This job tonight is for a hundred bucks. Tomorrow I'll pay you all back. It's good to have friends to help you when you need it."

The next day came and went, but Frankie didn't pay us back. Instead he hocked the new horn and by nightfall was in Bellevue fighting snakes. It seemed as if the jazz world was about to lose one of its better trumpet players. Various people, including me, gave benefit parties and concerts to raise money for him; and in fact several thousand dollars came into the pool to take care of his needs.

The doctors persuaded him to go somewhere and try to get himself cured of the drinking habit. He lost a lot of weight, but somehow the zest never returned to his trumpet playing. I lost track of him about that time; but when he died in about 1954, I heard it was of malnutrition induced by too much alcohol.

Jack "Papa" Laine

It seems unreasonable that I could have had any sort of relationship with Jack Laine when you consider that he led the first documentable jazz band in history as early as 1892 and that he retired from music in 1910, long before I was born. His Reliance bands spawned such talents as the members of the Original Dixieland Jazz Band, the New Orleans Rhythm Kings, and the Halfway House Orchestra. The fact is, I spent many rewarding days and hours in his company during the 1950s. From him I learned much about the history of ragtime, jazz, and even about my native New Orleans. (He died in 1966 at the age of ninety-two.)

I say that he "retired" from music in 1910. For three or four years after that he led bands in carnival parades, especially the fireman's band. Except for these occasions, though, he removed himself entirely from the musical scene. He had so many other interests in later years that it was hard for him to focus on the fact that he had once been a musician and a bandleader. He thought of himself first as a black-smith, for that was his trade, then as a fireman—who loved the excitement, the fraternal life and camaraderie of the fire house. He acknowledged his role in early jazz, looking back on it as a bit of frivolity not inconsistent with youth and callowness. He never saw the music as an avenue of artistic expression; it was just a way for young people to have a good time. The day he put away his bass drum, he seemed to give up even listening to jazz.

My late friend and collaborator, Edmond Souchon (Sou), would join me from time to time in taking Papa on a day's or evening's outing. We'd take him to lunch at Commander's Palace, tour him through the old New Orleans neighborhoods. He especially liked to visit houses in which he'd once lived and places where he'd worked. We'd buy snowballs or coffee at the stands and share the esoteric joys common to natives of the Crescent City.

One Sunday evening we decided to take Jack into Bourbon Street where a dozen or more jazz bands could be performing at once in the various tourist traps. I hoped he'd be able to find a band that sounded closest to his own historic Reliance bands. *That* sound, unfortunately, had never found its way to the recording studios. During those years, Papa could walk quite briskly. (He continued to march with his firemen in parades until his mid-eighties.)

We parked in the lot at St. Louis and Royal streets, where the Royal Orleans Hotel now stands, and walked the block to Bourbon Street. Passing the Paddock, where Octave Crosby led the house band, I noticed that Papa didn't even turn his head. He was busy talking, but it was clear that the music playing inside didn't gain his attention. We continued to within earshot of Sid Davila's Mardi Gras Lounge where Sharkey Bonano's band was employed. Papa stopped talking and listened alertly. I asked if they sounded anything like Reliance.

"Hell, no!" he assured us positively. "We could never play that good!"

Davila, the proprietor, himself a superb jazz clarinetist, greeted us cordially. At break time, along with the bandsmen, he joined us at our table. Papa already knew Sharkey and Harry Shields, though he couldn't remember their names.

"Your Daddy used to play in my band," he told Martin Abraham, Jr. He asked Li'l Abbie Brunies if he was any kin to Henny, Richie, Abbie, Merrit, or George. Li'l Abbie was happy to acknowledge the relationship.

"There wasn't no bands in my time to play as good as youse guys," Jack complimented, "but that's what we was tryin' to do."

Next door to the Mardi Gras, on the corner of Bourbon and Conti streets was (and is) the Famous Door. Paul Barbarin's band was on duty. On Sunday nights they spelled off the Dukes of Dixieland or George Girard's New Orleans Five, depending on which band had the night off. The instant Papa heard the sound of Paul's music, he said, "*That's* the kind of a band *I* had!" Considering his comments of a few moments before, this wasn't exactly high praise. In the fifties, Papa's vision was failing badly and he couldn't see the band until we got down front to our table. Then he turned to me and said in astonishment, "These guys is niggahs! They got all the *real* music jobs—the French Opera, concerts, all that. They never played our kind of music. They was too good. Now I see they taken it up!" He obviously found that amusing.

Papa invariably spoke of his own musical progeny as though most of them had not won world renown. He was unimpressed by the successes of the Original Dixieland Jazz Band, even though they had made the very first jazz record and had performed for more than a year in Europe. I asked him about Nick Larocca, the leader of the ODJB.

"Oh, sure!" he reported. "You know I had as many as six bands at the same time. But even so, some nights I'd have seven jobs, so I'd hire Larocca. I paid him just like anybody else. Of course, he was a potato man."

"A potato man?" Sou asked. "What's that?"

Papa explained. "Suppose you got a parade job for, say, thirteen, fourteen men, but you can't get four trumpet players, see. So you got the extra man, see; but you put a potato in his horn so he can't play nothin'. That's a potato man."

Sou laughed so hard he had to stop the car to get his breath. He couldn't see through the tears. When he recovered we drove by a fire-house where Papa knew the company; many were old friends of his. He introduced us around, and I talked to some of them. They were only dimly aware that Papa had ever been a musician.

Sou asked Papa about his first music job and he told how Dave Perkins (who was black though you couldn't tell it) had bought most of the instruments when the Mexican Military Band went home after the 1884–1885 World's Fair. They could replace them very cheaply in Mexico.

"I rented instruments off him," Papa recalled, "and I took a band on Robinson's Floating Opera House on the river. That's the first time we ever got paid for playin'. It was a private what-do-you-call-it—a stag party—a smoker. God! The place was full of Customhouse Street whores! Lulu White. You ever hear of her? My God, you shoulda seen what she done that night!" (My forthcoming biography of the redoubt-able Lulu contains the account of her horrendous exploits on that historic night as told by Papa and one other eye-witness.)

We didn't hesitate to ask Papa about the effect of segregation on the music world of his time, Sou reminding him that at least two Creoles-of-color, Achille Baquet and Dave Perkins, had worked in his bands. "Them guys played so good," Papa Jack told us, "we couldn't tell what color they was."

As for Buddy Bolden, Papa gave us his very best blank look for a moment, then said, "I don't believe I ever hired him, but I used so many musicians. What instrument did he play?"

Since nobody had ever recorded Jack Laine playing his drum, in the sixties Johnny Wiggs got together a group of top-flight jazzmen and got Papa to agree to play on the session. At Tulane University they recorded enough for one side of an LP. Though nearly ninety then, Papa kicked that bass drum as well as the best I ever heard. I tried to buy the tape to release, but then I learned Johnny had done it without a union contract.

Bill Russell

Like thousands of others, I admire Bill Russell, the dean of jazz researchers and archivists, who, almost single-handedly, brought about the jazz revival that began in the 1940s. His American Music Records company put on wax a host of jazz stars whose sounds would have died with them. A superb musician himself, Russell plays the violin in the New Orleans Ragtime Orchestra. He also fritters away endless hours playing with the restoration of superannuated musical instruments when he should be completing his definitive biographies of Jelly Roll Morton and Bunk Johnson. He's sitting on virtually all of the documentary material on these two jazz giants, and I keep telling him that at seventy-eight he hasn't got much time left for procrastinating. But you can't rush Russell—and that's not his only idiosyncrasy.

Russell is an animal lover. An Eagle Scout by temperament and habit, he has determined that it's important to be kind to all living things. That's okay as long as it's not carried to extremes. But when Bill gets mice in his apartment—which, incidentally, makes Armageddon look like a Japanese garden—he doesn't trap them. He feeds them!

Now, in the sixties Russell became the parent to a parakeet, which he permitted to fly freely around the apartment, despite the discomfort of his occasional visitors. One of these unhappy guests was me. I would rail at him about his damned sport-model sparrow, and he would chide me for being insensitive and brutal. Nevertheless, he would then be considerate enough to round the abominable thing up and herd him into his cage so he wouldn't fly about my head. Then he would waste a lot of our valuable time relating to me all the clever things this damned budgie had said that day.

"You're a fool, Russell!" I chided him. "That creature doesn't say a thing. He never has when I've been here. You just imagine these things."

"If you weren't such a narrow-minded dolt," he insisted, "and if you'd keep quiet long enough and listen when I put him up near your ear, you'd hear him. After all, he's only a little bird with a little voice and he's not amplified."

I agreed to participate in this demonstration. Russell held the bird next to my ear and said, "Talk to him, baby!"

Clearly and impeccably the bird told me, "My name is 'Pretty Boy.' I live at 600 Chartres Street."

I said to Russell, "See! That stupid bird doesn't even know you moved!"

Russell didn't speak to me for many months.

Mezz Mezzrow

When Mezzrow got out of jail, where he spent some time because of his indiscretions with illegal substances, he was broke and had no prospects for work. I produced three concerts just so he'd have a little encouragement. If you've read his autobiography, *Really the Blues*, you know all about his travails and that most of his problems were brought about more by stupidity than by criminal character.

In Harlem, Eubie Blake told me, "You could get in real trouble hangin' out with that guy. That guy ain't *finished* gettin' in trouble."

I insisted Mezzrow had learned his lesson, that he'd do anything in the world to stay out of prison, that he'd never go near the stuff again.

Eubie just said, "Don't say I didn't warn you." He found my confidence in Mezz's intentions naïve enough to be funny.

"Don't worry about *me*," I said, "I never even take aspirin." But Eubie wasn't convinced.

About those concerts, though. The truth is I normally wouldn't ever have hired Mezz to play. He wasn't a very good clarinetist. To play it safe, I engaged Sidney Bechet, too. Mezz and Bechet liked each other. In a weak moment, at Mezz's request, I also hired Bill Coleman for one of the concerts. Although Bill was an excellent musician, he just wasn't involved with my kind of music and didn't fit well with bands I presented. But this was all for Mezz. I wanted him to get his confidence back, and if he wanted Bill we'd have Bill.

You might well ask why I'd go to all this trouble for a guy who wasn't a close friend and who wasn't really much as a musician. It was because I knew, as did all authentic jazz musicians in those days, that Mezzrow had almost single-handedly kept the fire burning through the dark ages of this music. He had scrabbled for jobs and found them for dozens of musicians. He'd found things to sell to get their instruments out of hock—and sometimes he'd found things before they were lost. He shared anything he had with any colleague that needed it—food, clothing, housing. Among the many legendary things about him the most legendary were his generosity and his total devotion to the music we called jazz.

After these concerts, Mezz did feel better and he went on to an unexpectedly successful late career playing in jazz bands and, surprisingly, as the proprietor of King Jazz Records, which produced some better-than-average discs. But right at the time I'm talking about, Eubie was unconvinced.

Eubie and I were having dinner in the Theresa Hotel, Harlem's showplace, when Mezz walked in scanning the place. I realized he might be looking for me. As the only other paleface in the crowd, I wasn't hard to find. He came over to our table and paid his respects politely to Eubie. Then he handed me a square package, about the size of a deck of cards.

"This is just to show my appreciation, Pal," he said. "I just want you to know I'm stayin' straight and I'm going to do the best I can to stay out of trouble and play jazz."

Eubie said, "Anybody who's playin' jazz is *already in* trouble."

I thanked Mezzrow and wished him well. He said, "Don't open the package until you get home." Then he told us goodbye and left.

"Put that *away*, Shazzam. (That's what Eubie and some other people called me in those days.) It's probably some kind of dope." I laughed and so did Eubie.

When I got home, though, which was in Philadelphia at that time, I opened the package and found a beautiful sterling silver cigarette case full of—you guessed it—marijuana joints. Or, as they called them in those days, "muggles." I called Eubie on the phone. "I opened Mezz's package and what do you suppose it is?"

"I already told you, Shaz. Dope."

"Yeah," I admitted. "But how did *you* know?"

He said, "What else would Mezzrow give to somebody he really liked? Don't smoke any of it. It ain't good for you."

I confess that I *did* smoke one—first time in my life. It scared the hell out of me and I flushed the rest. I had seen enough muggles smoked and knew how to do it. I did get high and it did feel good. After all, it was Mezzrow's celebrated "golden leaf." But I knew I didn't want to do that anymore.

Bobby Hackett

We were having coffee in a cafeteria on Sheridan Square in the Village—Pee Wee Russell, Bobby Hackett, and I. I just happened to meet them in there. They were due on the bandstand at Nick's in forty minutes or so, and Hackett had promised Miff Mole he'd keep Pee Wee out of Julius' Bar across the street from the job. I was just in for a hamburger. I had a really strong stomach in the late thirties.

Hackett says, "Anybody hear anything from Bunny [Berigan] lately?"

Pee Wee says, "Not since they put him in jail for beating up his wife. She couldn't take it any more. I guess that's why she called the police in."

Hackett was aghast. Pee Wee could say things like that completely dead pan. You couldn't tell he wasn't serious—but anybody who knew Bunny had to know he was the least likely wife-beater in the universe. And anybody who knew Bobby Hackett knew how easy it was to take him in with such a story and that he himself would never utter a word of gossip or censure against anyone.

I said, "You never know what quiet guys like Bunny are liable to do."

"For God's sake!" Hackett began wildly. "How badly is she hurt, the poor girl—and my goodness—how terrible for Bunny! Shut up in jail for God's sake!"

Pee Wee said, "Her arm is broken and I think her pelvis, too, from his throwing her down the dumbwaiter shaft."

I said, "The electric fan he threw down after her must have weighed fifty pounds. I don't know how it missed her. He's been treating her like that for years. It's a wonder she's still alive. He deserves whatever he gets, the skunk!"

Pee Wee continued to lay it on. "Oh, yeah, I almost forgot that he cut her throat and tried to saw her in half with a bread knife."

Bobby's eyes popped with this detail.

I said, "In time she may get some vision back in her left eye, and they said they could repair her jawbone."

"What hospital is she in?" Bobby asked, the faintest trace of suspicion beginning to dawn in his innocent face.

Pee Wee told him, "She's in the mopery ward at St. Moishe's." Hackett patted the sweat from his brow. He always had an exaggerated response to the misfortunes of others.

"You fellows haven't heard from Bunny at *all*, have you?" he accused.

I shook my head. "Not for the past year or so."

And Pee Wee said, "Bunny who?"

Alphonse Picou

Anytime you hear someone play the clarinet solo in "High Society" it's either a copy or an adaptation of the original treatment created by Alphonse Picou. Picou crafted it himself, out of the piccolo part in Porter Steele's classic. For the rest of his life Picou reveled in the flattery of imitation.

He was already a vain old man when I first talked with him. He drank more whiskey than could possibly have been good for him, a habit which was not alleviated by his ownership of a bar on the corner of St. Philip Street and Claiborne Avenue in New Orleans.

Though he identified himself with the black community, Picou's complexion was very fair, his eyes a twinkling blue, his features delicate. He had a high-pitched little voice that always seemed to be coming from another room, as though it were being thrown by a skillful ventriloquist.

"Pike," as fellow musicians called him, was a part of the earliest jazz scene, having broken in with a nondescript musical group led by Bouboul Valentin in 1892.

"It wasn't what you call a ragtime band," he recalled. "But they done some fakin' jus' like anybody else. And they taught *me* how to fake. I could already play the clarinet when I was twelve years old."

Pike spoke in accents Orleanians identify instantly as "Creole"— not French, or not pure French. He used French words like *banquette* for sidewalk and *gallerie* for porch or veranda.

His bar, in those segregated days, was for blacks only. In fact, interracial fraternization such as might normally have occurred was actually prohibited by local ordinance. The police were very rigid in their enforcement policies, too, which meant that a pale-face like me actually ran the risk of arrest for merely being the dinner guest of a black family. All this was still going on as late as the mid-fifties, unbelievable as that may now seem.

A movie star named Zachary Scott, who died quite young but who was an avid jazz fan, called me one evening, told me he was in New Orleans at the Roosevelt Hotel (now the Fairmont), and asked if we might be able to find some old-time jazzmen. He even mentioned Picou by name as a special interest. I told Zach that Alphonse played at the Paddock with Papa Celestin on Tuesday nights only, but that he sometimes played at his own bar during the week.

After checking with Picou, who said he was going to host a "li'l jam session" in the afternoon, I picked Scott up. We parked on St. Philip Street at 4 P.M. and walked inside. I noticed that a trumpet man named Walter Blue was blowing on the little bandstand. Since there weren't many people there yet, we found a good table and sat down. We were the only whites in the place, but we weren't in there long. Within two minutes, the police had entered and arrested us. Of course, I was indignant, but Zach thought it was very amusing.

Anyway, I called the mayor, Delesseps S. Morrison, to whom I was distantly related, and told him where I was and what had happened and who was with me. Chep Morrison was committed to anti-segregation, but in those days it was an uphill fight. He asked to speak to the district police captain, who quickly became contrite, even sheepish. He let us go forthwith. But the flap following Scott's arrest while in pursuit of the innocent joys of jazz was enough to effect the repeal of certain relevant ordinances. After that it became the least bit easier to socialize with musician friends regardless of their color. Thereafter I would stop by to see Picou occasionally to pass the time of day and to remind him, the police, and others that I wasn't breaking any laws by just being there.

Late in the fifties, after the Tulane Jazz Archive was instituted, its first curator, William Russell, was collecting interview tapes of the surviving early jazzmen. One evening, I think in 1958 or 1959, he told me he was having difficulty getting a taped interview with Picou.

"I've had several appointments with him in the bar," Bill explained. "He's always very polite. He lives upstairs above the bar. When he gets up he comes down the stairs into the barroom. Then he comes over to the table where I've got the recording equipment set up and he says, 'Good morning, I'll be with you in a minute.' Then he goes over to the bar, sits on a stool, and gets so drunk he forgets I'm there, and by then he's in no condition to interview." He asked me if I had any ideas and I did.

Bill had a young Canadian friend in town, Ralph Collins, who was studying clarinet with exceptionally little success. I suggested that we bring Ralph and his clarinet to an appointment with Picou. By prior arrangement with Alphonse, the three of us got to his bar at the appointed time. Bill set up the recorder and pretty soon Picou came downstairs. He came to the table and said, "Good Mawnin', gennelmen, I be wit' ya in a minute," and proceeded to his customary barstool.

I told Ralph to get out his clarinet and play the solo from "High Society." Ralph did his best, but the resulting squeaks and squawks were as villainous an assault as that passage had ever been called upon to withstand. Even Ralph was embarrassed. Picou turned on his barstool, drink in hand, got up, and approached us.

"Turn on the machine," I instructed.

The first thing on that tape is Picou's tiny voice saying, "That ain't the way, boy!"

The interview itself turned out to be a comedy classic, sounding as though Picou and I had rehearsed it as a vaudeville routine. As the playback shows, Alphonse didn't want to talk about jazz; he wanted to reminisce about the amorous exploits of his salad days. He was eager to add to the record an explicitly detailed account of his most memorable forays into many boudoirs. In each tale, just as he approached the end of his story, after weaving a complex fabric of suspense, I— loth to waste the opportunity to document some scrap of jazz history—interrupted, steering him back to the subject. So intent was I on realizing our pristine purposes that it never entered my head listeners might possibly be as interested in Picou's lurid accounts as in anything he might have had to say about music.

The net effect of all this was to frustrate both Picou and his listeners regarding the endings of his accounts of adulterous derring-do and to abort our serious efforts to find out much of what we wanted to know about early jazz.

Picou died and was buried during the 1961 Mardi Gras season. His enormous funeral attracted large numbers of international journalists. Russell invited them to crowd into his little record shop on St. Peter Street opposite what is now Preservation Hall, to listen to the tape.

The interview affected them like a Mack Sennett two-reeler. Roars of laughter could be heard out in the street; it was an act that could have been a hit in Minsky's.

Many of the newsmen refused to believe the whole thing hadn't been set up for laughs. I was widely congratulated for my till-then-unknown ability as a straight man. The tape remains at the Jazz Archive, available to all listeners. It may be one of the greatest all-time jazz-comedy classics. Listening to it ten years later, I found that it had lost none of its spontaneity. But I also found myself wondering how those erotic recitations of Picou's might have come out if I hadn't been trying to redirect his comments.

Irving Fazola

Irving Fazola was a physical wreck by the midforties. (He was only thirty-seven when he died in 1949.) He had already established himself in the front rank of all-time great jazzmen. A student of classic teacher Jean Paquay, who was a mainstay of the French Opera Orchestra in New Orleans, Faz's real name was Prestopnik. Because he was the only one among the musical kids he grew up with who could really read music, they called him "Fa-sol-la." That's how he came to be Fazola. Those same kids formed a highly successful band, led by twelve-year-old trumpet virtuoso Louis Prima and featuring Faz, age eleven, on clarinet. His clarinet already had that mature New Orleans tone which was the envy of musicians everywhere, jazz and classical alike.

Eventually, Faz became famous for his irresistible records with Bob Crosby's "Bob Cats." He didn't live long enough to realize his full musical potential, succumbing to the pleasures of the flesh at what should have been the beginning of his prime. By the time he died he weighed over three hundred pounds, despite a short, stocky frame. He often drank himself into complete insensibility and consorted with as unsavory a class of ladies-of-the-evening as the tenderloins of the northeast could muster.

Once he invited me to his room in the Picadilly Hotel in Manhattan where I found him *en deshabille* in bed with a pair of seriously battle-worn chippies. A third superannuated Venus slept noisily on a nearby rollaway bed. Faz generously let me know I was welcome to participate in the festivities, but I explained that I had too much business to take care of. I managed to get him out of bed long enough to say, "Look, Faz. You're supposed to play a concert for me in Philadelphia a week from Friday. That means you don't drink anything that day, understand? No beer, no wine, no whiskey. Nothing!" I reminded him how scarce jobs were and vowed that if he showed up with alcohol on his breath I'd never hire him again.

He favored me with a stream of selected, uniquely New Orleans-style expletives, the utterance of which was his second most noteworthy achievement. But in the end he pledged himself to abjure all intoxicants on the Friday in question. I didn't hesitate to remind him of the times he had reported to me in no real condition to perform, and although, in justice, I freely admit he was never an actual embarrassment to me, he didn't play those dates like Faz could play.

Came the Friday evening of the concert. At about 7 P.M. I got a call from a Horn & Hardart's Automat Restaurant—the one an earlier generation of Philadelphians had nicknamed "The Heel" for reasons not known to me. The manager was on the line and wanted to know if *I* knew a Mr. Fazola. He went on to explain that Mr. Fazola had eaten more than he had intended and as a result had found himself wedged, apparently forever, in one of those captains' chairs. He apparently could not be pried loose, even with the efforts of the manager and a strong pair of busboys. I immediately sent an ambulance to "The Heel" and hurried over there myself. It was only a few blocks away.

The manager hadn't exaggerated. There was Fazola, clearly jammed into the chair. "What the hell happened?" I demanded, concerned for his condition and for my concert.

"Well, I gave you my promise," he reminded me, prepared to put as much of the blame as possible on me for the inconvenient circumstance. "I told you I wouldn't drink nothin' today and I didn't." But he went on to tell how he'd gotten into town on the train a little too early and had just decided to while away the time over a hamburger or two.

"How many did you eat?" I asked him.

"Thirty-six," he admitted. "I still feel okay. I just can't get up out of the chair."

So the two ambulance attendants, the two busboys, the manager, and I carefully loaded him, *with* the chair, into the ambulance, drove to the Academy of Music, and unloaded him carefully right at centerstage of the auditorium. I paid everybody off and sent them on their ways.

Patrons of Journeys Into Jazz who remember that night may recall thinking it odd to come to their seats promptly at 8:30 and see one of the great stars of jazz sitting contentedly on the stage putting his clarinet together. Those who were present may be pleased to know, at last, how that came about.

During the first half of the concert, Faz kept his seat—playing magnificently, but not standing for his solos as was customary. At intermission time, pianist Joe Sullivan, a trombone player named Munn Ware, and I pulled him loose. The second half of the concert went off without a hitch, though I did substitute a chair without confining arms. Faz then got up to do his solos, and nobody could tell we had started the evening with an emergency.

After the concert, Faz sheepishly suggested he'd like to go somewhere to eat. I took him to Billy Yancey's. (He was once a black major league baseball star.) And Faz ordered—you guessed it—hamburgers.

Once back in New Orleans, Faz was relieved to be away from the pressures of music in the east and of what he saw as the restrictive environment of New York. At home, though, his beloved red beans and rice, Creole hot sausage, and gumbo got the better of him. He had some decent music jobs, but that great New Orleans cooking in those huge quantities, that alcohol, and the ravages of his indiscriminate amours brought his career and his life to an untimely conclusion. His proteges and admirers have kept the sound of Fazola from vanishing into the mists of history. Listening to Pete Fountain playing the blues, you sometimes feel you might as well be listening to Faz.

Oran "Hot Lips" Page

"It's all in the lip," he explained. "You see these valves and all this plumbing—the only thing you really *need* is the mouthpiece." If that had been anyone but a really great jazz trumpet man like Lips Page speaking, I probably wouldn't have been paying the close attention I was.

We were sitting at the bar in George Brodsky's saloon in Philadelphia. The place was named after Harlem's more famous Cotton

Al Rose, 1936. This is the suit, the tie, the collar, etc.

Jack "Papa" Laine was the leader of the first documented Jazz Band (1892). Here, at eighty-eight, he had a difficult time remembering he'd ever been in the music business. *Photo by Johnny Wiggs.*

Dan Burley could do many things well, including running a newspaper. The other guy liked the way Dan played piano.   *Photo by David Hawkins.*

Dan Burley shows Beryl Booker the sound of *real* jazz piano in my living room in Philadelphia, in 1946. She got famous playing the other kind.

In the 1950s, Percy Humphrey was the leader of the Eureka Brass Band. He said, "Being the leader sounds good, but that's a music word for book-keeper." *Photo by Mary Mitchell.*

Al Rose and Percy Humphrey, some years earlier. *Photo by Joe Marcal.*

Young George Girard was on his way to the jazz summit, but he was just twenty-seven when I went to his funeral.   *Photo by Mary Mitchell.*

Eubie Blake said of nineteen-year-old Morten Gunnar Larsen, "I been sittin' here all afternoon waitin' for this kid to make a mistake."   *Photo by Diana Rose.*

Morten Gunnar Larsen, the debutantes' delight, came to New Orleans from Norway and at nineteen was spellbinding audiences with his interpretations of Jelly Roll Morton, Louis Moreau Gottschalk, and Scott Joplin.   *Photo by Joe Marcal.*

Merrit Brunies was a redneck sheriff in Biloxi, Mississippi, but you wouldn't have known it from the way he played valve trombone.   *Photo by Joe Mares.*

Doctor Leonard V. Bechet, Sidney's brother and an excellent trombonist, filled my cavities as well as he filled out a harmonic chord. *Photo: The Second Line.*

Don Marquis and I won the only two Louisiana Library Association annual awards given for books on jazz subjects. His *In Search of Buddy Bolden* won in 1978, and *New Orleans Jazz: A Family Album*, by Edmond Souchon and me, won for 1967. *Photo by Joe Marcal.*

Not Napoleon, but pianist Bob Doyle, who always tuned the pianos for my New Orleans recording sessions. He would never play on them, though, because his brother-in-law, Armand Hug, was too good. *Photo by Joe Marcal.*

Don Perry's behind-the-scenes work in the jazz world made many things happen that wouldn't have been possible without him. We always needed a friend in TV. *Photo by Joe Marcal.*

During my second appearance on Joe Franklin's TV show in New York, did Sammy Kaye and I talk about our current projects? Hardly. We reminisced about how I had gotten him into the above mess with Philadelphia Eagles backs, Bosh Pritchard and Steve Van Buren. Sammy, center, failed to score. *Photo by Nick Alexakis.*

Sammy Kaye, looking more like himself. *Photo by Nick Alexakis.*

George Schmidt gained fame in the forefront of the New Orleans art world with his paintings and hotel murals. But he's also the guy who sings those art deco vocal choruses with the New Leviathan Oriental Fox-Trot Orchestra.   *Photo by Joe Marcal.*

Johnny Wiggs insisted that I could play the piano—and you never argued with Johnny Wiggs. He hated to play cornet alone.   *Photo by Mary Mitchell.*

Al Rose and Johnny Wiggs.   *Photo by Johnny Donnels.*

Paul Crawford's first recording session. You can see I was more confident than he was. We turned out the best "Tishomingo Blues" I ever heard.
Photo by Edmond Souchon.

Real skiffle music for a public library function. Raymond Burke, on the left, is playing a piece of bamboo and a funnel with a sax mouthpiece. You can't see the bell of Paul Crawford's plungerphone, but you can guess what it is. Art Marshall is doing rhythm on a suitcase that's hidden in the shrubbery, as is the washtub at the end of my rope. (I swear I can make an octave and a half.)
Photo by John Kuhlman.

Four museum pieces—from left to right, Al Rose, Johnny Wiggs, Joe Mares, and Bill Russell—at the New Orleans Jazz Museum when it was in the Royal Sonesta Hotel.   *Photo by Justin Winston.*

Most record sessions don't look like this one in the Esplanade Room at the Royal Orleans. Sherwood Mangiapane, bass; Armand Hug, piano; the impresario himself; and Bob Lawton, the electronic genius who made most of the tapes for the state of Louisiana sessions; then Paul Barnes and Alvin Alcorn. The kid is my son Rex, and on the far right is trombonist Wendell Eugene, wondering if he's come to the right place.   *Photo by Johnny Donnels.*

Kerry Price (Gower) is celebrated as a singer of authentic blues, but she's as good a jazz band pianist as there is in the world. In this picture, as usual, my wife has come between us. *Photo by Joe Marcal.*

Stevenson Palfi, on the right, is the TV producer of such successful documentaries as "This Cat Can Play Anything" and "Piano Players Rarely Get to Play Together." I'm hiding behind a post at the Miami Seaquarium, but Diana laughs at killer whales. *Photo by Polly Palfi.*

Club, but shared no other characteristics. George did, from time to
time, bring in some New York musicians. He really loved the sound
of jazz.

There had just been a Journeys Into Jazz concert at Town Hall,
and Lips had invited the musicians and me down to his place to un-
wind. It wasn't commercial opportunism. He closed the place as soon
as we came in and let us know all drinks were on him.

"All that fancy fingerin'," Lips was saying, "'course you can do a
few frills with it, but *here's* where the music is." He was removing his
mouthpiece from his coat pocket. "See?" He put it to his lips, reached
for an empty beer glass, and began to blow the hottest, dirtiest blues I
could remember. Very quietly, of course. You can only get so much
volume out of a beer glass. If anybody had been talking, that music
would have been drowned out. Baby Dodds found two swizzle sticks
and began to tap rhythm on the bar. He decided it was too loud and
covered the spot on which he was tapping with a wine list to muffle
the noise. The complicated, whispering beat was just perfect. Elmer
Snowden had removed his banjo from its case and was playing beautiful chords more softly than I thought a banjo could play.

Then Dan Burley sat down at the piano, and I thought that would
break it up. But he pedaled the upright down and just hit an occasional note with one finger—in exactly the right place. I felt as though
I'd been waiting around all my life just to hear this one blues. With a
"two can play this game" look in his eye, Jimmy Archey joined the
group, his mouthpiece working on an entirely appropriate trombone
part. For perhaps three quarters of an hour, George and I listened to
the kind of music that makes it all worthwhile.

The musicians didn't have to signal to each other. They only
communicated with the music. Lips sang a verse in what I can only
describe as a melodious whisper.

> If you lose yo' money, don't you lose yo' mind,
> Papa if you lose yo' money, don't you lose yo' mind.
> If you lose yo' woman, don't mess aroun' with mine.

When it was all over nobody said anything for a while. George
refilled the glasses, and I was still hearing it all in my head. I had the
feeling all of us were still hearing it. It was that jazz magic that comes
upon us very few times in our lives. After maybe twenty minutes of

quiet drinking, Lips spoke up in an ordinary conversational tone that boomed like thunder out of all the silence. "It's all in the lip."

Lips Page was an easy guy to like. Drunk or sober he was relaxed and friendly, always generous and considerate of others. There was a nobility about him that inspired trust and confidence. He had all of the leadership qualities except ambition, and there was nothing he loved as much as an audience. He worked many concerts for me, even though he limited my style because he didn't know most of the old tunes Journeys Into Jazz audiences loved. But then there was nothing wrong with just sitting and listening to Lips playing the blues all night.

I've always avoided comparing musicians. Many that I know do the particular things they do better than anyone else in the world can—like Art Hodes doing "Davenport Blues" or Harry Shields playing "Tin Roof." But as great as Satchmo' was—and *he* could do *anything*, when it came to the blues—Lips could match him thrill for thrill.

He came out of the Kansas City crowd, from Bennie Moten to Count Basie, but all that music was too mechanized to provide the showcase that would let the world know how outstanding he was. He walked with confidence and dignity; he had the bearing of a man determined to be free, and he was free of everything but the damned whiskey that laid him low in 1954. He was only forty-six.

Tony Parenti

The concert was around 1946, at the White Horse Bowling Academy in Trenton, New Jersey. I just can't remember whom I brought besides Tony Parenti, Max Kaminsky, and the drummer, Arthur Trappier. This wasn't an auditorium, just a place set up with tables and chairs. It seems to me that drinks were served, but I could be mistaken after so many years. Anyway, it wasn't a typical Journeys Into Jazz environment. I don't even recall how I happened to put that particular gig together. But what keeps it in my mind is the fact that it was the first session I ever recorded on wire, and I was overwhelmed with the possibilities of this ingenious device. I couldn't have guessed how quickly the technique would become obsolete.

Parenti, whom I had literally known all my life, had the daily racing form spread on the table before us and was busy with his pencil in the endless process all horseplayers know so well. "Have you ever thought," I asked idly, "how rich you'd be if you'd never heard of horse racing?"

Parenti had to play music every day whether he wanted to or not just to keep ahead of the sheriff. He was always broke or in hock and never had anything to show for his labors, though he stayed as much in demand as any musician in New York.

"All of life is an illusion," he told me grandly. He was not above an occasional muddled philosophical observation. "I have the illusion that someday I'll parlay a half-dozen of these nags into a fabulous fortune. It keeps me going."

I was paying him sixty dollars plus transportation for the evening—big money for a jazzman in 1946. In his mind that broke down to ten five-dollar bets, breakfast, and money to get into the track.

"You always get a better shot at Belmont," he averred. "When the horses are running clockwise they're not used to it and that kind of equalizes them." (It seems that all other race tracks run counter-clockwise.) Then he said, "You never play the ponies, do you?"

I confessed I'd never seen a race, never been to a track.

"Hell!" he said. "The races are beautiful to see even if you don't bet! You'd really enjoy it!" He proposed that I join him on the morrow just for the novelty of it. Somehow at that moment, in the smoke-filled atmosphere of the White Horse Bowling Academy, the idea appealed to me. I said I'd go.

Next day I hired a car and a chauffeur. I still didn't know how to drive in 1946, and you could still afford that kind of luxury then. It cost me, maybe, thirty dollars—about half of what Tony would have spent by day's end. At about 11:30 A.M. I picked Tony up at his place in Long Island, and we proceeded to Belmont. Once inside the gate, I came upon a gentleman I knew whose name was Winfrey (of the Winfrey Stables). He was a horse owner of some stature in the sport, as I learned later, but I knew him through his enthusiastic interest in ragtime. Tony broke away from me to get to the betting window in time for the first race. When he returned, I introduced him to Mr. Winfrey, who then excused himself, explaining that he had business in the paddock.

"You know him very well?" Tony wanted to know.

"Well enough," I answered, noncommittally. "He was thrilled to meet an authentic jazz legend like you."

"He have anything interesting to say?" Tony pursued.

"Nothing special," I told him. "We talked about music and the weather, you know."

"I'll bet," Tony said, suspiciously. If I'd told him he wouldn't have believed I didn't know Winfrey was a horse owner. I followed Tony to the rail. To this day I don't know whether we had seats or not. Going to the track with Tony was an all-day marathon between the rail and the betting window. You wouldn't think of sitting down. Tony's horse, by the way, was far back at the finish but he was undaunted.

"You're not going to place a bet?" he asked incredulously. He couldn't imagine a race going by that you wouldn't have something on. Unthinkable.

"Maybe later," I told him. "I just want to watch 'em run for a while. You're right, it is beautiful."

"Somehow," he confided, "I don't get any kick out of it if I haven't got a little something riding."

Tony lost the first four races and took to muttering curses at the horses and the jockeys. By the time the fifth race came around, I told him I'd decided to place a bet. On the day's program, I noticed a horse named Microphone." Since I had just begun my radio series, Journeys Into Jazz, this seemed like a felicitous choice. I told Tony what I was betting on, and he explained to me why Microphone had no chance that day. Having observed the results of Parenti's expertise in the earlier races, though, I was not deterred. He instructed me in the betting procedure, took me to the window, and I played $10 to win. Then we went back to the rail, Tony supremely confident that his choice would make him even for the day.

Microphone came in by at least ten lengths, paying $160 for my $10.

"You son-of-a-bitch," Tony addressed me. "I might have known. You come in here, and the first thing I see is that you know Winfrey personally and, for all I know, all the other owners at Belmont. What the hell did he tell you?"

"I told you," I reminded him. "We talked about music, you, the weather."

"Bullshit!" Tony insisted. "He gave you a horse! Great 'jazz legends' like me he can hire for what he spends on cigars in an afternoon. You could have given me that horse, too. You're supposed to be my friend!"

"If I had that kind of information, do you suppose I would only have put ten bucks on it?" I challenged.

He thought about that for a while, but he never said anything.

Later he asked me if I had any information about the feature race. I told him I didn't, but that I might put a few dollars on it. "It's true that having a little money on a horse does make the race more exciting."

We went to the paddock to size up the horses. I saw one I liked the looks of. He was kind of grey, and I still remember his name—Sunvir.

"I'm playing this one," I told Tony. We went to the betting window where I placed a $20 bet, and Tony followed me with $10 of his own on my horse.

Sunvir came in and returned about $200 for my bet and $100 for Parenti's.

"You're still telling me with a straight face that Winfrey didn't tell you anything?" he demanded.

"Not a damn thing," I insisted.

"Well, anyway," he said, "thanks for letting me in on this one. It put me ahead for the day." He didn't buy my disclaimer for a minute.

We had a great dinner that night in Luchow's. I paid off the driver and Tony went on a gig. I didn't see him for a couple of years after that. I bought a home in Hollywood, Florida, and shortly thereafter Tony left New York and moved to Miami where he worked in Preacher Rollo's excellent little band. I'd drive down to see him from time to time. (If you decide to live in Florida, you *have* to learn how to drive.) His job didn't pay too badly, but Hialeah and Gulfstream Park were siphoning off his money. He'd ask me occasionally, "Do you know any owners down here?" and I'd tell him I didn't think so, which was true. I'm the kind of a guy that goes to Hialeah just to look at the flamingos.

I sold my Hollywood place and moved back to New Orleans in 1954, and about that time Tony called me. "I'm sick of this place," he announced. I assumed the Florida racing season was over. "I want to go back to the city [New York], but I'd like to spend a few weeks in New Orleans. I haven't been home for twenty years. You think you could find me a job for a couple of weeks?"

It so happened that the Bourbon Street scene was in flux at the time, and I arranged with Frank Assunto to feature Tony on clarinet with the Dukes of Dixieland at the Famous Door. "He can stay with us as long as he wants," Frank said. "It's an honor to have him in our band."

When Parenti arrived, I picked him up at the airport and the very first thing he wanted to do was to go to Felix's Oyster Bar in the French Quarter. "I've been dreaming about this for years," he told me, as the two of us put away seven dozen oysters on the half-shell. "Nothing in the world like New Orleans oysters." Since the New Orleans track was closed until Thanksgiving, he could save up a little money to get to New York.

After that I'd see him around, either in New York at Jimmy Ryan's where he worked for some time or at jazz festivals in New Orleans or places like Manassas, Virginia. Some years later, maybe in 1965 or so, Edmond Souchon called to tell me he and Tony and Knocky Parker were going to make a ragtime band session for George Buck in Columbia, South Carolina. He wanted to know if I could be there. He said he didn't think George Buck had ever run a session of his own before. Since I was due at the University of Georgia for several weeks at about the same time, I agreed to drive over to Columbia in case I could add anything to the session. He told me they were planning to do a dozen or so classic rags.

I arrived at the high school auditorium where George was recording before Tony did. I greeted George and the musicians and then drove out to the airport to meet Tony's plane. He was his usual dapper, businesslike self, and he was carrying a briefcase. He was very happy about doing this LP, because he dearly loved to play the old rags, music of the pre-jazz era.

"Hey!" he yelled. "I'm glad to see you on this date. I didn't know you were going to be here. I'm always worried that these record people don't understand rags. Anyway, I've got it all here. Right here." He patted his briefcase.

"You've got all *what* right here?" I asked, innocently.

"The arrangements," he told me confidently. "The charts."

I suppose I laughed when I told him I didn't think he could use them because the great ragtime piano player, Knocky Parker, couldn't read music. And neither, for that matter, could Doc Souchon. I said I didn't know about the other musicians. (The others were Larry Conger, trumpet; Charlie Bornemann, trombone; Pops Campbell, drums.)

"You never stop putting people on!" Tony complained. "Why are you telling me Knocky Parker can't read music. The man played a Scarlatti concert in Hollywood Bowl, for heaven's sake. He's already recorded the complete piano works of Scott Joplin and James Scott. You can't play that stuff without being able to read."

I continued to insist that Knocky couldn't read until Tony said, "What's the use of talking to you. You're so thick-headed. Ah, well, if you were a musician, you'd know he has to read!"

When we arrived at the high school, I introduced Tony and Knocky. "All the way down here," Tony reported to Knocky, "this guy has been trying to tell me you can't read music. He doesn't understand that if you can't read, you can't play this stuff. It's not like the blues or something. If I didn't know he always put people on, I'd have been plenty worried. Imagine going into a ragtime session with a piano player that can't read!"

Knocky broke the news as gently as he could. "It's true, Tony," Knocky said. "I can't read music."

"You guys made all this up between you!" Tony charged, trying to laugh. "That can't be."

Once the fact sunk into his brain I thought we'd lose him. Of course, Knocky can't read music, and the session came off magnificently—one of the most satisfying orchestral ragtime LP's ever. In the beginning, I thought Parenti's fears might scuttle it all. But he was fine, beaming in fact, after the first number.

In 1971 I was planning a complicated session to be entitled "The Oriental Twenties," featuring Harry Shields on clarinet. Harry related so well to those far-Eastern tinged numbers that had been very popular when he started playing jazz in the taxi-dance halls of New Orleans. Before we actually got around to making the record, though, this irreplaceable jazzman passed on. I postponed the session, of course, to think out what kind of adjustments I'd need to make. After a couple of months, I decided to invite Parenti down to cut the disc for me. But once more I was too late. Tony died on April 17, 1972.

I abandoned the project.

Dan Burley

I don't know how many jazz fans remember Dan Burley. He came out of the rent-party tradition, which in Chicago spawned such stars as

Pinetop Smith, Meade Lux Lewis, Albert Ammons, and Jimmy Yancey, besides Cripple Clarence Lofton, Pete Johnson, and so many more. Dan, though, was different. He didn't play jazz for a living, though he was always a concert attraction and made many exciting records.

Dan Burley was a newspaperman whose résumé included editorial stints on *Ebony* and *Jet*. In Chicago he worked on the *Daily Defender* and at the time of my association with him he was editor-in-chief of the *Amsterdam News*, Harlem's big-circulation daily paper. He was also the author of a hilarious and informative little book entitled *Dan Burley's Handbook of Harlem Jive*. During the forties this volume was "in." It sought to establish etymology and lexicography for the fugitive jargon that virtually became a complete and arcane language.

Besides recording for me, he was also on Decca with Lionel Hampton, and he made some great Circle records for Rudi Blesh with Pops Foster and Brownie McGhee. We did a few things that included Pops, Danny Barker, and Jimmy Archey.

Dan and I would frequently convene late at night with the great jazz piano players of the world at Jimmy's Chicken Shack, where he'd occasionally take a turn playing his distinctive "skiffle" music, as he called it. Others who often turned up there were the stride giants, Eubie Blake, Luckey Roberts, James P. Johnson, Willie "The Lion" Smith, and, on some memorable nights in 1939 and 1940, Fats Waller. Unbelievably, there were times when they all showed up at the same time. For a time, the house pianist was Luckey Roberts, who later opened a posh place of his own. On some Saturday mornings, just as the sun came up, we'd all leave the Chicken Shack and trail after Fats, who had a deal with St. John the Divine Cathedral where they let him play on their pipe organ from 6 to 7 A.M.

I can't convey how exciting Harlem was during these years. There were several weeks when I was involved with Dan in the promotion of various enterprises, both his and mine. During these times I stayed in the Theresa Hotel, the lone Caucasian on the premises. I was there with Dan's endorsement, so if the other people had any prejudicial attitudes concerning my presence, I never felt them. Many black show people sort of headquartered at the Theresa. Cab Calloway, the Mills Brothers, and bandleader Lucky Millinder were frequent breakfast companions in the coffee shop.

One Friday night I checked in and had barely reached my room when the telephone rang. It was Dan.

"I need a favor, Shaz!" he said tensely. "Will you go out in the hall and turn left. There's a window at the end. Hurry to the window, put your head out and look down. Then hurry back and tell me what you see. I'll hold."

I assumed I had just become a reporter as I ran through the hall. Down in the street I saw a shocking spectacle; but I took in as many details as seemed pertinent, then dashed back to the room and breathlessly picked up the phone.

"There's a woman lying on the sidewalk on her back. Lots of blood. I'm sure she's dead. She seems very well-dressed—a fur coat, I believe. But I'm on the fifth floor and I can't make out details too well. There are lots of cops, lots of sirens. I think an ambulance pulled up just as I left. Maybe five hundred people around the scene."

"That's the problem," he said. "I can't get a reporter through the mob."

"Anyway, I'm sure she's dead," I told him.

"You sure enough so that I can stick my neck out and *write* that she's dead? Hold on. I'm going to be dictating this so I'm not always talking to *you*. Okay?"

I said okay. My door was open and there was a lot of excitement in the hallway. "Hang on just a second," I told Dan. I went out into the hall. By now it seemed news of the suicide had permeated the entire hotel. I found out who the lady was and got back on the phone.

"It's Billy Daniels' wife," I reported. "She jumped out of the window."

I heard him relaying this information. Then he said, "See you at ten o'clock. Wait in the lobby. I guess we've got room on the paper for one ofay reporter." And he hung up.

The next morning when I saw the headline about the suicide of the famous singer's wife, I felt like it was *my* story.

Dan, when I first met him, was as racist as a black can get. He endorsed the utopian ideals of Marcus Garvey for a National Black Republic, and he was sure that whites were sadistic, untrustworthy, savage, greedy, and, most of all, stupid. His column in the *Amsterdam News* referred to nonblacks as "greys," and he was always writing polemics against Harlem nightclub owners who catered to white "slumming" parties. I take great pride in having played a part in modifying and perhaps even curing this extraordinary man's bigotry. By the time he left New York to return to Chicago, he had a host of white friends; and he had stopped attacking people in print just because of their color.

The most memorable time I spent in his company was on Christmas eve in 1946, when he threw a party, mostly for musicians, in his apartment on Edgecomb Avenue on what was called "Sugar Hill" by envious Harlemites too poor to live in that kind of luxury. It turned out to be the night of the biggest snow storm in the history of the city. Before the night was over we were as snowed in as you could ever get at the North Pole. Drifts were up to the second story of the buildings, and getting out the front door was out of the question. No traffic, of course, could get through. You couldn't even see the tops of the parked cars in the snow.

Dan had plenty of liquor on hand, but very little food, especially not for a siege like this. Among the guests were Albert Nicholas, Pops Foster, Lips Page, and an editor of the New York *Daily News* whose name was Macdonald. There was also a reporter, Ted Poston, who had once been an alto sax player who recorded with Jimmie Noone on those Apex Club Orchestra records. There was only one woman present, Una Mae Carlisle, the only female ever to sing on a Fats Waller record. After it was past the time when we all should have been gone, our resourceful host began a game by singing the first two lines of a blues as he played the piano and challenging anyone who could remember the last line to sing it. The winner got to sing the first two lines of another one. It's my recollection that this went on for several hours. We all enjoyed it despite our mounting hunger. In the process of fooling around with the music, Dan and Lips Page and I put together a tune and a lyric that would later enjoy a substantial popular success. It was titled "They Raided the Joint" and was recorded by various artists on a half-dozen different labels.

Una Mae sat in the bay window with a writing tablet and composed a piece which she sang and played for us that very night. Called "Walkin' by the River," it was destined to be the biggest hit of the following spring.

By now, the sun was shining brightly. Baby Dodds was just sitting and gaping out the window. Suddenly he yelled, "What's that?"

Dan opened the window and hauled in a huge basket of provisions that some good Samaritan had thoughtfully lowered either from the roof or from an upstairs window. I never did find out who our benefactor was. Una Mae and Dan understood about pancakes, and they spent a couple of hours feeding them to people, along with real maple syrup, apples, and coffee. Bill Chase, the *Amsterdam News* society editor was pleased that he could *now* write that it was a great party. The black thespian, Wardell Saunders, said he'd heard about starving actors but never expected to *be* one. We were able to leave at about three in the afternoon. The snowplows had done their work, and the inevitable subways still ran.

I always enjoyed going with Dan to the Harlem after-hours spots where performers gathered for their own recreation, when the theater lights went out and the night clubs closed. It wasn't easy for whites to get into these places, and I was fortunate to have Dan's sponsorship to make my admission comfortable. It was in just such a place, the Monroe Club, that he presented me with a small trophy proclaiming me Harlem's champion free-style rib-polisher after I had effectively attacked some barbecued ribs. The entertainment wasn't programmed, but we saw and listened to Milt Jackson and his quartet, which I think was the house band. We also heard Hazel Scott playing her piano boogie woogie and saw Pearl Primus, the modern dance sensation of the day, perform. Bojangles came in and said hello, but he didn't go on.

In later years, Dan wrote me occasionally from Chicago. I got a wedding invitation, and toward the end of his days he became a father. I always had a hard time picturing Dan Burley as a family man.

Allan Jaffe

In the jazz world I've known all kinds of musicians—hustlers, pimps, drug addicts, band managers, entrepreneurs, and booking agents. I've met my share of dilettantes, philanthropists, political proselytizers, politicians, cynics, and innocents. And very few people don't belong under one or another heading. There were and are people for whom I have felt deep and abiding personal respect, people who remain in my personal gallery of saints. For none of these individuals do I feel more admiration and affection than for Allan Jaffe, the proprietor of Preservation Hall and now the best jazz tuba player in New Orleans. He's one of the rare ones who thinks of a whole lot of other people before he thinks of himself.

I met Jaffe and his lovely wife Sandra the first week they were in New Orleans in 1961. They were newly married and Allan was fresh out of the University of Pennsylvania. He was just beginning his career as an efficiency expert in D. H. Holmes Department Store. Larry Borenstein owned the building that is now Preservation Hall; he had but recently invited me to take the place over and run it as a jazz "kitty hall." I persuaded him, quite properly, that there was no way I could make a success of it. I didn't have the patience, the business acumen, the inclination to relate to people in the fashion that was necessary to build Preservation Hall into the international shrine it has become. Allan Jaffe did, and I shared Larry's pride in watching the Hall grow in world stature and become an economic bonanza in Jaffe's hands. I could never have established the personal loyalties the musicians feel for Jaffe. I don't have the temperament to share their lives, their deaths, their domestic difficulties, to steer them through devastating illnesses and other personal crises. Jaffe doesn't tell, but *I* know the medical bills he's paid, how he's buried them and how he's helped their families financially afterward. And I know that my telling all this will embarrass him. But it needs to be told. I've seen talented but duplicitous musicians, knowing Jaffe wouldn't retaliate, doublecross and exploit him. They've flagrantly violated contracts, stolen jobs, ignored agreements when it suited them to do so—only to have Jaffe forgive and forget. He's able, apparently, to overlook any fault if the guilty party is a great jazzman.

I share with him the historian's interests, the social views, and the collector's passions. We have, for instance, had lots of fun going to auctions, rarely bidding against each other, but enjoying the game and acquiring treasures. One of our biggest laughs we found at an unclaimed freight auction where everything is in sealed, unmarked boxes. I think this one was at the Railway Express warehouse in New Orleans. One was not permitted to open any purchases on the premises. I bought a rather large box for fifteen dollars that contained a high-quality leather suitcase worth, today, maybe $150. I found in it a sterling silver cigarette case, which I later sold at auction for $70; a half-dozen superb Sulka neckties; a quart of Ballantine's 30-year-old scotch whiskey; and two quarts of Beefeater Gin.

Jaffe went to twenty dollars on a larger carton, approximately five cubic feet in size. He and Sandra took it home—all of us, of course, curious about the contents. Later in the day he called me and told me he had bought six thousand pairs of chopsticks. He was giving away chopsticks at the Hall for months afterward.

Once in 1970 I asked him to rent me the Hall for my wedding reception. Characteristically, he wouldn't permit me to pay him. Apparently one doesn't offer Jaffe money for anything. I'm happy for him that he can afford to refuse. Diana and I haven't thrown *that* big a party since. There were jazzmen everywhere. Alvin Alcorn led the band and Bill Russell recorded all the music.

Punch Miller didn't stutter when he sang, only when he talked, and he sometimes got out of hand in casual conversation. But there was never a stammer when he talked about Jaffe. "That man! I don' know—he's like a father, a son, a brother. I love that man. He got the *feelin'* when somebody else hurts. My God, the things he done for me!—what I *seen* him do for other people—not even musicians—. He come from heaven, Allan Jaffe. What would we all be *now* without him?"

As a kid in Pottsville, Pennsylvania, Allan used to listen, he tells me, to Journeys Into Jazz on his radio. I take more than a little pride in having contributed to the taste development that led him to settle in New Orleans and establish the framework that has provided a new life and prosperity for so many aging jazzmen.

When the history of the last days of authentic jazz is written, I have no doubt that the authors will think of those years and write of them as the Jaffe years. If all of the people who brought jazz to the public in the past had had Jaffe's qualities, jazz might still be a lusty and thriving art form.

Louis Prima

Outside of the years I spent in college, a few of my adult years were spent in Philadelphia. In 1946 and 1947 I was doing the Journeys Into Jazz radio shows and concerts there, supporting these vices by working in the advertising and publicity business. My favorite account was The Click, an enormous nightclub that contained the world's longest bar. The proprietor of this huge posh enterprise was the legendary Frank Palumbo, celebrated among band musicians as the most generous of all saloon keepers. He engaged me to publicize the place a couple of months before its opening on Labor Day of 1946.

My old New Orleans friend, Louis Prima, was booked as the opening attraction. The Click had a revolving stage, and its policy was to have two bands, for continuous music. As part of my initial public relations salvo I created the Frank Palumbo Award to the most valuable Philadelphia baseball player. After I went over the details with Frank, he said, "Hell, if you can get them to accept an award publicly from a saloon keeper, go ahead and do it."

As it happened, it wasn't all that easy to do—but I managed. I polled the sportswriters on the four daily papers, and they selected a pitcher, Schoolboy Rowe, for the honor. I had hoped they'd select one of the Phillies. The town had two major-league teams then, and the Phillies were going to be playing at home on Labor Day. I wanted to have Louis Prima make the presentation and play the Star Spangled Banner. All of this was fine with the Phillies.

I then went to Frank Dailey's Meadowbrook, a primary big-band spot in Caldwell, New Jersey, to talk over my plan with Louis, who was filling an engagement there. I hadn't seen him in quite a few years, and when I entered his dressing room he looked pale and exhausted. He was cold and withdrawn and it occurred to me that he might not recognize me. I was about to refresh his memory when his face brightened with the realization that I was someone from home.

"Al Rose!" he told himself. I nodded and we shook hands. He acknowledged that he wasn't feeling too well. Then he said, "I need to do a set before I come to life. Stay and watch and we'll talk later."

It was never easy to get used to the suddenness with which Louis' personality changed the instant he stepped on stage. He suddenly became an energy bomb, a whirlwind of action. His performance was always in high gear, filled not only with music but with wit, slapstick comedy, and at times some acrobatics. When he came off he was soaked with sweat, calm, and even sleepy looking.

I explained that I'd like for him to come into Philadelphia early enough to make the double-header so we could execute the ceremonies as planned. He agreed without apparent enthusiasm, though he was certainly aware that this kind of publicity could do him nothing but good. He was just exhausted after his appearance.

Back in Philadelphia I let the papers know he'd be on hand to play the national anthem at the game. But as soon as the paper came out the union called and told me he wouldn't. There's a rule that an out-of-town artist may only appear in the one place he's booked for. After some frantic telephoning, I actually got through to the czar himself, James Caesar Petrillo. "It's just the damn Star Spangled Banner!" I complained. "Who the hell listens to the Star Spangled Banner? The publicity will do Prima as much good as it does us."

Petrillo offered a compromise. "You got a decent reputation," he complimented me. "I know you never promote any nonunion jobs. I got a suggestion. He can walk out on the field. He can carry his horn. He can *sing* the Star Spangled Banner. The union has no jurisdiction over singing. That way the people get to see him and hear him. He can give away the car or the golf clubs or whatever. Okay?"

It was a tolerable compromise, and that's how the baseball fans got their first look at Louis Prima. I had arranged with sportscaster Byrum Saam to avoid radio commercials while our thing was going on. Between games I got out to the pitcher's mound and blew a police whistle to call the players into an infield conclave. They surrounded Louis and Schoolboy Rowe while the news photographers clicked away. A plane passed overhead trailing a streamer that announced, "Tonight . . . Louis Prima . . . The Click."

That night, 38,000 people triggered the electric eye counter at the entrance to the saloon, 3,000 more than the attendance at the ball park. Louis said, "When you were a kid I never thought you'd have the guts to pull off something like this."

"When *you* were a kid," I replied, "I didn't think you'd ever be able to memorize the Star Spangled Banner."

When Louis was very young, perhaps 17 (he was four years older than I), he was already a featured soloist in a theater pit orchestra. I can't remember whether it was Loew's State or the Strand. He was already the boy wonder of New Orleans jazz. I remember sitting in the theater and watching the single spot pick Louis up as he blew his hot chorus of "The Sheik of Araby." Later I asked him, "Have you ever thought of having a band of your own?"

He answered, "I already *had* that."

Adrian Rollini

All jazz collectors know the name of Adrian Rollini, who was not only an expert bass-saxophonist and xylophone virtuoso but also had the knack of getting jobs for himself and whatever group he happened to be performing with. For a time he was the proprietor of Adrian's Tap Room, a thirties jazz spot in New York. Some spectacular records that included Wingy Mannone were issued under the name of Adrian and His Tap Room Gang. He made countless records with Red Nichols, Bix Beiderbecke, and the California Ramblers. Toward the end of his musical career he was featured leading his own cocktail trio in New York at the Roosevelt Hotel. (Guy Lombardo was in the main room.)

On more than one occasion he told me he was going to "quit the music business and go fishin'." Since I'd heard that story from scores of musicians who never seemed to actually do it, I paid him no attention. However, Adrian did leave New York, and I never heard any more about him, musically.

In 1960, I bought a house in Key Largo, Florida, on Buttonwood Sound. I could catch snapper, grouper, tarpon, and lobsters from my dock. I was living alone at the time, which has always been easy for me to do as long as I had something to write on. I'd been in the place for maybe a week when I found it necessary to drive to Tavernier, about twelve miles down the road, to a tackle shop. On the edge of town I was startled to see a fairly large sign that advertised Adrian Rollini's Fishing Camp.

On my way back from the store, I pulled off the highway and took the indicated road to his place. He must have been out fishing. The premises were deserted and there was a padlock on the door. There was also a note that just said "7 PM." I left a note, too, telling him I'd been there and would stop by one day soon. My phone hadn't been installed yet, so I couldn't leave a number.

Several times I stopped by, taking a chance on catching him, and at last I did. I couldn't believe how different he looked. In his playing days, he worked so much you rarely got to see him in anything but a tuxedo. He wore his hair slicked down and parted in the middle, very shiny. His mustache looked like it had been made with an eyebrow pencil. He was the typical jazz age sheik, right out of a John Held, Jr., cartoon. Looking at this unshaven face under a disreputable fishing hat, I couldn't believe it was the same Rollini.

By that time I wasn't drinking anymore, but he was. We talked awhile about old times and our mutual friends. As we talked, I realized that he had really put the music business out of his mind. What he was genuinely interested in was fishing.

So here he was, renting small boats and equipment, apparently having the time of his life. After that we'd see each other now and then. Once we went to a bowling alley in Tavernier, but after we got there he changed his mind about bowling. I think, though, that it was the atrocious music on the public address system that chased him away. We spent a lot of time fishing off my dock, and several times we went bonefishing in one of his skiffs. He was quite expert and much more animated than in his performing days.

"Ah, the music!" he said one day. "The music is gone. The people who could play it, the people who *understood* it—they're all gone. The dancers are gone. What they want now is Beatles. You ever hear those four schmucks? But money! They can make more in a night than I made in a year. It would be different if they could play or sing or any goddamn thing. Ah, well. Whatever it is, we went through it before with Rudy Vallee. But no—this is something else. It's like a sickness, and this time I'm not sure the world will cure itself for a long time. In ten years you won't be able to find any real jazz—just a few schmucks with clown haircuts singin' stupid songs out-of-tune and making millions."

History has, of course, proven him a prophet. It had to be disillusioning to spend a lifetime making creative and beautiful and most of all *happy* music, to assume you were an organic part of a great cultural process, expecting to find your proper niche in the pantheon of musical gods, and then to watch the economic and aesthetic structure of the society crumble before the mindless and greedy huns who have come to dominate it.

So we fished. We put mullet heads on our hooks and fought it out with many a tarpon on the silent night waters of the Gulf of Mexico or in the calm South Atlantic. There were times when our muscles ached from hauling in and releasing the big fish. Some went over a hundred pounds. We never seemed to get tired of the sport and we hardly ever talked about music anymore.

Many months later I had to leave for a couple of months on business. From Tuscaloosa, Alabama, I read in the New York *Times* that Adrian Rollini had been brutally murdered in Tavernier. I'll not recall here the especially grisly details. His body was found in his pickup truck, and that was the end of his exciting, pioneering career. The crime was never solved. When I got home to Key Largo people were speculating that he had been killed in retaliation for robbing other people's lobster pots. But anybody who had known Adrian would have known that kind of thing wasn't in his character.

I didn't get to know many people in the Keys, and I missed his company. I wish I could tell you things he said about Jean Goldkette, Eddie Lang, Bix, and some of his other musical buddies, but the truth is we just never talked much about all that.

Stephane Grappelle

Hugues Panassie introduced me to Stephane Grappelle in the winter of 1936. Panassie was the first patron of jazz in France and the author of *Le Jazz Hot*, the first book ever written to acquaint the public with this art form. He organized the Hot Clubs of France, which produced the celebrated quintet records on which Grappelle and Django Reinhardt made their recording debuts.

Panassie picked me up in the eighth arrondissement where I was staying with Parisian friends. He had a congenitally deformed foot and walked laboriously with a cane. He took me to a place where the quintet was rehearsing for a session. There I met Charles Delauney, a quiet man who was then working on his "Hot Discography," the first such effort ever attempted.

We all went out to a large, low-priced, busy place to eat. My French was very rusty and the musicians spoke little or no English, though Reinhardt and I spoke Spanish and he translated some of the discussion for me. Django wasn't a stimulating personality; he was one of those vague and languid types who never think about anything besides music. Grappelle, on the other hand, was a dynamic, actively curious person, with a remarkable grasp of facts and contemporaneous events. He was Jewish, and he had what seemed to me then a morbid concern for the future of his nation, for the future of Jews throughout the world. I never for a moment thought that Adolf Hitler posed much of a threat to anybody except Germans.

Grappelle said, "These animals are a threat to the entire world—not only to us Jews, but to you, too. We must prepare ourselves for our defense—even survival. Anyone who thinks our French politicians, our generals, will protect us against the inevitable Nazi invasion doesn't understand that most of them are Nazis in their hearts." Three years later, exactly as he'd predicted, we saw the vaunted

Maginot Line crumble and watched the treachery of General Petain and Pierre Laval as they turned Paris over to the brown-shirted beasts.

Having been, in those days, a labor activist and militant anti-Fascist, I was in a position, during the worst days of the French occupation, to hear reports of the activities of the French underground. In the jazz world many of us came to know that Grappelle, a stupendous musician, was even more important as a hero of the resistance. This frail fellow endured torture, imprisonment, illness—more than anyone could have foreseen—not only to survive but to save many other lives by helping his compatriots gain freedom from Hitler's oppression. When I saw him again in 1949 and expressed my admiration for his heroism, he said it was only natural to protect oneself and one's own.

The last time Grappelle and I talked, in New Orleans in 1980 on the gallery of Johnny Donnels' photographic studio overlooking Royal Street in the French Quarter, those black days had receded in our memories and we could talk of our work, his violin and my writing. It crossed both our minds that the freedom to pursue our arts was a luxury we couldn't always guarantee ourselves.

At this 1985 writing, Grappelle is seventy-three and still doing the concert circuit, drawing substantial crowds. His virtuosity on the violin hasn't been approached by anyone in the jazz field.

George Cvetkovich

The young man told me that as a civilian he'd been a professional jazz saxophonist. I never did hear him play, but it was clear from his talk about life in Baltimore that he knew all the right people, that we shared many friends. From his manner I had no reason to doubt that he was involved with the music world.

He weighed whatever was the minimum required for someone to be drafted into the United States Army, and he told me how he'd starved himself in the weeks before his physical in an effort to become ineligible. He was also the shortest soldier I served with during my tour of duty, a service I approached just as reluctantly as he did. Through our six-week basic training course, Private Cvetkovich occupied the bunk next to mine in the dismal barracks at Fort Leonard Wood, Missouri, which, as any G.I. knew, was the American Siberia.

George and I got to know each other well. He needed me—not just to keep his morale up by talking of the delights of the jazz life, but also to help him to his feet when his eighty-plus pound field pack caused him to fall backward to the ground. We were required to wear these loads strapped to our backs for the ten-mile regulation saunters into the hustings. We shared a contempt for the unattractive terrain, the army, its institutions and customs. We were both against American involvement in World War II and had participated during our civilian days in active skirmishes with the law and against the Communists over the political issues involved.

Cvetkovich's concerns were two. One was finding a way out of the army, and the second was discovering a source of supply for Cannabis Sativa, which was as illegal a substance then as it is now. My exclusive concern was getting out of the army, by fair means or foul. That I achieved this with an honorable discharge was pure happenstance. Certainly I wasn't about to be picky about *what* kind of discharge I got.

Before we were shipped out of that legal concentration camp, we did manage to get one three-day pass with which we went to the nearest town, Jefferson City, where we set out in search of wine, women, and jazz. We found a form of the last being performed abominably in some establishment that was aspiring to be a dive. Somebody agreed to lend George a saxophone so he could participate. I didn't hang around. Bad music hurts me, and in certain circles my antipathy to saxophones is well known. Besides, seeing George absorbed in the awful music we were hearing made me realize he had a long way to go before he could ever be a jazzman. So I left. We got back to camp separately on a Sunday night, and George displayed with some enthusiasm several packets of cigarette papers he'd managed to acquire against some anticipated windfall of marijuana.

One miserable morning as we headed out in trucks for the rifle range, I heard a sharp intake of breath from him and I turned to notice an unaccustomed gleam in his eye. "I found it, Jack!" he whispered excitedly.

My name, of course, isn't Jack, but my diminutive Serbian colleague called *everybody* Jack, like you'd say, "Buddy" or "Kid."

That night he sneaked out of the barracks and didn't get back for a couple of hours. It was still dark. He whispered, "Hey, Jack! You awake?" I told him I was. "I found it, Jack!" he announced exultantly.

"I got it hid in a safe place to cure. By Friday you and me can get high enough to forget we're in the army."

During the week he disappeared many times for short periods, sometimes barely making it back in time to answer the endless bugle calls. He wasn't ready on Friday, but on Saturday night he announced that his magic carpet was ready to put in gear. I didn't feel any compulsion to smoke any gage (as we sometimes called it then), but I suppose I was ready for anything to relieve, even briefly, the miseries of a conscript. And so as the rest of the platoon passed the time in what our officers called, with straight faces, the recreation hall or did the jock thing on the lighted athletic field, Cvetkovich and I went into a nearby wooded area for a smoke. He was breathless with anticipation, already high with the prospect of things to come. I, less zealous, was certainly interested. George produced a rolled-up parcel that contained cigar-sized cylinders of his processed weed. We lit up.

The taste and aroma proved intolerable. For a moment I assumed that my tolerance for this stuff was demonstrably lower than George's. But then I noticed he had ceased to puff on this mini-haystack and was contemplating it with marked distaste.

"Shit!" he announced fervently. "This ain't it, Jack."

When we were shipped out of camp it was to different places. We wished each other early discharges. I told him I hoped he'd keep me posted about his musical career and that he'd find some proper marijuana before his stint was up. I did get one post card from him just before he went overseas. All it said was, "I got it, Jack."

Sidney Bechet

Reading Sidney Bechet's autobiography, *Treat It Gentle*, I had to accept the fact that the Bechet he was writing about had little in common with the Bechet I knew so well. His Bechet and mine both played soprano sax and clarinet. The kindly old gentleman in his book was filled with charity and compassion. The one I knew was self-centered, cold, and capable of the most atrocious cruelty, especially toward women.

As much as I admired his artistry, I couldn't help being appalled by his character. Toward his fans, his attitude ranged from indifferent to contemptuous. He could have been the prototype for what is now called "male chauvinist pig." I never discovered anything he wouldn't do for money; to my knowledge, he had absolutely no ethics, no principle or loyalty.

In 1937 I arranged a number of Journeys Into Jazz concerts in some of the Ivy League schools so people would get a chance to hear Bechet in person. The whole tour was for only ten days or so. We had appearances at Amherst, Tufts, Princeton, Brown, and Yale on the schedule. The band also included Muggsy Spanier, Jimmy Archey, Baby Dodds, Pops Foster, and Joe Sullivan. In the back of my mind is a banjo player, too. It would have been either Danny Barker or Lee Blair, though I don't remember which. Bechet was just off the road playing in Noble Sissle's orchestra in vaudeville. In the universities, I usually did a little historical commentary and the band played appropriate, illustrative pieces. We were sponsored by the music departments of the schools we performed in.

Every now and then Bechet showed a flash of humanity. Once we were getting ready to leave our hotel suite in New Haven. He was waiting for me to put on my tie, a function that took me an inordinate amount of time back in my days of sartorial impeccability. Sidney said, "You sloppy son-of-a-bitch—you got no tie clip?"

I confessed I rarely wore one.

"So," he pursued, "you gonna let your goddam tie flap around in the wind?"

There hadn't seemed to be any unusual breezes. He fished around in a little leather case on his dresser and came up with a goldstone tie clip which he handed to me. "Put it on!" he instructed. "Any son-of-a-bitch goes anyplace with Sidney Bechet gotta look like a gentleman."

On reflection I had to assume this was Bechet's way of proffering a gift, and I thanked him warmly for this gesture.

"Shit!" he said. "I give you that for *me*. When you ain't with me I don't give a shit whether you wear a tie clip or not!"

I wore it, I think, in 1970 at the ragtime festival in St. Louis. Walt Gower, the clarinetist with the Mothers Boys Jazz Band of Detroit, was expressing his admiration for the work of Bechet. He said he was sorry he never had the chance to hear Bechet when he was alive. I told him about the tie clip and took it off and gave it to him. Walt still wears it, whether he's sporting a tie or not.

In concerts I was always in arguments with Sidney about his soprano sax solos. No matter what other stars were on the stand with him, he always assumed the audience wasn't interested in them. "Tell Muggsy not to play so loud behind me. I don't need no other horns with me."

It was my rule that Sidney was only permitted to play a single soprano specialty in each half of the concert. (I grant that a large portion of the audience would have been grievously disappointed if he hadn't.) The rest of his time on the stand he had to play the clarinet. I never heard anyone who could play clarinet better in the front line than Sidney.

Bechet resented any restraints and never stopped complaining. "What you think them people is payin' to hear? Bechet! Not no fuckin' piano player [Joe Sullivan] or some half-assed trombone tooter [Jimmy Archey]. They want Bechet! You hear! Bechet!"

I never even gave him star billing—just more money than he'd make anywhere else at the time.

He had this hit record out, Gershwin's "Summertime." It was very good for what it was, and he played it with some hot overtones. But he worked it like a rhapsody and it didn't have any real jazz character, though it was a perfect vehicle for his unchallenged virtuosity. Bechet played it at every performance. And—just to irritate me, I think—he would take two or three additional improvised choruses, breathtaking and dazzling, that would drive the crowd crazy. On these occasions, they'd applaud wildly, stamp their feet, and whistle loudly. He'd look offstage to me for permission to do an encore and when I was certain the crowd noises would not abate, I'd grudgingly signal for him to continue. Once in Philadelphia, I let him take two encores.

"I want them people to remember me," he told me. "That's the onliest way I'll ever get into the big money. Them other musicianers, they gone as far as they can go. But not Bechet! You wanna get any-place in this world, you gotta look out for number one."

I must mention that Bechet had a consuming hobby, photogra-phy. I know he liked to take pictures of naked ladies, a preference consistent with his exploitative bent toward females. He seemed, even on the bandstand, to be constantly clicking the shutters of the cameras that always hung from his neck. One evening the two of us were standing on the steps of the Philadelphia Academy of Music waiting for an attendant to come and unlock the doors. I was holding his instrument cases, and he was weighted down with enough accoutrements to film an edition of *National Geographic*. As a younger man, similarly laden, walked by, he and Sidney recognized each other and exchanged greetings, though Sidney displayed no sign of cordiality.

Pointing to one of the man's cameras, he demanded, "How much you want for that?"

"I don't want to sell it, Sid. I just got it," the man replied.

Bechet turned away and the man introduced himself to me. His name was Emmett Matthews, no mean soprano saxist himself and a member of the internationally acclaimed Red Caps. He tried a little small talk on Bechet; but since Sidney ignored him, he left us with polite goodbyes. I mentioned to Sidney that he hadn't treated this acquaintance very considerately.

"He wouldn't sell me his camera!" Bechet pouted, with irritation. "He ain't got nothin' else I want and I don't need him to give me sax lessons."

Bechet never showed me any of his photographs, even the ones he took of me with various musicians. He promised to have a set made for me, but he never bothered to do it.

One night after a concert, I paid him his thirty-five dollars. Then after counting the exceptionally high box office receipts, I handed him an extra hundred. He didn't even thank me, though I never failed to thank any musician when he finished a concert of mine. The next time I called Bechet for a gig he said, "I ain't comin' unless I get seventy dollars."

Now, nobody in the world valued Bechet more as an artist than I, but I knew there were limits to his box-office value. My musicians were always guaranteed scale, and they got bonuses according to the night's take. I asked Bechet if he ever worked a job for me that hadn't brought him more than seventy dollars. He told me he didn't remember.

"You want to take this job for a flat eighty bucks and no extras?" I pressed.

He hung up on me.

For that concert I hired Edmond Hall.

Tom Brown

The music we have come to call Dixieland made its debut north of the Mason-Dixon Line under the leadership of Tom Brown, born in

New Orleans on June 3, 1888. He and his Band from Dixieland made their bow at Lamb's Cafe in Chicago in 1915, and that started it all. Tom played a thoroughly satisfying trombone, and his influence on succeeding sliphorn players was universal. He was not merely an innovator but a protean performer capable of filling every ensemble hole, in and out of his register.

He was also as thorough a bigot as the sunny South ever produced. He provided leadership to a tiny group of peanut-brained musicians, many of whom, I must say in fairness, were among the greatest jazzmen New Orleans ever produced. But this crackbrained coterie effectively kept black and white musicians in the Crescent City from playing together for two generations. Not that there weren't some outstanding white jazzmen, like Johnny Wiggs and Armand Hug, who had no prejudice. Nevertheless some of them refrained from performing with black musicians for fear of being blacklisted by their colleagues. Raymond Burke, Harry Shields, and Boojie Centobie, a trio of super clarinetists, were indifferent personally to the color line; but except for recording sessions, they refused to work mixed band jobs for me, though Raymond never objected to sitting in informally with black musicians.

Yet Tom Brown, except for this neurosis, could be a charming, friendly fellow. We did do a few things together in the fifties. But since he was nearly illiterate and, where music was concerned, opinionated to the point of rejecting any concept he hadn't initiated, the potential for a working relationship was very narrow indeed. For a time, late in his life, he attempted to operate a small job-printing business. But he was frequently handicapped by his inability to spell simple words. I gave him a job once over the phone—printing personal cards for me—but he spelled the street I lived on then "St. Louse Street" and insisted I should have spelled out "St. Louis" over the phone if I was going to be so picky.

One Monday evening in 1954, I was managing the regular monthly meeting of the New Orleans Jazz Club in the University Room of the Roosevelt Hotel. I invited Tom to sit in with a group of his peers. He said, "I've got my mouthpiece, but I ain't got my teeth," a fact I could plainly see. "But if y'all don' mind," he offered, "I might take a crack at it."

And without teeth he played as beautifully as any trombone man you ever heard. In fact, for interested collectors, if you own the

Southland album (reissued on GHB) of Johnny Wiggs and his Jazz
Kings with Tom Brown on trombone, you have a textbook performance of trombone in the jazz band. Tom didn't have his teeth in for
that either.

His ethnic hostilities were apparent in virtually every musical
comment he ever made to me—as though he, personally, were constantly under attack by racial groups other than his own.

> Them foreigners don't want to hear no jazz unless a nigger's playin' it.
>
> You notice how the dagoes get all the hotel jobs? You ever hear Castro
> Carrazo at the Roosevelt? He can't play nothin'.
>
> It ain't like the old days. They got Jews movin' uptown.
>
> There's niggers in De La Salle High School. Now they wanna eat
> in white restaurants and sit in the white section of the trolley cars, the
> movies—everywhere.

Once I mentioned a concert I had presented in New York and
mentioned that Albert Nicholas had been playing the clarinet. He
snorted and reminded me, "Come on, Al! You know niggers ain't no
good on clarinet. Them thick blubbery lips can't make no decent
tone."

I pointed out that Nick didn't have thick, blubbery lips. But Tom
replied, "That ain't the only thing. They ain't smart enough to tell
where the harmony is, neither. After all, they niggers." Thus was my
understanding of ethnology augmented by the wisdom of Tom Brown.

Even now, a quarter-century after his death in March of 1958,
this attitude survives among some white jazzmen of New Orleans.
It is, of course, encouraging to see it declining, but I can't guess how
long it will be before that brand of stupidity vanishes from among
the very people for whom it is least appropriate.

George Girard

It's impossible to write of any phase in the history of jazz, most especially a first-person account, without finding oneself constantly dealing
with bigotry, meanness, and the gross insensitivities that are just as
prevalent in jazz as in the rest of our society. Such character flaws are
not, of course, restricted to white, southern musicians. And from time
to time, I've even made the joyful discovery that not all southern jazzmen are cast in this mold.

One of the noblest young men New Orleans jazz ever produced was George Girard, who died in 1957 at the age of twenty-seven. George played the trumpet and was the original leader of the Basin Street Six in which teenaged Pete Fountain played the clarinet. His trumpet sound, admittedly inspired by Bunny Berigan, had reached an exceptional proficiency, and its superior quality was matched by his entertainment skills. Representative of the musical school identified with Louis Prima, Wingy Mannone, and Sharkey, George was a true gentleman—thoughtful and considerate, concerned for the welfare of others.

One night in 1954 I was preparing the usual all-star session that was part of every monthly meeting of the New Orleans Jazz Club at the Roosevelt Hotel. One of the members, Don Perry, met me on Royal Street and mentioned to me that Lee Collins was in town. "It's a shame we can't have him playing at the meeting," Don said.

"Why not?" I asked, with the naivete that has oftentimes enveloped me.

My esteemed colleague was surely skeptical about my astonishment in learning that we were operating under an unwritten segregation law. But since I had for years been presenting Journeys Into Jazz concerts in more civilized climes, I had failed to notice that a color line survived in this one. I'd been away too long.

I promptly invited Lee Collins to attend and to perform. I even arranged to pick him up myself and to see that he wasn't required to go upstairs via the service elevator. With Lee ensconced backstage, I had a talk with George Girard. I planned to bring Lee out during George's forty-minute stint, and I asked if he'd mind going to a little trouble to make the old maestro comfortable.

"A great musician like Lee Collins!"—and I was shocked at an actual tear in George's eye—"to think you'd have to ask a jazzman to treat him like a human being!" The tear ran down George's ample nose. He was an emotional kid.

I made no prior announcement to the audience. My plan was just to bring Lee on, let him play, then wait to see who raised an objection. Lee told me he'd heard that black musicians never played at the Jazz Club. I decided that if I got any flack from the board, I'd just resign with a public—and published—statement of my reason. The more I contemplated the confrontation, the more hostile I became.

Then I found myself on stage. Turning my head, I could see Lee Collins standing in the wings. George and his New Orleans Five stood behind me as I was saying to the crowd, "And now, friends, here's an unscheduled treat to delight you. We have with us tonight one of the great masters of hot trumpet. It's been my pleasure in the past to introduce him on some of the most prestigious stages in this nation. And it's an honor and a privilege now for the first time to present him in my own home town—and his. Ladies and gentlemen, Mr. Lee Collins." I thought I could hear some sharp intakes of breath, but in a split second I was conscious of applause behind me. As I turned and joined in, I could see George and his band clapping their hands vigorously and smiling broadly. Then the audience joined in the swelling crescendo as Lee walked sedately to the center of the stage, carrying his brilliantly polished, golden horn. He was, as usual, beautifully groomed and poised, with all the confidence you'd expect of an outstanding performing artist.

I don't remember what he opened with or what his program consisted of. I do recall that it was all superb. But even more, I remember George Girard submerging his well-known ebullience to concentrate on playing magnificent, skillful, and deliberate second trumpet, using his horn to showcase every nuance of Lee's performance. Lee, of course, was both musician and showman enough to be aware from the start of George's intent and the masterful effectiveness of his efforts. The combination of his gratitude and affection reflected itself in every phrase Lee played. The audience, whatever the philosophical flaws of some of its members, was enthralled by the overriding beauty of the performance. They responded with volcanic applause.

At the end, George embraced Lee—even kissed him. Louis Scioneaux (now Sino), the trombonist, stepped up to shake Lee's hand, and the rest of the band filed by to do the same. George thanked me for giving him the opportunity to play behind Lee.

As I left the stage, George Blanchin, who was president of the club that year, said to me, "Another great show, Al!"

I never heard a critical word. After that we had mixed groups on the stage right along, and nobody thought anything of it. Their comments always pertained only to the quality of the music.

I wrote George a personal letter of appreciation, expressing my admiration for his handling of this delicate circumstance. Now he's been gone for a quarter-century, and I continue to think of this fine young gentleman with the same warmth and affection, wishing all jazzmen shared his personal generosity and sympathetic understanding.

James P. Johnson

There's a kind of piano playing I never could work up any enthusiasm for. I can't label it "stride," since I was always transfixed by the performances of folks like Luckey Roberts and, later, Don Ewell. On the other hand, Fats Waller, Willie "The Lion" Smith, and Art Tatum, despite their unquestioned brilliance and dazzling virtuosity, always seemed to me more engaged in solving problems of their craft than in bringing to the audience the kinds of thrills that I think should be at the core of every jazzman's art.

Even though my personal taste rebelled against it, I nevertheless frequently employed James P. Johnson to play in my concert jazz bands. I'm sure many will agree that James P. left a lot to be desired as a band pianist, but there's no doubt that, especially in solos, his proficiency was outstanding. I never could understand why, but Journeys Into Jazz audiences never seemed to get enough of James P. My musician friends, notably Eubie Blake and Luckey Roberts, had a boundless admiration for his pianistics.

Irrespective, though, of my musical appraisal, I found James P. to be grossly unreliable. When I stopped hiring him it wasn't because of the way he played, but because I couldn't rely on him either to show up or to be in satisfactory condition when he did. But I've been in audiences that included Don Lambert, Luckey, Eubie, and Willie "the Lion"—all mesmerized by James P. at the piano.

One night in Philadelphia in 1946, I had a concert going on at the Academy of Music. As curtain time approached it became increasingly apparent that I would have to face the crowd without a piano player. James P. was nowhere to be seen. I looked out through a slit in the curtain to see if I could see any competent keyboard star who might have come in as a paying customer. In the past, in similar exigencies, people from the audience like Frank Signorelli or Arthur Schutt had come to my rescue. This time I saw no musicians I recognized. Backstage, I told the members of the band what we were up against. There wasn't time to call the union and get a replacement sent over. Then Max Kaminsky, whom I had engaged to play the trumpet that evening, said, "I brought a friend along as my guest. He's not a professional musician, but he's a very good piano player. He can handle it."

It didn't seem likely to me that there was anybody in the world who could "handle it" that I wouldn't already know about. I said, "My audiences expect to see the best jazz musicians in the world—that's why *you're* here. I just can't sit anybody on that piano stool. I don't want this to sound like a high school band."

Max seemed a tad indignant. "I wouldn't have suggested it if I wasn't sure he was good enough!"

So I asked Kaminsky to find his friend and bring him to me. In a few minutes he was back with a short, stocky, wavy-haired lad who looked more like a freshman in accounting school than a jazz piano player. Max said, "Al, I want you to meet George Wein."

I said, "Do you think you can play with this band?"

"I think so," he said, matter-of-factly. "I've played with Max and some of his friends before. Not for money, though."

"Well, here goes," I thought to myself as I went on stage to greet the audience and introduce the musicians. Among them that night were, I think, Brad Gowans and Pee Wee Russell.

"And on piano," I heard myself saying, "in place of James P. Johnson [Groan], who was supposed to be here and isn't [Groan], a young man from Connecticut who has established himself, etc. etc. . . ."

George Wein was sensational. As a band piano player, I found him infinitely superior to James P., though, naturally, he couldn't match the master's solo virtuosity. The crowd was extremely responsive, and I have to believe the young man was heartened by the enthusiastic acceptance. For my part, I was massively relieved.

As the first half ended and I came on to announce the intermission, there was James P. sauntering down the center aisle toward the stage. He was profusely apologetic, had obviously been drinking, but didn't seem as bombed out as I'd had him before. I announced that James P. had turned up, introduced him, and told the crowd he'd perform during intermission.

In the second half, I didn't ask him to play with the band, frankly because I found Wein's performance more satisfactory. At the end, I paid James P. off for the whole night's work, promising myself he'd never again appear on a stage under *my* auspices. I paid George Wein the same amount and thanked both him and Max for saving the day. As for George Wein, he impoverished jazz both by quitting the piano and by producing his festivals. James P.? Of course I never hired him again, though there were occasions later when he asked me to. The last time I talked with him, we were in Tom Delaney's club in Harlem and I heard him say, "All this *jazz* business. I always wanted to be a musician—not a jazz musician. Any son-of-a-bitch can play that!"

I thought to myself, "I know one son-of-a-bitch who can't."

Chris Burke

There have always been magical people in this world, individuals found in unlikely places, catalyzing their environments into something infinitely better than without them. With an aura of indestructibility, agelessness, magnetic charm, they make legends. Two such flowered in Nottingham, England; one was the romantic and elusive Robin Hood, who gave the sheriff fits, stole from the rich, gave to the poor, and in general comported himself like a carefree adolescent in springtime. The other is the elfin and resourceful Chris Burke, who, by 1985, had become a fixture in the world of New Orleans music.

I became aware of Chris sometime in the early seventies. I'd see him around with other musicians during Jazz Festival time when so many Europeans mill around Preservation Hall to hear and talk to— possibly play with—the old-time New Orleans performers who are featured nightly. To my knowledge, nobody ever hired Chris to play his clarinet or saxophone, for the acceptable reason that he sounded miserable. But he really had something going for him. Not prepossessing to look at, short and slim, he nevertheless attracted young girls with a kind of magnetism much envied in jazz circles. His quick wit and geniality make him an ideal master of ceremonies. He could as well have been a stand-up comic as anything else.

He would seek me out to satisfy his insatiable thirst for information about jazzmen and the history of the music. He was much interested in my reaction to his musical performance, which I gave him with all the tact I could muster. And because he was really serious about his music, he wasn't offended, but rather always seemed to be paying close attention to what I said. In any case, we became good friends and he graciously invited Diana and me to visit him on our next trip to England. We did go in 1976 and, after spending a week or so in London, we proceeded to Nottingham to see the castle, Sherwood Forest, and Chris.

Chris proved to be a superlative host. He showed us the sights, including Yeats's Tavern, where a superannuated gentleman with an excellent violin and an elderly lady sitting at the piano played popular music of a bygone era—even before my time. When they learned that Americans were present, they honored us by playing perhaps the only yankee tune they knew, "Old Black Joe." We had occasion to listen briefly to Chris playing his clarinet with a couple of superb local musicians—Maggie Kinson, an outstanding pianist who has since made her home in New Orleans, and a trumpet man, Teddy Kullick, easily the best we heard in Europe.

Our next proposed stop was at Stratford-Upon-Avon and Chris, when he heard that, spontaneously volunteered to take us there in his van. He told us of his beautiful sister (a stand-in for Elizabeth Taylor) and her husband, the set designer for the BBC series "Upstairs, Downstairs." They had recently purchased the grand Eddington Manor, which dated back to the eleventh century and had eighty bedrooms. The trip devoured most of a day, including stops on the highway at some of the very worst eating places into which I've ever ventured. The English stoutly defend certain things as edible which, I submit, should at the very least be called controversial. A glutinous mass they lightly call "trifle," contrived of wallpaper paste and thin milk, seems to be legal, even though it can reduce strong men to catatonia.

We spent the evening in what had been the great dining hall of Eddington Manor and which had been converted into one of the most satisfying pubs to be found in the civilized world. Five young men sang beautiful English folk ballads in exquisite harmony, and then we went to bed in a room as cold as the tone of Perez Prado's trumpet.

Sometime afterward I had occasion to hear Chris perform again in New Orleans, and I noticed at once that his facility in the lower register showed marked improvement, as did his tone. I recall lecturing him a time or two on the role of the clarinet in the authentic New Orleans jazz band. He told me he'd taken some lessons from Barney Bigard, and they'd obviously helped. Then Barrie Martyn, the superior English drummer and impresario, had hired Chris to go on the road with his Legends of Jazz for a European tour as band manager. Chris wrote to me frequently about their progress and his delight that Barney was one of the "legends." The aging maestro apparently helped Chris a great deal.

Chris came back to New Orleans and married an American girl (whose name is Chris, too), and became a citizen. Early in 1985, while in New Orleans, I stopped by the Gazebo in the French Market where he was playing with the best band I'd heard in many years. He gave me a copy of a new LP they'd made, which I've played perhaps thirty times by now. Chris, happy as can be, has become part of the city's jazz establishment. His dress is more subdued, and he's divested himself of his golden earring. And even though this appraisal is sure to embarrass him, there's no doubt in my mind that he's become the best jazz clarinet player in New Orleans, that his taste and understanding of the form will eventually win him a pedestal in the pantheon of Crescent City jazz gods.

Eddie Condon

We were walking together toward our rooms in the Downtowner Motor Inn in Manassas, Virginia. I was the only one sober enough to count that there were three of us on that winter night in 1969. There was me, for one. I was in Manassas to attend Johnson McCree's annual jazz bash at the local high school. I also counted Bob Greene, the shadow of Jelly Roll Morton, but not the Johnny Walker he was carrying. And finally I counted Eddie Condon, who was, by this time, no longer speaking, but dedicating his not inconsiderable powers of concentration to getting his room key out of his pocket. Our three rooms were situated in a row, with Eddie's in the middle. We told each other goodnight and retired. It may have been two in the morning.

Since it takes me no time to get to sleep, I'd gotten a full hour of shut-eye when a sudden loud and eerie noise set me rigidly upright in bed. I went through the process of satisfying myself that I was in a motel room. A little added attentiveness retrieved for me the fact that I was in Manassas. And with the noise level increasing as it was, I deduced that someone had broken into Condon's room and was in the process of pulling his fingernails out.

I immediately put on my bathrobe and charged out into the frigid night to rescue our little friend from the demented attackers. Once outside, I noted that Bob Greene, too, had emerged from his room. We faced each other in front of Condon's door and I tried the knob. No dice. Bob knocked. The painful groans and screeches continued unabated. I stepped back, preparatory to charging the door with the intent of breaking it down. Just as I was about to make my initial lunge, we saw Phyllis, Eddie's wife, coming our way down the walk and carrying what looked like an overnight bag.

"Good morning, boys," she greeted us, reacting not a tittle to the howls and screams we knew she couldn't help hearing. "Trouble getting to sleep?"

"Eddie's in trouble!" Bob shouted excitedly.

Phyllis had her room key out. "No," she said calmly. "He's all right. He's just singing. He sings in his sleep." Phyllis explained that she was the one who always checked them in at hotels. Without telling Eddie, she always rented an extra room so *she* could get some sleep, too. Then, early in the morning, she would join him in his room and he would never know the difference.

We still insisted on looking inside after she opened the door, just to make sure that this time it wasn't mayhem instead of music. We saw Eddie, flat on his back, still fully dressed, emitting these terrifying sounds. Having satisfied ourselves that he was indeed alone, we left Phyllis with him and returned to our rooms. The last thing I said to Bob was, "Everybody Loves My Baby."

We met Eddie in the coffee shop at noon, and I began to report to him the events of the early morning. Halfway through the recital, he interrupted, turned in his chair, and stared squarely into my face. "Who the hell are you?" he demanded.

Now it's true that we hadn't seen each other for many years, and it's also true that in that long interval my appearance had changed far more than his. I said, "Wake up, Eddie. I'm Al Rose."

He said, "The hell you are! Al Rose is a tall, skinny guy with glasses—and he's got no beard! Who the hell are you?"

Bunny Berigan

By 1937, Bunny Berigan had already hit the big time. He was still playing with Tommy Dorsey, but the fans had begun to note his name. And among his peers he had achieved optimum status as a sideman.

What we did together, mainly, was drink. We had our favorite places in the Village. He wasn't a very social person and didn't associate much with other musicians. He wanted to talk about philosophy, infinity, psychology, or anything else that made him feel he was untangling the riddles of the universe. He wanted to know why he, or anybody else for that matter, was alive, and whether it was worth it. These considerations often made him irritable, and his impatience with the stupidity around him was ever apparent.

He was always looking for quiet places where there was no music—places where one could talk. Although we shared an avid interest in the opposite sex, we never went on double dates. Our forays into the saloon life of downtown New York were always "between dates."

Bunny's custom was to carry several packages of chewing gum in his pocket, not because he was addicted to the vigorous mastication of chicle. He had an even more practical use for the stuff. He'd put three or four sticks of gum in his mouth as we approached a boite with liquor in mind. Once inside, we'd sit at the bar and order our drinks. Then he'd excuse himself, promising to come back in a moment. He would walk purposefully off, to the men's room I assumed incorrectly. Early on I discovered that what he was doing was finding the jukebox, putting a wad of Wrigley's Doublemint through the coin slot, then pushing the slide in to assure the device's inoperability for at least as long as we'd be there enjoying our drinks. He'd return to the bar secure and relaxed in the knowledge that our ears wouldn't be assaulted by bad music. Later on I took to doing that myself.

Bunny had a statement to make on that entire subject. "There's no reason in the world why some stupid son-of-a-bitch with a nickel should have the right to impose his tastes on a room full of people."

During the late thirties most big cities had one hotel with an entire floor reserved for the personnel of the big dance bands that succeeded each other week after week at the main theater or night spot in town. In New York it was the Manger (now renamed the Taft); in Chicago, the Stevens; in Cleveland, the Morrison; in Philadelphia, the Ritz-Carlton. Bellhops, prostitutes, and liquor vendors took a great interest in knowing which band was "in" during any given week. A sedate group like, for example, Sammy Kaye's, traveled with wives, played bridge, and created a kind of mobile suburbia—no whores, very little alcohol, no festivity. That meant reduced increments for the hotel force and the local ladies of the evening.

There were a couple of celebrated bands in that era that were composed entirely of gays. (They didn't call them "gays" in those days.) The leader of one of these, who happened to be straight himself and well-known for his unusual trombone solos, explained that it was easier to travel with a gay band. They rarely got in any trouble and usually just hung around in the hotel together. It's no secret in the hotel business that gays don't tip very well as a rule.

But the purveyors of the elemental vices always had a field day when Berigan came to town. Then you needed a written pass to get off the elevator at their floor. Some of the most orgiastic nights of my life were spent in this select company in New York and Philadelphia. Those evenings gave me a new slant on living. How the musicians survived through an entire tour, with every night given over to this sort of merrymaking after putting in a gruelling night's work, I'll never know. There were a few other bands that followed this pattern. Wingy Mannone's was considered to be runner-up to Berigan's in free-style high jinks. For a brief spell a crew led by Johnny "Scat" Davis screamed like a comet through the beds of the nation's hostelries. Gene Krupa's band earned an honorable mention from bell captains everywhere. But with *them*, Berigan reigned supreme.

Berigan never really made it economically with his band, despite his enormous success with his theme, "I Can't Get Started." He had no business sense whatever and he was a soft touch for anybody with a hard-luck story. Drummer George Wettling played with that band at its peak. He once said to me, "You see, it's possible for as smart a guy as Berigan not to have any sense at all."

Bunny died in 1942 while in the employ of Tommy Dorsey. They called it pneumonia, but he really died from not having any sense. But there's no doubt he had some great ideas. I *still* carry chewing gum.

Alvin Alcorn

The year was 1976—the American Bicentennial. Alvin Alcorn and I sat on the deck of a bateau in the Seine and I said, "Back in the late thirties—I think that must be when we first met—could you have dreamed that one day we'd be sitting here on a boat in Paris with you telling me that you and the band had to fly back to Louisville tomorrow to play for the Kentucky Derby but that you'd be back here in Paris on Monday?"

"You didn't do no flyin' nowhere in them days, let alone across the ocean!" he reminded me. "And lookit you! You be goin' with Averty to the National Palace to autograph books for the *president*. . . . And you don't even *play* nothin'."

I pursued the pleasant subject. "And parading down the Champs Elysees with fourteen New Orleans style jazz bands? What a week! Speeches, TV cameras, thousands in the streets."

Alvin just shook his head and said, "We must have done somethin' right."

The Republic of France was celebrating Louisiana Week. Alvin, with his Imperial Brass Band, and I were guests-of-honor through an endless series of exciting events. There were a few other Americans around. Rotund Phil Johnson, WWL's television newsman, displayed unexpected agility running the streets with his shoulder camera, making what would become an award-winning documentary. There was impresario John Shoup, looking dazed and happy with his part in organizing the celebration. And I thanked my stars for one-time sax player Pierre Salinger, who came to my rescue when I got stage fright while presenting the Key to the City of New Orleans to Madame Jacqueline Boudrier, the Minister of Communications of France. I lost confidence in my rusty French, and Salinger, magnificently bilingual, translated my remarks to the distinguished audience.

Through this hectic week, Alcorn surveyed the scene as impassively as a sphinx. The years, which seem never to age him, had put him in countless unexpected situations—like playing a bit in a James Bond movie. In the first scene of *Live and Let Die*, Alcorn sidles quietly beside an unsuspecting parade watcher and sticks a knife in his ribs. After that we called him the "Baby Faced Killer."

He and his band joined my wife Diana and me at Kennedy Center in Washington, D.C., in 1980 to supply the music for the opening of our traveling exhibit, "Played with Immense Success," which toured under the auspices of the Smithsonian Institution through the three subsequent years. (That was a social history of New Orleans from 1840 to 1940 as shown in its published sheet music. Diana and I wrote the text with Vaughn Glasgow of the Louisiana State Museum.)

Alvin looks like a sun-tanned "Poppin' Fresh, Pillsbury Doughboy." He's got more friends and is more respected than any other musician in New Orleans. When I have guests visiting me and I'm showing the Crescent City off, Alvin is always on my tour. I think the guest who enjoyed him the most was my late friend Louis Alter, whom I took to Commander's Palace for Sunday brunch so Alvin could play a tune Louis wrote. Alvin put his mute an inch from Alter's ear and whispered his version of "Do You Know What It Means to Miss New Orleans." Alter, though he'd written the piece thirty-five years earlier, had never been in the city before. When he got back to New York he wrote me a letter in which he said, "*Now* I know what it means to miss New Orleans."

Way back in 1954, during a rehearsal for a recording session of the Papa Celestin Orchestra, I said to Papa, "The 'Li'l Liza Jane' piece is going to need a hot trumpet chorus, probably. Are you going to play it?"

He answered, "No. I got Alvin Alcorn comin' in to do that. When I make records, I need to have a *real* trumpet player."

Alvin's professional attitude is relaxed. When you play music for a living you have to perform some real garbage. But Alvin always loved to play genuine New Orleans jazz with a half-dozen of the city's finest on a record session. We had one such afternoon in the Royal Orleans Hotel's luxurious Esplanade Room, which manager Archie Casbarian had thoughtfully made available to us. I was producing one of the records for the State of Louisiana Department of Commerce and Industry series. We had on hand not only Alvin, but trombonist Wendell Eugene, Harry Shields on clarinet, and a matchless rhythm section consisting of Armand Hug on the piano, Danny Barker on the guitar, Chester Zardis playing bass, and Josiah "Cie" Frazier on drums. We opened with "Wang Wang Blues," all driving rhythm and tight ensemble play. When it was over, Alvin set his trumpet down and said, "*That's* what we used to call jazz!"

Muggsy Spanier

The Ochsner Clinic in New Orleans is world famous for its cancer research and for alerting the nation to the extreme dangers of tobacco. Smoking, of course, is not permitted in the hospital. Dr. Alton B. Ochsner was very specific on that point.

Muggsy Spanier, the great jazz trumpet star, though his entire musical career was spent outside the South—Chicago, New York, and California—headed for New Orleans when he was in need of physical rehabilitation. It is to that fact that we owe such recorded classic blues titles as "Relaxin' at the Touro," which pays its respects to the renowned Touro Infirmary where I, as well as scores of other jazzmen, was born.

The last time Muggsy was with us, during the sixties, he was ensconced in a prime room at Ochsner; and whatever his symptoms, he was in the best of spirits. Edmond Souchon and I visited him shortly after he was admitted. After he asked me to shut the door the very first thing he did was to fish into his bathrobe and come up with a package of cigarettes and some matches.

"This is the last pack I've got," he told us. "They took away all I had in my suitcase. They've got a smoking rule in this place. I don't know how I'm gonna get through the next ten days."

I tried to get him off the subject, asking him how he liked living in Sausalito. He told me of the glories of California's Garden of Eden. I asked him if he ever saw Henry Miller, whom we both knew from New York, and he said he'd seen him a time or two. Then he told Sou a hair-raising story of a time nearly twenty years earlier when I'd called him at the Picadilly Hotel in New York, where he was living, to ask him to book a room for the week-end for the refugee playwright, Ernst Toller. Toller had fled his native Austria after having been, for a brief period, through a freak of circumstances, the dictator of Bavaria. New York was full of conventions, and there was not a room to be found. I had been delegated by a mutual friend to secure housing for this man who had a hit show on Broadway at the time entitled "Re-union in Vienna." It just happened that Muggsy was going to be out of town himself that week-end and he generously offered to let the author use his room. He'd warned me that the place might not be too neat, but said he'd notify the desk clerk to give me the key.

I brought Toller to the Picadilly, took him up to Muggsy's digs, and left. By the time I got down to the lobby in the elevator, Toller had made it a faster way—jumping the fourteen or so floors from Muggsy's window to the sidewalk below. I saw the mob in the street when I left the hotel, but never suspected that the playwright, whom I had just met that evening, had chosen that moment to end his life. I read about it in the papers the next morning.

Muggsy called me soon afterwards and said, "Don't bring me any more of your friends." Muggsy was a good storyteller and Sou was fascinated.

We had a friendly, pleasant visit. But as we prepared to go, Muggsy said, "If you guys are really my friends, one of you will smuggle a carton of butts in to me before you leave. I'll die in this joint without cigarettes!"

For me the request posed an obvious ethical dilemma. While I was weighing in my mind the rights and wrongs involved, Sou, who was an eminent physician, said, "Wait a minute. I'll be right back."

He returned some fifteen minutes later carrying a well-camouflaged carton of cigarettes and handed them to Muggsy with a conspiratorial grin. Muggsy immediately hid the carton under his blanket. We said goodbye, promising to come back soon for another visit. When we were back in Sou's car I asked, "Do you really think it was right to bring him those cigarettes?"

"I'll tell *you*," he said, "but don't let it go any further. The cigarettes now won't make any difference. I'd do anything for him that will make him more comfortable."

Not too long after that I had further reason to respect Sou's diagnostic abilities.

Wild Bill Davison

They don't call him "Wild Bill" for nothing.

The reference is not to his playing style, which has won him an international following for the past forty-five years or so. He's just, well, *wild*. The oldest incorrigible brat in the jazz world, his misdemeanors were magnified exponentially when George Brunies was still alive to urge him on to more heinous atrocities. According to most recent advices, Davison, at eighty, has lost neither the drive nor the obstinacy that made him famous and infamous, respectively.

Wild Bill is a genuine scholar in American history, with a specialty in the Civil War, about which he knows absolutely everything. I had occasion to observe the depth of that interest at three o'clock one very frigid February morning in Manassas, Virginia. We were all staying at the Downtowner Motor Inn to participate in Johnson McCree's annual jazz bash. Needless to say, most of us were asleep after an exhausting day. It was in 1970—the year after Eddie Condon roused me and Bob Greene by singing in his sleep. I'd have thought that at the age of sixty-four, Wild Bill would have known better than to ap-

Stephane Grappelle doesn't speak much English, and my French needs too much help. But we both remember when, a half-century earlier, Django Reinhardt interpreted for us in Paris. Django's English wasn't much either, but he and I both spoke Spanish.   *Photo by Johnny Donnels.*

John Hammond, left, never looked this bleary-eyed. The fellow on the right was Glenn Miller's main male warbler, Ray Eberle.   *Photo by Nick Alexakis.*

An afternoon in the fifties in Joe Mares's alligator warehouse. Kneeling, from left to right, are Martin Abraham, Jr. ("Little Chink Martin"); Martin Abraham, Sr. ("Chink Martin"); Stanley "Happy" Mendelson; and Raymond Burke. Standing, left to right, are Harry Shields, "Li'l Abbie" Brunies, Jack Delaney, Joe Mares, Al Rose, Sharkey Bonano, Tony Parenti, and Armand Hug. *Photo by John Kuhlman.*

Mayor Moon Landrieu of New Orleans, reading the dirty parts of *Storyville, New Orleans* to, from left to right, Armand Hug, Raymond Burke, Danny Barker, Al Rose, and George Deville. *Photo courtesy of Winston Lill.*

Sherwood Mangiapane, one of the best jazz bass players in the world, reminds me of things we did a half-century earlier.   *Photo by Joe Marcal.*

If you saw the Rex parade in 1967, this is the band you heard on the band-wagon. From left to right are Al Rose, director; Leonard Ferguson; Sherwood Mangiapane; Bill Humphries, kneeling; Paul Crawford, Dr. Henry A. "Hank" Kmen, Jack Delaney, Raymond Burke, Jack Bachman, George Finola, Stanley Mendelson, and Harold "Shorty" Johnson.   *Photo by Edmond Souchon.*

Una Mae Carlisle was gorgeous, sang like a meadowlark, and composed the big record hit of 1947, "Walkin' by the River."

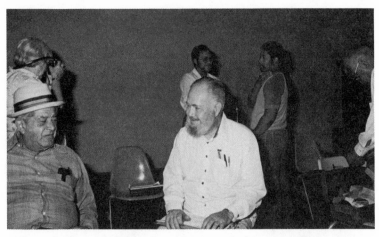

Willie Humphrey is telling me he remembers when I wasn't old enough to play a typewriter. Behind me is clarinetist Joe Torregano. Freddie Lonzo is wearing an undershirt of a type that Orleanians call "esplanades." *Photo by Joe Marcal.*

The shade of Sidney Story telling how it was in the red light district. The theater audience gave the live model an ovation. The professor at the piano is Morten Gunnar Larsen. *Photo by John Shoup.*

As far as Bob Greene, right, is concerned, Jelly Roll Morton *lives*. His concert tour, "Jelly Roll Morton Revisited," brought that music from coast to coast. The guy in the hat, whose name is Neal Unterseher, is a banjo player from the Razzberry Ragtimers. Johnny Donnels only took this picture to show himself on the wall with Jack Nicklaus, who blows a great nine-iron.

Local boy makes it in the movies. Al Rose, as Sidney Story, reads the ordinance establishing the red light district to the board of aldermen in *Storyville*.

I kept telling Louis to stop fooling around and get down to business (*ca.* 1946).   *Photo by Harry Romm.*

The beginning of the Louis Armstrong All-Stars in the mid-1940s. By now you recognize the guy on the floor. The others are, left to right, Earl "Fatha" Hines, Satch, Barney Bigard, and Arvel Shaw. Missing from this shot are Jack Teagarden and Sid Catlett.   *Photo by Harry Romm.*

Eubie looked at Claire Spangenberg and said, "I wish I was ninety again."
Photo by Johnny Donnels.

Some of my best friends play ragtime piano, especially Max Morath.
Photo by Joe Marcal.

Edmond Souchon and I were swamped with customers when the first edition of *New Orleans Jazz: A Family Album* came out in 1967. Even jazzmen like Monk Hazel (in the checked hat) showed up for copies. *Photo by Maison Blanche staff photographer.*

Karl Kramer founded the Music Corporation of America and booked King Oliver and Jelly Roll Morton. In this photograph, we're on the deck of the *S.S. Goldenrod*, anchored in the Mississippi River for the St. Louis Ragtime Festival in 1966. *Photo by Dr. Charles Riley.*

Live and direct from the French Quarter in New Orleans. Left to right are the emcee, Blue Lu Barker, Harry Shields, Martin Abraham, Sherwood Mangiapane, and entrepreneur Joe Mares.   *Photo by John Kuhlman.*

Dixieland bands were unknown outside of New Orleans until Tom Brown took his Band from Dixieland to Chicago in 1915.   *Photo by Mary Mitchell.*

When I was very young I was known to associate with saxophone players like Eddie "Lockjaw" Davis who went on to international fame. *Photo by Nick Alexakis.*

The youngster is Allan Jaffe. Preservation Hall had just opened in 1961, and he didn't look old enough to operate it. If he'd followed my instructions, the place would have closed in three weeks. *Photo by Grauman Marks.*

These days you've got to pay 'em to rehearse, but back then you couldn't stop 'em. From left to right are Raymond Burke, your Eminent Authority, Harry Shields, Chink Martin, and Monk Hazel. *Photo by Mary Mitchell.*

Alan Lomax (with glasses), dean of American Folk Musicologists. Bill Russell told me, "I'll never call you a musicologist again if you promise not to call me one." *Photo by Joe Marcal.*

If you think *this* wasn't long ago, look at the playback speaker. This record session was at Steinway Hall in New York in the mid-1940s. Left to right are John Hardee, a saxophonist; Herman Mitchell, guitar; Jimmy Archey, who said, "They don't throw trombone players back if they're under five feet tall." Then there's Dan Burley, enjoying his own sound; the Paymaster; Danny Barker, still with a little hair; and Pops Foster, who couldn't remember being on this gig, plays bass. *Photo by David Hawkins.*

Mitchell Ayres's "New Fashions in Music" was a household phrase in the 1930s. He was musical director for many hit radio shows. This one was "Juke Box Jury," 1948. A speeding auto ended his life. *Photo by Nick Alexakis.*

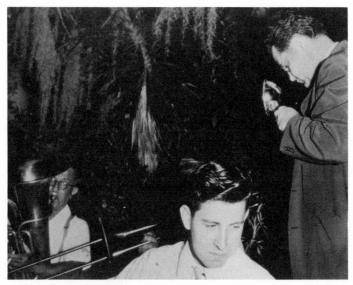

While I try to take a picture of Chink Martin, a sixteen-year-old banjo prodigy is playing like a veteran. Thirty years later, he became the ranking studio bassist, backing up all the big-name pop stars on LPs. His name is Bill Huntington.

A typical Journeys into Jazz concert might feature, as this one did, left to right, Sammy Price, Baby Dodds, Albert Nicholas, Wild Bill Davison, and, way down at the end, Bunk Johnson.   *Photo by Nick Alexakis.*

pear on the balcony in 7° weather, clad only in his boxer shorts, to play a very loud trumpet solo of "I Wish I Was in Dixie."

When the initial raucous strains pealed out, Diana and I hurriedly got into our bathrobes to find out what was going on. I was of the opinion that none of that was really happening, but I was going along with the gag my subconscious was playing during my most vulnerable sleeping hours. Once outside in the lividly cold air, I noticed a hundred or so other folks, many of whom I knew, were sharing my bizarre dream. But for the temperature, I could have been convinced positively that Morpheus still had me, especially when George Brunies stepped out on the same balcony with only *his* boxer shorts on.

Wild Bill, having assembled his troops, proceeded to remind them that we were here in Manassas, the site of the historic Battle of Bull Run. He also described the unfortunate quirk in the action that had led the yankees, damn them, to victory and shouted that the wrongs could yet be righted and that at least a paragraph of American history could yet be rewritten if we in the patio would but take the offensive, follow his fearless leadership, and retake the battlefield in the name of Jefferson Davis, Robert E. Lee, Stonewall Jackson, and the Confederacy. Brunies, meanwhile, apparently having arrogated to himself the role of adjutant, was yelling, "Right on! Yeah! Rise again! Way to go!" and other less genteel exhortations, all of which had not yet approached their crescendo when the security people arrived, put down the rebellion, and took its fervent leaders into custody.

The next day at breakfast I told Wild Bill I was surprised he didn't get pneumonia. He said he never did anything like that without antifreeze. Then he demanded, "Where were you when we needed you, you son-of-a-bitch? You too goddamn old to be drafted? I know you're over the hill because somebody told me you came here with your *wife*, for Christ sake!"

I reminded him of a balmier night a generation earlier, when we had stood together on the raised railway station at Princeton Junction, after a concert at the university. With us were Sidney Bechet, George Brunies, Sammy Price, Pops Foster, and Baby Dodds. We had almost two hours to wait for the train to New York.

It was always Wild Bill's restless way to explore every inch of his immediate environment for objects that interest him. On this particular night he found an emergency case, with a glass door, behind which was a fire hose. I don't know what he used to open the door, but it seemed only an instant before he had the hose nozzle to his lips and was playing what I had to concede was some very hot music. Remonstration was to no avail. I told him to put the hose nozzle back, but he patently assumed that my authority had ended one second after the finale on stage. Regardless of the merits of my protest, there was no doubt that what he was playing was hot and exciting. Brunies couldn't resist opening his trombone case, getting his horn out, and supplying counterpoint. It doesn't take jazzmen long to act once they've taken a notion, and before a whole chorus was over, everybody was playing except Baby—and that only because it takes a few minutes more to set the drums up.

The dorms were deployed in a semicircle around the trestle, and their windows began to light up one by one until the entire area was illuminated. Students began to emerge from their buildings. In a matter of minutes the terrain was alive with bathrobed undergrads. The concert was even more brilliant than the one we'd had inside. Since I alone was aware that train time was approaching, I reluctantly began to exhort the musicians to pack up and get themselves ready to board. They ignored me. I took the nozzle away from Davison and put it back in the case. In the end we were all scrambling to get Pops' bass fiddle back in its case. Baby's drums we had to drag aboard, item by item, plus the cases. I think we got on the train with everything because Baby never mentioned missing anything.

When we were well out of the station, Wild Bill proudly displayed the hose nozzle, which he produced from his coat. After I reminded him of the incident a quarter-century later there in Manassas he said, "You do things like that when you're young."

Joe Mares

Strictly speaking, you couldn't really call Joe Mares a musician, though I know for a fact that he did play a little clarinet in his youth and once or twice might even have been paid for it. But he did have the opportunity frequently to sit in with the key members of the New Orleans Rhythm Kings—Leon Ropollo; Joe's brother, Paul, who was the leader; George Brunies, the trombonist; and the bass player, Steve Brown.

However, somebody had to carry on the family business, so Joe directed his attentions to the buying and selling of furs and alligator hides, from his location at 520 St. Louis Street in the French Quarter. The musty old warehouse contained within it a large studio that was the office and musicians' lounge of Southland Records, which was Joe's pride and joy through the fifties. He divided his time between dealing with Cajun trappers and hosting and recording the great stars of New Orleans jazz.

I was fascinated by the men coming in from the Louisiana swamps with their bundles of gators, and I enjoyed the selling and buying game Joe played with them. Gator skins are bought by length, and Joe had a calibrated table with a spike on one end to facilitate measurement. The trapper would slap the snout of the saurian onto the spike. Then he had the prerogative of pulling the tail of the reptile as far on the board as it would go without splitting. If it split, he'd only get half-price for it. The trapper usually brought a consultant with him, whose role was to advise on whether the hide was extended to its maximum length or if there might still be an inch or two before the breaking point. The dialogue would go:

"What you t'ink, Placide? You t'ink maht be wan, two mo' inch in dees sunnumbitch?"

"Lemme see, Telesfore. Lemme see if he twang." Then he'd pluck the sunnumbitch like a harp string. "She tight, dat goddam bastidd. Maybe you tak' you money on dat wan, you."

Joe would pay them off, gator by gator, as they repeated the ritual. No running a tab. Cash per gator.

This phase of Joe's daily operation usually took place in the morning. Afterward we would retire to the studio, which was decorated with blown-up photographs of his favorite things—the Bob Cats, his brother Paul, George Girard, naked ladies, Louis Armstrong, Irving Fazola. Musicians would begin to arrive—Santo Pecora, Monk Hazel, Sharkey, Johnny St. Cyr, Raymond Burke, Stanley Mendelson. They didn't play at that early hour; they just sat around and talked about their jobs of the previous night. The joke-tellers told jokes. Joe is good at that. They reminisced. Joe would send out to Johnny's Po' Boys across the street and the incredible sandwiches and drinks would appear. He never let the musicians pay for anything. If they'd get to talking about something musical, Stanley or Armand Hug or Jeff Riddick might go to the piano and play a chord or two—maybe Raymond would by now have his horn together, its parts maintaining unsteady liaison with each other with the aid of rubber bands and chewing gum—and run down a melody, maybe helping someone to associate a tune with a title.

All this might end up in a snappy treatment of "Underneath Hawaiian Skies" or some such esoteric melody, performed by a jazz band that would command a fortune at a concert in Copenhagen or Kyoto. At its conclusion, Joe might say, "You guys know 'Of All the Wrongs You've Done To Me'?"

There'd be much shaking of heads. Jazzmen don't remember titles well. Raymond, of course, knows every tune ever played. Sherwood Mangiapane might nod and say, "It goes like this," then whistle it. Sherwood is a great whistler. Then maybe somebody would ask, "How does the bridge go?" and Sherwood would whistle *that*. Finally, Joe might say, "Let's try it out and see how it goes. You know, it could be pretty to have the whistlin' in it, too. That sounded nice."

So then whatever musicians were present might have a go at it. On the particular occasion relating to this tune we had three guitars— Edmond Souchon, Danny Barker, and Johnny St. Cyr. There was a bass fiddle, Sherwood; a tuba, Chink Martin; a pair of clarinets, Raymond Burke and Harry Shields. Raymond also had his soprano saxophone with him. Jeannette Kimball played the piano. Not your typical jazz band instrumentation by any means. But this assemblage of master jazz artists could never feel any limitations. Sherwood whistled. The effect was so captivating that it expanded itself into a truly rewarding LP.

Joe Mares could maintain this kind of informal, relaxed, creative environment that produced such little masterpieces. Jeannette, superbly gifted as a band pianist, sang on that LP, which is remarkable because Jeannette doesn't sing.

Joe was always proud to have the Who's Who of New Orleans jazz on his label, but he was equally delighted to be able to put some extraordinary musicians on wax for the first time. Mike Lala, Al Hirt, Dutch Andrus, Pete Fountain, and Kid Avery all made their recording debuts on Southland, as did the gospel star, Sister Elizabeth Eustis. Tom Brown and Johnny St. Cyr both had their first records with themselves listed as leader under Joe Mares' auspices. He also brought Papa Celestin back to the recording studio after a hiatus of decades.

One of the hottest and most charming tapes he produced couldn't be released for contractual reasons. Rosemary Clooney, while she was playing at the Blue Room in the Roosevelt, expressed the desire to hear herself on records with a genuine New Orleans jazz band. Joe invited her to do just that. She came to the warehouse and sang a half-dozen things, with accompaniments she had never dreamed were possible. Joe, in his customary generosity, offered to present the tapes to Columbia if they'd issue them. But Mitch Miller, then their talent and repertoire director, felt that the record wouldn't be consistent with the image they were trying to build for her and thus commerce frustrated art once again.

That kind of thing isn't easy for Joe to understand. He relates to the music with an intensity you never see among musical entrepreneurs and rarely even among fans. Many a time I've seen him weep copiously in response to really well-performed music. I'm satisfied that he's never motivated except by his own taste. He developed into a real master recording director by knowing exactly what he wanted. His superb musical ear proved to be the best instructor, and he learned the mechanics of balance and tone in an era before electronics and multitrack devices homogenized and sterilized the nation's music. The atmosphere around Joe was brought home to me one night in the fifties when he gave a wedding reception for Li'l Abbie Brunies and his bride, Jerri. His patio was alive with the great names in the New Orleans jazz world, many in from faraway places. They milled around eating Helen Mares' renowned crab salad, jambalaya, gumbo, and red beans and rice. Tony Parenti sighed with satisfaction over his third plate, turned to me and said, "It's good to be home."

Harry Truman

Sometimes things happen that don't take very long and they're so far outside of your regular routine that in retrospect they seem unreal. Such events seem more frequent among jazz people than among the members of saner society. I mean the average working citizen can live an entire lifetime without anyone ever calling him from the State Department. One Friday morning I received such a call. It seemed that there was going to be a sort of social function at Blair House in Washington, D.C., that night. Blair House was where visiting VIP's were usually put up when the President had them as guests, but right then

Harry and Bess Truman were in residence there while certain re-modeling was in progress across the street in the White House. What the President wanted me to do was to put together an all-star jazz band to perform. It was then 9 A.M., and we were expected to be at Idlewild to be picked up by a government plane at 7:30 P.M.

I may have stammered a little, expressing less than complete confidence that I could put such a band together on that short notice. My communicant, however, ignored my reticence. When I suggested he call and ask Satchmo' he said he'd done that. He said Satchmo' was booked and had proposed that somebody call Al Rose, who always knew where everybody was and could surely accommodate the President of the United States.

That's how it came about that on a chilly evening in 1947 I shook hands with a State Department attaché in the unimpressive air terminal of Idlewild (now Kennedy) Airport and introduced him to Muggsy Spanier, George Brunies, Pee Wee Russell, Brad Gowans, James P. Johnson, Lee Blair, Pops Foster, and Baby Dodds. We were guided into a luxuriously appointed plane and turned over to a half-dozen gorgeous flight attendants. (Pee Wee said later that they were so beautiful he almost forgot they were the ones that served the gin.) The trip took no time at all.

So now we're set up in the Blair House. There's a little bandstand, possibly set up for the occasion. Baby went about putting up his drums, a process that took him longer than any other drummer I knew. James P. ran a few arpeggios on the grand piano and said the action was okay. The tuning-up process began, and a very pleasant, formally gowned lady whom I recognized at once as the First Lady approached me with a few welcoming remarks. Then she said, "You know, nothing in the world would make the President happier than a chance to play the piano with your musicians."

I assured her that we'd be delighted to have him sit in.

On the way over in the plane, I'd asked if anyone knew "Hail to the Chief" and was met with blank stares. However, Brad said he knew "Kansas City Kitty." He took out his valve trombone and played the melody. Muggsy and Pee Wee recognized it at once, so we decided that when the President came in, we'd play that.

At about 9:30 P.M. there was a flurry of secret service men at the entrance. The band had been playing for maybe a half-hour, and an impressive assemblage of dignitaries, including Vice-President Alben W. Barkley, was standing around and really enjoying the music. A few couples were dancing including, if my memory is working, Congressman and Mrs. Richard M. Nixon.

So in came the President, beaming jovially and shaking hands with everyone within reach. My practiced eye told me that he'd already begun the party somewhere else on the premises, possibly with no guests present. Bess whispered in his ear and he nodded. Then she spoke to what appeared to be a head secret service man and *he* nodded. Then he came over to talk to *me* and *I* nodded. The band continued to play "Kansas City Kitty." I told James P. to go to the bar and make himself comfortable, explaining that the President was going to sit in. It wasn't the kind of a suggestion that would displease James P.—not if there was a free bar set up.

The President, escorted by two large gentlemen, approached, extended his hand, and said, "Hello, Mr. Rose. I'm Harry Truman."

I introduced the musicians to the President, proposed that they start with "Kansas City Kitty," which he would, of course, know. Then I turned to the audience and said, "Ladies and gentlemen, we have a guest artist with us tonight, sitting in on piano . . ." and I was drowned out by applause, laughter, and cheers as I retired from the makeshift bandstand.

Harry Truman knew "Kansas City Kitty" and he kind of knew the "Missouri Waltz." After that it was straight Stephen Foster. Anyway they played those two tunes for perhaps two hours. Truman appeared to be in heaven, and Bess stood by beaming at his obvious delight. She said, "I don't know when I've ever seen him so happy."

Anyway, the evening ended. We were all roundly thanked, praised, congratulated, and patted on the back. The President shook hands warmly with all the musicians and especially made his apologies to James P. for having hogged the piano all evening. James P. blearily told him it was a pleasure.

So they took us to the plane—these same State Department folks—and we fastened our seat belts. I was sitting next to Dodds, who was always preoccupied and I'm convinced never thought about anything else but rhythm and music. After we were in the air, I turned to him and asked, "How do you feel, Baby? Did you enjoy the party? Have a good time?"

"Oh, sure!" he answered, "but that little fellow with the glasses couldn't play much piano."

Jack Teagarden

As far as the musical arts were concerned, the middle thirties were years of drastic changes. The swing era started effectively in 1935 with the startling success of the Benny Goodman Orchestra, which achieved popularity by dumping the prime essentials of authentic jazz and borrowing the solo concepts of what was called "Chicago style," showcasing them in elaborate arrangements for thirteen pieces. Anyone who wanted to get rich in the music business had to abandon the idea of doing it in a genuine jazz band and scramble to catch on as a "sideman," or featured soloist in a swing orchestra. Some, equipped with special personality and appearance requirements, could become leaders like Artie Shaw, Glenn Miller, and the Dorseys. Jack Teagarden decided he was one of these.

Now, "Big T" was certainly personable enough, certainly talented enough to overwhelm an audience. He had a pleasant singing style, and his trombone artistry was already a legend. But Jackson couldn't attend to business. He didn't know how to get serious. He was lazy and he had a short attention span. The only things that really interested him were jazz and railroad trains, either the real thing or the Christmas toys. He had been talked into being a bandleader, but it didn't come natural to him. I've seen him stand with a baton in his hand and gape at his sidemen as they wove their ways through their solos— and he had sidemen like Irving Fazola and Sterling Bose. He'd just forget to wave the stick and become part of the audience, and he'd even applaud them just as the fans did. When it came time for his solo, though, he didn't lose track of things. He'd lift up his horn and transfix his listeners for as long as he wanted to.

Back in 1936 I got some musicians together to play a concert for the Philadelphia local of the American newspaper guild. I hadn't thought about it at the time, but this was the very first time people ever bought tickets to sit in a room and listen to authentic jazz. No food. No drinks. Just jazz. The first jazz concert. Sidney Bechet, Sidney De Paris and friends. It was in Mercantile Hall on North Broad Street.

No cheapskates, the guild had also engaged Jack Teagarden and his Orchestra to play on another floor of the building for dancing. But that's not the way it worked out. By ten o'clock all the dancers were downstairs listening to the jazz. Teagarden, Fazola, and Bose had joined the front line and excitement was high.

I had an unexpected thrill that evening. I was just a twenty-year-old kid with literary pretensions, and during a brief break I was standing with Big T when a baggy-looking fellow came by and greeted him with real enthusiasm. T said to him, "This is the kid who got these folks together, Al Rose. Al, I'd like you to meet Damon Runyon."

I doubt that I contributed much to the subsequent conversation. I knew I'd be telling generations yet to come that I had personally shaken hands with Damon Runyon. Big T was on first name terms with the great and famous—not just musicians, but movie stars, a king or two, big industrialists. But he considered that the most important person he knew was Mr. Van Sweringen of Cleveland who built and owned the Nickel Plate Railroad. If there was ever anybody in the world he envied it was this man who had been able to build and operate his own railroad. Jack did a brief concert tour with me one time. St. Louis, Minneapolis, and Cleveland. He couldn't wait to get to Cleveland. Maybe he only came with me because he was sure Mr. Van Sweringen would let him ride in the cab of a locomotive.

Working with jazzmen you get inured to all kinds of idiosyncracies and after a while nothing surprises you. That Jack knew the owner of a railroad well enough to call him on the phone and ask to be permitted to ride in the locomotive was credible to me by that time. What wasn't credible was that when T got ready to go for his ride he was able to pull a motorman's hat out of his suitcase. I discovered he wore that to drive his car, too. Even more astonishing was the fact that Mr. Van Sweringen joined him for the ride in the cab of the locomotive.

The way things worked out, I saw him frequently in the years after that, during many of which he was, of course, playing in Satch's all-stars. I moved back to New Orleans, more or less to stay, in the fifties. It was with great pleasure that I noted he had been booked into the Dream Room on Bourbon Street. He called me from out-of-town, told me he'd be staying at the Prince Conti Motor Inn, and asked if I'd take him by the old railway stations and roundhouses while he was in town. I said I'd be happy to do that, but we never got to make that particular tour. Jackson died in the Prince Conti motel during his engagement.

Eubie Blake

I knew Eubie Blake so well, and for so long, that I still can't believe he's gone. As his official biographer I put almost all the Eubie stories in that volume, *Eubie Blake* by Al Rose (Schirmer-Macmillan, 1979), but not *all* of them. Some were withheld in deference to Eubie's wife Marion, who was always offended by any mention of his many—and I mean many—amours. She was very generous in the matter of supplying photographs, but she absolutely refused to turn over any, no matter how innocuous, that showed him with another woman—even his first wife Avis, who died before he began his courtship of Marion. Eubie had an extended string of affairs from his extreme youth, through both his marriages, and the last of them when he was in his nineties. I asked him when he was ninety-seven, "How old do you have to be before the sex drive goes?"

He answered, "You'll have to ask somebody older than me."

Eubie wasn't a man to pursue the ladies, but he was certainly quick to yield to temptation. After all, when "Shuffle Along" became a smash on Broadway, he was rich, talented, and personable. He was an international celebrity; his songs like "Memories of You," "I'm Just Wild About Harry," and "You're Lucky to Me" were part of the main body of American music. The ladies, especially the show business ladies, were all over him. He was lionized.

Certainly everybody knew he was in love with Lottie Gee, his "Shuffle Along" ingenue. The cast knew it, his partner Sissle knew, his wife Avis knew, and all of Broadway knew. Both Avis and Lottie were jealous as they could be, and Eubie's attitude was one of complete helplessness. He never felt he was cheating on anybody. It was just that all women were always taking advantage of the unfortunate fact that he couldn't resist them. He once confessed to me, "I been gettin' away with that act for sixty years."

He told me that every time he left his house, Avis would insist on making love to him until he climaxed and then when he left Lottie in the apartment he kept for her, she'd do the same thing; then, he added, ruefully, "there were the *other* girls." The roster of Eubie's lady friends read like a directory of black soubrettes, ingenues, chorus girls, and showgirls. That, he said, was the *big* thing about being a success in the music business. He was saddened by the girls—and there were several—who committed suicide over him, two who were killed by their husbands—yet he discussed all these events as an outsider, as one who had exercised no initiative in these matters. He viewed it all as an innocent bystander.

"Listen," he explained. "You got to understand how the world is. I wasn't foolin' with jail bait. These were all grown-up women. They were in the theatrical world, and a woman in the theatrical world needs to know it ain't the same as the rest of the world. Show people think a certain way. They act a certain way—and what I did was what show people did. Maybe I did it more than most of the others—but it wasn't the kind of thing you just decide you're gonna do! It just comes up on you and there you are. I treated Avis good and she was the first to say it. And Marion, too. A guy like you, you been in it and you understand it, but women—even show business women—they might understand it if it's somebody else. But if it's *them,* hah!"

But then he told me a story that seemed to tell me he thought Avis was really above all that, too. I wrote it in the manuscript of his biography, but Marion raised so much hell I took it out. It seems that this girl friend of Avis' came to visit her, to recite his list of misdeeds. The girl friend appeared scandalized with Eubie's adulterous conduct, saying, "Avis, that niggah you married to, he got an apartment for a chippie in his show. An' that niggah goes up there to be wit' her every day. You might be a saint, Avis. You shouldn't have to put up with a niggah like that."

Avis reportedly led her informant to the window and pointed down to the luxurious new automobile. "You see that car, Honey?" she asked. "That niggah just gave me that car. And inside of that car there's a chauffeur sittin' just waitin' to see if I want to go anywhere." Then she led her friend to the closet, opened the door, and said, "You see these fur coats? This one's mink, this is sable. That's a beaver, that's a silver fox. That niggah gave me all those things. Now, *tonight,* after the show is over, where do you think that niggah's goin'? He's comin' right back here where he goes every night and," indicating the bedroom with her thumb, "gets into that bed next to this niggah," indicating herself.

Eubie never told me how he knew about this incident but I have to assume one of the ladies involved reported it to him.

Although he lived to be a hundred, Eubie was always young, always planning new things to compose, even considering writing one more show. But many of his attitudes were old-fashioned. He deplored, for example, the modern public attitude toward homosexuals. Eubie had always been willing to work with them, because he was prepared to accept genuine talent wherever he found it, but he wouldn't, to his knowledge, associate with one. He hated for show-business men, even straight ones, to hug him or kiss him as is the common practice in the theater these days. As he grew older, the problem got worse and his aversion increased. By the time Eubie got into his late eighties it seemed as though every man, woman, and child wanted to embrace him. He didn't mind the women and children doing it, but he pulled away from the men as though they were preparing to give him a tetanus injection. ("Stand over here, Shazzam—and if you see one comin', head him off.")

Back in the late thirties and early forties he and Noble Sissle, as well as many other Harlemites, called me "Shazzam" because Sissle said I looked like Captain Marvel, a comic strip character of that day who frequently entered the scene in a kind of explosion that spelled out in jagged letters SHAZZAM! As we all got older I guess the resemblance vanished.

Diana and I went to New York for Eubie's hundredth birthday celebration, which was held at the Shubert Theater. Max Morath, the super entertainer of our times, and Eubie's long-time friends Robert Kimball and Phoebe Jacobs organized the party, but he was confined to his bed in Brooklyn listening to the proceedings over a telephone hook-up to the stage of the theater. He heard messages from the President and the governor, as well as countless other friends. Mayor Koch was present in person. The stage and the audience were peopled with celebrities.

When it was over some of us went to Max's new studio on 42nd Street at his kind invitation and reminisced about Eubie. Norma Morath and their three adult children were skillful and patient hosts as Rudi Blesh, Bill and Joanie Bolcom, Dick Zimmerman (the ragtime magician), William Albright, Ian Whitcomb, and I don't know how many others toasted Eubie's happy life.

Five days later, on my car radio in Athens, Georgia, on February 12, 1983, I heard the news of Eubie's passing. It was hard to be sad over the completion of as successful a life as his.

The Original Dixieland Jazz Band

The ODJB's importance in the history of jazz can't be overstated. Those musicians made the very first jazz record ever issued (1917). And they ultimately made *jazz* a household word with early records that were enormously successful just after World War I and with tours both in the United States and abroad. The recorded performances that earned the band its fame, though, sounded little like the prerecording ODJB. Since 78 rpm discs were limited to three minutes of performance, the band had to play far too fast to get the entire piece tracked. As a result much of the subtle and artful improvisation had to be sacrificed. Subsequent audiences, of course, wanted to hear the band sound the way it did on its records. Thus the ODJB had to say goodbye to the real jazz and give the public what it wanted.

"What could we do?" Nick Larocca, the trumpet player and leader, asked me in 1955. "That's how we made those records and everybody in the world was copying *us*. The only thing *we* could do was to copy our own records."

When I met Eddie Edwards, the trombone player, in the 1950s, he was no longer the slim, handsome figure I had known from photographs, but a jolly old gentleman of enormous girth. He was making a Commodore record session with Johnny Wiggs, and they ran through a piece in rehearsal that was real and satisfying. Wiggs was gleeful over Edwards' sound. Then Eddie said, "Yeah, Johnny. That was great—but we can't do that on the record. It'll put everybody to sleep." Unfortunately, his view proved to be accurate.

I noted that Edwards didn't speak with the characteristic New Orleans dialect and I mentioned it to him. "You don't sound at all like a yat," I said. (Orleanians tease each other for using the phrase "Where y'at" as a greeting, and thus call each other "yats.")

"I never heard it at home when I was young," Edwards said, "and my mother was always correcting my speech. So I guess I just never picked it up. It used to be hard for people from home, when they met me up North, to believe that I was really from New Orleans."

Larry Shields came home from California for a brief visit just before he died. I took him and his brother Harry to lunch at Tujague's on Decatur Street. (Larry remembered the place nostalgically and observed that it hadn't changed in forty years.)

When I asked him if he thought he'd picked up his clarinet style from someone who had gone before, he shook his head and said, "Style! I didn't have any style! I just blew like hell the best way I could and only hoped I could keep up. When people talked about my style I never knew what they meant. I could never play much clarinet. Not like the kid, here. [Younger brother Harry was then fifty-two.] If *he'd* been playin' he would have been the most famous clarinetist in the world." But Larry's testimony notwithstanding, listening to those old records is enough to show that Larry wasn't the tyro he made himself out to be.

I never knew Harry Ragas, the original piano player with the band. He died when I was three years old, but I had the opportunity to speak with J. Russel Robinson, who made many early records with the band, and he said, "I suppose you could say that I've played with better musicians in my life, but that's only true in a way. For originality and spontaneous music—and for just plain *fun*—that was it. I never had a better time in my life."

Frank Signorelli, who also played with the ODJB in its early years, recalled that he was completely disoriented during his first rehearsal. "Those guys didn't know any music, but they always knew what they were doing. I knew all about music, but I didn't have any *idea* what I was doing. But they just showed me. They didn't *tell* me. They *showed* me. God, it was great." Signorelli worked for me a time or two, and I was impressed with his professionalism and flexibility. I couldn't believe that someone who had never played in New Orleans could have fit in so well.

I used to love to have Tony Sbarbaro (Spargo) on my sessions, not only because he kept the authentic beat going as naturally as he did, but also because he was always oriented toward having a happy time. A New Orleans lady I knew who lived in Philadelphia could make red beans and rice with hot sausage in true French Quarter style. If Tony was playing for me in New York, I'd bring a bucket of this specialty with me. And if he was going to be doing a concert in Philadelphia, I'd call Tante 'Nette and we'd eat at her house. He was full of talk about ancient drummers he had admired: Kid Totts, Ragbaby Stephens, and a man named Alfred L. Jaeger from the Orpheum Theater Orchestra.

Emile Christian didn't appear on the early ODJB discs—or any that were made in America. But he did make the European tour with the band and played the trombone on all of the British sides, since Edwards had elected to stay in New York for personal reasons. Christian's association with the ODJB, though, preceded Nick Larocca's. He was, in fact, the group's original trumpet man. But for the vagaries of the music business he might have been the one credited with the band's meteoric rise. It's doubtful, though, whether Emile would ever have had Nick's presence or acumen. But he was a magnificent musician.

One of my most exciting recollections is of an evening in 1959 on the stage of the Shryock Auditorium at Southern Illinois University in Carbondale. Emile was sixty-four years old, ailing, and suffering foot trouble that made it painful for him to wear shoes. I had persuaded him to make the trip, anyway, as a replacement for Jim Robinson, who had, in his customary careless manner, double-booked himself for the date. It was truly a great all-star band with Johnny Wiggs playing the cornet, Harry Shields playing clarinet, Jeannette Kimball playing piano, Danny Barker on the guitar and banjo, Chester Zardis playing bass, and Louis Barbarin as the drummer. I had Blue Lu Barker to sing her incomparable specialties, plus a delightful member of the psychology faculty who was also a fabulous entertainer, Jeannie Kittrell.

When I introduced Emile, I supplied all the historical build up, telling how, despite his advanced years, he continued to play with the verve and excitement he had been known for a half-century earlier. Then I brought on this frail, emaciated, white-haired old man wearing bedroom slippers and obviously having great difficulty making his way to center stage, even with a little help from me. The people applauded, but could have been expected to take my encomiums with a grain of salt after watching his laborious progress to his chair and observing his ancient figure.

I'm so happy that that concert was recorded! Nobody would have believed the old man could come up with that riotous, ingenious, and vital trombone. It only took four bars to make you forget his age and condition. He drove the crowd wild.

Fourteen years later I tried to get him out to make a final appearance on wax, but he told me, "I've given all that up, man. I give away my horn, too. After all, I'm seventy-eight years old. A man can't keep doin' that forever. It's hard work, you know."

"But it's fun, though, isn't it?" I asked.

He replied, "That's easy for *you* to say. You ain't doin' the playin'."

Emile died on New Year's Eve of 1973, and that was the end of the Original Dixieland Jazz Band.

Armand J. Piron

How I wish I could recreate this scene for you and the feelings of this nine year old, as he sat on the bank of Lake Pontchartrain in the light of the full moon, watching the flickering bulbs of the amusement rides of Spanish Fort in their perpetual multicolored pattern changes, and listened while A. J. Piron and his orchestra played for dancing at the end of Tranchina's Restaurant Pier. The strains of "Purple Rose of Cairo" or "Dreamy Blues" seemed to take on an added dimension by drifting languidly across the easy ripples on the surface of the lake. There was even the illusion that the occasional mullet that jumped out of the water was part of the arrangement. Piron's Orchestra was a New Orleans institution. In these years, the band was at its musical peak with the legendary Lorenzo Tio, Jr., playing the clarinet and Peter Bocage on trumpet, occasionally joining the leader in a violin duet. Old man Louis Cottrell, Sr., played the drums in that band, and Steve Lewis played the piano, with Johnny Marrero and his banjo. "Dreamy Blues," which was then the band's theme, was to have a devious history, ending when it was published in 1930 as "Mood Indigo" and carrying the names of Barney Bigard and Duke Ellington as composers. But all of us in New Orleans knew that tune, and we knew it was Tio's.

It was a great thrill for me, then, in 1939, while I was headed north from Mexico to Philadelphia, having stopped for an extended visit in New Orleans, when Peter Bocage suggested we go by and visit with Piron. We walked from the French Quarter to the impeccable little white house in the 1400 block of Derbigny Street. Piron was ailing at the time. He was still in his early fifties, and I never had known what his physical problems were, but he only lived four more years after I met him.

Edmond Souchon was his attending physician, and he just happened to be present when Bocage and I arrived. In fact, that was when I met Sou for the first time, too. He was just leaving when Bocage and I got there.

I was impressed by the manner in which Piron and Bocage greeted each other. It was all very Creole. "Evenin', Peter. You lookin' might' prosperous, sir. The family fine?"

"Evenin', Arman'. I hope you res' well this mawnin'."

Not at all the kind of meeting I was accustomed to among jazzmen, but this particular breed was reared in gentility. Their soft voices and mild manners were relaxing, comfortable to be around.

I asked Piron about a piece that was copyrighted in his name, "I Wish I Could Shimmy Like My Sister Kate," noting that Louis Armstrong had recently said Piron had stolen it from him. Piron's attitude toward Satch' was patronizing, but understanding.

"Of course," he assured me, "that's not Louis' tune or mine or Pete's either. That tune is older than all of us. People always put different words to it. Some of them were too dirty to say in polite company." He sang me one brief and obscene version. "The way Louis did it didn't have anything to do with his Sister Kate":

Gotta have 'em before it's too late,
They shake like jelly on a plate.
Big 'n juicy, soft an' 'round
Sweetes' ones I ever found.

"That's the way Louis sang it, his words. Well you know, there's just so many places you could do a number like that. Not in *my* band, you know. We never did anything like that. Now it's true we used the "jelly on a plate," but who knows if Louis made that up himself. The published words—at least the title—Peter made up. Most of the rest of it was Steve Lewis and me. Steve worked out the band routine."

Bocage nodded along with this recital. They both made a number of comments about the extraordinary talents of Steve Lewis, talked about the success of Pete's "Mama's Gone Goodbye," which had been recorded very recently by a number of bands and was having an unexpected revival. I asked him if he thought the kind of music he played with his orchestra would ever become popular again. He shook his head and told me, "You know, back when I started to do that, it was something new. It was way ahead of the jazz guys. So very few of the jazz guys could play well enough to work in my band, and I always had the cream—the very best. Well, now you see these new fellows, these swing bands—Benny Goodman, Tommy Dorsey—they're even more ahead of me than I was ahead of the jazz people. I listen to their records, and I can't believe musicians can play that well. But still, when you'd hear Tio play 'Aunt Hagar's Blues' or 'Liebestraum,' well, you might wonder if music ever got any better than that."

I asked him if he ever played his violin anymore.

"I fool with it some," he admitted, "but I was never what you'd call a great violinist. Pete, here, could give me a run. He can really play it—I mean *play* it—not like some of these banquette fiddlers you throw pennies to by the Cabildo. We still do a job here and there, but out in public I'm satisfied just to wave the stick. It's lucky there's still some good men to wave it in front of."

I asked Peter after we left if he knew what was wrong with Piron. He said, "Armand was never very strong. He doesn't have a lot of bad habits—used to drink a little wine years ago, but I don't believe he even touches that anymore. He doesn't smoke. And as pretty as he always was, you'd think he'd be a big lady's man. But that's just not his way."

The Candy Man

In our times, you may have noticed, there's been a proliferation of "old time ice cream parlors." Even the very young now associate that white-topped table, those ice cream chairs, the gayly striped awnings, and the Tiffany-style light fixtures with fifty delicious flavors in cones or dishes. I must admit that entering certain of these establishments strikes a nostalgic note in my head. And it's amazing how closely some of them come to reproducing the real thing. (Only the decor—never the ice cream.)

But in New Orleans, the ice cream parlor—at least the more popular ones—didn't stop at merely serving ice cream and imaginative sundaes and sodas. They also offered floor shows. Can you believe a floor show in an ice cream parlor? There was no cover charge. You just paid your dime for the sundae and permitted yourself to be entertained by some outstanding talent.

At the moment, I'm recalling the rather large emporium at Old Spanish Fort Amusement Park, which was called Brown's Ice Cream Parlor back in the 1920s. The house piano player during the afternoon—before he went to work as the pianist in Piron's Orchestra at Tranchina's Restaurant at night—was Steve Lewis, composer of many tunes that Piron made popular. The energetic dancer and blues singer, New Orleans' Willie Jackson, was the principal entertainer, sometimes the only one. He would later have his singing preserved on commercial records. But *I* always hoped that one of my visits to Brown's would coincide with one of the unscheduled appearances of the "Jacobs Candy Man."

The Jacobs Candy Company was a local manufacturing firm that turned out boxes of quality chocolates, frequently in ornate metal boxes bearing the legend

JACOBS CANDY
"Made Last Night"

Freshness and flavor were their prime selling points. In order to convey this message to the sweet-toothed public, the company employed a song-and-dance man whose function was to visit the city's many ice cream parlors regularly and do his act, replete with remarks about the excellence of Jacobs Candy, "Made Last Night." He would pass out samples, and for the young ladies he carried a pocketful of lapel buttons that he'd pin on their dresses or blouses. The buttons said, "Made Last Night."

A number of entertainers succeeded each other as the Jacobs Candy Man. Among the most noteworthy were songwriter Billy Price Augustin and Al Bernard, whose multiple careers as a composer ("Shake, Rattle, and Roll," "Blue Eyed Sally"), TV show host, and vaudevillian earned him great distinction in the world of show business. (Bernard was also the only male singer to perform on records with the Original Dixieland Jazz Band.) Another Jacobs Candy Man was Wilbur Leroy, who traveled the theater circuits with his own revue. (He was the uncle of the great jazz pianist, Armand Hug, who called him "Uncle Dewey.")

I think it was this very same "Uncle Dewey" that I was familiar with. I remember him singing and playing and dancing to "He Was a Nice Boy (But He Ain't No Relation of Mine)" and "He's Just a Cousin of Mine." He played some really *hot* piano, and Armand would sometimes play little things for me "the way Uncle Dewey did it."

Bunk Johnson

There may have been a variety of earth-shaking events going on in the world on that particular spring day in 1922, but only one thing mattered in the sun-drenched town of Perryton, Texas. It surely didn't look as though it were participating in Mr. Coolidge's prosperity, with its dusty streets and its one-story buildings with two-story fronts. But nevertheless, all its flags were flying, flamboyant bunting was draped over a speakers' stand, and the mayor was about to open the festivities observing the town's first anniversary by dedicating the new wooden sidewalks. To help celebrate the gala occasion, a unit of the Greater Holcamp Carnival Shows had set up in the vacant square upon which the optimistic townsfolk proposed to erect a grand City Hall.

I suppose my memory could play tricks on me. I was only six years old, and the lingering images in my recollections could be confused with the sets of Jack Hoxie or Ken Maynard western movies— what with the real Indians on horseback, the cowboys in their big hats, their lariats hung over the pommels of their saddles. I remember very well that most of the cowboys were black and that they fraternized freely with the white ones. I hadn't yet seen that kind of social phenomenon in my native New Orleans.

My father had acquired ownership of this unit of the Greater Holcamp Carnival Shows, and I do recall a visit from Mr. Greater Holcamp himself, a short, skinny, dyspeptic, youngish man in a golf cap (we call it a golf cap now) and a sweater with leather-reinforced elbows.

One of the feature attractions of this particular carnival was a real blackface minstrel show, complete with tambo and bones, the traditional interlocutor, and the pink top hats and gloves. Best of all though was the band, which consisted of five black New Orleans musicians. The leader's name was Willie, and he played the trumpet.

The music, of course, wasn't new to me, but it was a music that never failed to be exciting. I observed early that when this music was played, people listening couldn't keep still. They were impelled to dance, stomp their feet, and otherwise appear to have lost kinetic control of their appendages.

From time to time, when my parents were off tending to business, Willie would take temporary charge of me. It wasn't a difficult assignment for him, since I was a sober and sensible six-year-old, reasonable

enough to understand that there were surely dozens of things Willie
would have preferred to do. We carried on brief, desultory conversations, handicapped by the fact that I found it very difficult to penetrate
his dialect. I probably asked him a question or two about the music he
played, but I just don't remember. In any case, a season went by in
which I frequently found myself in Willie's company. I would have
to describe the relationship as sedate and uneventful. I still attended
every performance of the minstrel show, mainly to listen to the band.
I had, by this time, all of the routines and gags in my head, though I
had made no effort to commit them to memory.

Back in New Orleans, I resumed my accustomed lifestyle, and I
remained endlessly fascinated with the multifaceted French Quarter.
I remember feeling considerable relief when I learned that my father
had sold the carnival and that I wouldn't be required to repeat the
tour. (Some kids have no sense of adventure.)

Now two dozen years go by. I have, by that time, learned a lot
about this music and the people who played it. I had been producing my Journeys Into Jazz concerts for some time, and during 1946
and 1947 I had a regular Friday night series going in the Philadelphia
Academy of Music. I did very little advertising, because I had a mail-
ing list of devout followers of the music.

One day I got a call from Bob Maltz, who operated the Stuyvesant
Casino in New York, asking me if I'd like to book Bunk Johnson for an
appearance at one of my concerts. I had, of course, heard of the old
man, since anything that happened in the jazz community of those
years became common knowledge almost instantly. We all knew how
several months earlier Bill Russell and Fred Ramsey, on a tip from
Louis Armstrong, had discovered Bunk working in a canefield in
New Iberia, Louisiana. It has become a jazz legend now, how they got
Sidney Bechet's brother Leonard, a dentist, to make Bunk a set of false
teeth, how they got him a horn and inaugurated his heralded
comeback.

I thought my regular patrons would enjoy having a look at this
ancient relic, so I hired him. Naturally, I assumed that very little
could be expected of Bunk musically by now, and to be on the safe
side, I also engaged Wild Bill Davison to take up any possible slack.
The rest of the musicians I called were all New Orleans people, except
trombonist Jimmy Archey, who really understood authentic jazz. The
others were Albert Nicholas for clarinet, Sam Price for piano (come

to think of it, *he's* not from New Orleans, either), and Pops Foster for bass. (I never hired anyone else if I could get Pops.) Baby Dodds, my choice for greatest jazz drummer of all time, was present, too.

Anyway, on the night of the concert, perhaps forty minutes before curtain time, this old, old black guy, wearing a brown homburg hat and a long, tightly fitted, long out-of-style overcoat and carrying a trumpet case, walks down the aisle to where I'm standing on the stage. When I saw him I'm sure I must have looked like I'd turned to stone. When I recovered my equanimity, I said, "Willie! What are *you* doing here?"

"You got to know me a long time to be callin' me Willie," he speculated. "Most everybody calls me 'Bunk.'"

In a matter of seconds I realized that I had undergone dramatic changes in appearance since the time I was six, and I reasoned that it was perfectly logical that Willie—excuse me, Bunk—could fail to recognize me. After settling down to some coherent talk, we discussed who I really was and I saw a flicker of not-too-excited recognition on his face. We marvelled for a moment over the small world, and by this time other members of the ensemble had arrived.

Bunk said to Nick, "Remember we played in that carnival in Texas and Oklahoma in the twenties? You remember the boss had a kid that hung around the jig show?" (Sorry—that's what they called minstrel shows in that era.)

Nicholas remembered vaguely. Bunk told him I was that kid. My discussion with Nicholas over this bit of history was more animated. I already knew him well, but had no idea he had been the clarinetist in that early venture. As I took another look at him, I found I could match his middle-aged face with that of the twenty-two-year-old from that Texas spring. He then told me, "You know, Dodds, here, was with us in that band." I was amazed. The whole story was carefully repeated to Baby, who didn't remember the boss's kid. He also didn't remember the boss, the Greater Holcamp Carnival Shows, and was somewhat surprised to learn that he had ever been in Texas. He wasn't skeptical about it. He just expected other people to remember things for him. (Most of Baby's life was spent in an unfamiliar galaxy.) Bunk, however, corroborated Baby's presence on that tour. I was, of course, overwhelmed to learn that these great jazzmen had been part of my childhood.

Bunk also told me that we had had a one-legged blues singer and guitar player traveling with the show who had achieved a certain success in the music business. I remembered a fellow who answered to that description who was employed to perform in front of the sideshows to attract a crowd. Bunk told me this was Walter "Furry" Lewis of Memphis, the virtuoso of the bottleneck guitar. I had the opportunity to check that report out with Furry in later years when he came to stay at my house in New Orleans while filling a musical engagement. Amazingly, it checked out.

The concert that evening was beautiful. I got to record some of it on wire. It includes Wild Bill and Bunk playing together. Paul Mares turned up gratuitously for the session and was on stage with his horn. I thought he was playing along, but the playback reveals no trace of his sound. I played it for Joe Mares, too, but he could detect no trace of his talented brother's presence, either.

After the concert, Bunk and Nick and I went to Billy Yancey's to eat, and we talked about Bunk's revival. He had proved to be articulate and outspoken. Apparently my ear had matured sufficiently to be able to follow his speech patterns. Most musicians are careful to speak no evil about their fellow performers. Not so Bunk.

> So now I'm stuck with this band. They got me a trombone player, Jim Robinson. I swear he come out of some Hawaiian band. He don't know but three changes and he don't always make *them* in the right place—and he don't wanna learn nothin' new! You ever hear of a musician like that? An' a clarinet player! George Lewis, he knows how to play a little blues an' that's all. Like you see Nick here? He hears the harmony. You play him a lead, he plays you the harmony. But that guy? Them people, Russell and them, they found him an' I'm stuck with him. 'Course, Baby's okay. The li'l bass player got a good enough beat, but he don't make no changes. It might as well be a drum. I got 'em to get me a white boy, Don Ewell, to play the piano. He's a shark. The guy that come up here with me, Alton Purnell, is okay, too, but he really don't know the basics. I really enjoyed comin' here to play for you tonight. Real musicians. An' it was good to see ol' George again. [George Baquet, the great New Orleans clarinetist of jazz's earliest days, had come backstage to say hello to his old colleagues.]

I had occasion to see and talk with Bunk several more times before he died in 1949. I suppose he represented my earliest personal association with a New Orleans jazz musician. The four or five times I heard him in live performance before an audience, I came to understand his stature as a trumpeter and leader. His records reveal very little of his actual ability. They couldn't and didn't demonstrate the extent of his inventiveness, the firmness and facility with which his dominant lead drove the ensemble.

I also came to understand that for the most part his musical objectives had little in common with those of the musicians who had been assigned to make up his band. "People don't want to hear those same old numbers all the time. 'Panama,' 'Muskrat Ramble,' you know, 'When the Saints Go Marchin' In.' When I come up, we learned the new tunes soon as they come out. Musicians got to move with the times. Can't keep playin' the same thing all the time. People don't want that. They want to hear the new songs."

Not what I expected to hear from the dean of New Orleans jazz trumpet players.

Edmond Souchon

Over the phone, he said: "Man, I do believe my family's tryin' to *kill* me! I promised Marie [pronounced with a flat *a* and with the accent on the first syllable] I was gonna take her for a visit to California, and I swear, I'm too sick to go. I'm not over this damn flu yet. And it's not only my wife! My daughter Dolly Ann, too. They say, 'Get out in that California sunshine! It'll do you good. You'll feel better.' All that kind of stuff. Even my brother Harry is after me to go to California. I'm not well enough to go to California—or anyplace."

I happened to know there were good reasons for Sou not to want to go to California right then. Of course, he'd promised to go and he'd keep the promise if the ladies in his family insisted. I suspected, though, that he was using his recent bout with the flu to try to postpone the vacation. I said, treacherously, "Might be a good idea. The change could do you good."

"You, too, you son of a bitch?" he demanded. "You're all tryin' to kill me."

The problem was, of course, that we were all in on a secret we were keeping from Sou. He and Marie were to be the guests of Karl Kramer, one of the founders of the Music Corporation of America (MCA). Karl was to take him on a tour of the CBS studios and, once there, to steer him through a door that would bring him on stage and camera, face to face with Ralph Edwards, as the guest of honor on

"This Is Your Life." An all-star jazz band, including Eddie Condon and Muggsy Spanier, had been summoned to abet Sou's musical efforts, and I was one of the people the CBS researchers had contacted to help supply data and photographs. I was, of course, sworn to secrecy, because it was supposed to come as a complete surprise to Sou when the host said, "Doctor Edmond Souchon—*This* Is Your Life!"

I wasn't one of the people invited to make the trek to California, so I stayed home and watched on television. I saw the show open on a semidarkened hallway at CBS. Walking slowly in the hall were Sou and Karl. I saw Karl put his hand on a doorknob to open it, and I saw Doc lean toward him and say something the TV audience couldn't hear. Then Karl opened the door onto the TV stage where Sou, in the brilliant glare of the Kleig lights, stood nonplussed, realizing suddenly, I'm sure, the cause of the strange conduct of his family and friends during the preceding week or so.

Well, Sou did what he was supposed to do. He was affable and friendly, though I noticed he seemed ill at ease, a state in which he was rarely to be found. Nevertheless, he played his banjo and guitar, he sang, he listened as the host recounted the fact that he had dragged ten thousand infants, kicking and screaming, into this world. He accepted the accolades and the deluxe souvenir scrap book graciously. Then the show was over.

A week or so later we met for lunch at Commander's Palace to discuss the publication of our joint venture, *New Orleans Jazz: A Family Album*, for which we would ultimately win the Louisiana Book Award. I congratulated him on the tribute the TV show had paid him, and I commented that he hadn't looked as happy on camera as I would have expected. "You seemed uncomfortable," I said.

"How the hell would *you* feel?" he demanded. "You saw right at the beginning—before Karl opened the door—you saw me lean over to him and say something?"

I recalled that I had noticed that.

Sou explained, "What I said to him was, 'Is it possible that in this whole damn place they don't have a men's room?'"

Sou and I were natural collaborators. Both of us accepted a leisurely approach to work. We shared our musical interests, produced happy LP's together, stood in for each other as speakers. We'd call each other to pass along the news when some out-of-town jazzman was coming in, and together we'd do what we could to help him have a pleasant visit. We went to the ragtime festival in St. Louis in 1967, and I had the pleasure of hearing him perform a blues that I had written, to tumultuous applause. That took place on the riverboat *Goldenrod*, which has a rather large, conventional theater where melodramas are frequently presented. Sou sang "Mindin' Your Business Blues," which I wrote just for him and which he recorded a number of times. When he came to the last lines,

> I didn't rob no money—it wasn't nothin' that I done—
> I just give a gal some lovin' when she didn't crave it none.

it brought down the house. I'd like to think it was my deathless lyric that did it, but more likely it was Sou's irresistible delivery.

The two of us visited many ailing jazz greats in their last days. I remember when we left little Monk Hazel for the last time, Sou said, "There goes another one. Pretty soon it'll only be you and me."

When I wrote the book *Storyville, New Orleans*, he proved to have genuinely reliable firsthand recollections of the red-light district. And he was also able to direct me to people even more intimately involved with it, though he made me promise not to tell Marie about the misdeeds of his youth.

Not too long before he died Sou put together a fascinating autobiography, including a substantial selection of excellent photographs. He gave it to me to read before submitting it for publication. Because I'm interested in the social history of New Orleans, the book mesmerized me. But by the time I was finished I realized that he'd had virtually nothing to say about jazz or his role in it. The manuscript was the entertaining memoir of a successful physician—not exactly what the mass market was likely to storm the local bookshop for. In discussing the work I made this point, suggesting strongly that Sou add a great deal of material about his life in jazz. I myself was aware of and a witness to a variety of reportable events.

But Sou was hardheaded, never morbidly addicted to sweet reason. He sent the memoir to a publisher that found in it the same shortcomings I had. Pettishly, he suggested that I had raised these questions in their minds, though as a matter of fact I had never discussed the project with this publisher.

I did write a long piece about him in *Second Line* entitled "The

Wonderful Wizard of Oz A La Creole." (*Second Line* is the quarterly magazine published by the New Orleans Jazz Club.) Because of its fascinating subject, the article brought in more mail than the publication had ever received in response to a single article.

Sou died in August, 1968, just a few months after our *New Orleans Jazz: A Family Album* was published. He had been ailing—though hiding the fact—through all the time the volume was in progress. When we planned it, both of us conceived of it as a tax shelter. We reasoned that the processing costs for our photographic collections would be high enough to insure a substantial loss. It seemed obvious to us that the work could never return in royalties anything like what it cost us to deliver it. To everybody's surprise, our first period royalties ran into the thousands, and Sou said, "Now it's *really* gonna cost us!"

Both the second, enlarged, revised edition of 1978 and the even more revised and enlarged edition of 1984 continued to carry Edmond Souchon's name alongside mine. I wouldn't have had it any other way.

Pee Wee Spitlera

Only recently someone told me that Pee Wee Spitlera had retired. *Retired?* That little child, *retired?* Why it was only yesterday. . . .

He had a distinguished career as a clarinetist to Jumbo (Al Hirt) and developed a following of his own not only in Jumbo's Bourbon Street nightclub, but among the TV audiences that noticed there was something special in the tone of this roly-poly little fellow whose every note was pure New Orleans.

Okay. So he's retired. After all, I just looked up his age and he *is* forty-six. I suppose he saved his money while the pay was good. I suppose he made a few decent investments. Why not? Why shouldn't he retire?

I think back to 1954. In those days at 112 Royal Street in New Orleans, on the second floor, there was a place called the "Parisian Room" where the proprietor, trumpet player Tony Almerico, hosted a regular Saturday afternoon jam session to which jazz fans across the nation had become addicted, since they could tune it in on 50,000 watt, clear-channel WWL, which conducted a weekly live broadcast of the proceedings. Pee Wee then had a nice tone for a sixteen-year-old, and Tony would let him sit in with the band until the broadcast started. There were top musicians on those shows—Jack Delaney,

Deacon Loyacano, even, before he died, Fazola. People like Stanley
Mendelson or Bob Doyle might be on piano. Usually Tony stomped
things off at tempos that were too fast to make for the best jazz, but it
was a good-time place and a good-time party. It was always fun.

We used to tease Pee Wee because, even though he had reached
the advanced age of sixteen, he looked closer to eleven. He never had
any smart comebacks. He'd just look at you with those big, wide eyes
and apply himself to blowing the best horn he could.

The first week that Tony Parenti came back to town after an ab-
sence of two decades, Almerico called me and asked if I'd bring the
master clarinetist up to his radio talk show. I said I thought Parenti
would do that, and later Parenti agreed. We went up there and spent
an hour on the air, talking about old times and listening to records.
Then on Saturday, I was in the French Quarter with Parenti, eating
oysters at the Acme, and I suggested we go around the corner to the
Parisian Room for the jam session. I thought Tony might enjoy meeting some of his old friends. So we went up and walked in. Pee Wee,
his eyes shut, was wailing away on some war horse. Just as the number
was over, I brought Parenti up to the low bandstand. He shook hands
with bass player Joe Loyacano, an old friend, and greeted others he
knew. We came to where Pee Wee was standing. He had never seen
Parenti, of course. The maestro had been gone too long. But like
every young New Orleans clarinet hopeful, he knew the name and
was familiar with all the Parenti records.

I was saying, "Tony, this little kid is Pee Wee Spitlera—and Pee
Wee, I know you'll be happy to shake hands with Tony Parenti." Pee
Wee's reaction was instantaneous. With a motion quick enough to
rival the great Houdini, he whisked his clarinet behind his back so
Parenti wouldn't think he'd have the presumption to attempt to play
it in the great man's presence.

Parenti was at his benign best. He chuckled at Pee Wee's ingen-
uousness and said, "Don't worry, kid. You sound good. I heard the
last chorus you played and you're okay—and you're gonna be even
better. Now on the next number, you and I are gonna play a little
duet. You know 'Cecilia'?"

Pee Wee knew it and Tony made arrangements with the band.
"Now you just play the melody, kid. Don't let anything get you off the
melody. And then don't worry. You'll see. It'll sound great."

So the grand master of New Orleans clarinet and the new kid got into it. Pee Wee didn't feel like he was doing anything but it sounded like the angels, and I always had the feeling the kid learned a lot from the five minutes they were on the stand together. The audience, naturally, was ecstatic. Later Pee Wee told me, "I always thought a great man like that would be, well—hard to get to know. But he's just like anybody else. Whew! I was scared to be standin' there alongside him and tryin' to *play!*"

And that's the little kid who has just *retired?*

Morten Gunnar Larsen

Morten Gunnar Larsen is one of the great jazz and ragtime pianists in the world. His only problem is that he lives in Norway, apparently on purpose. Now in his mid-twenties, he devotes himself to concert work in Europe, playing mainly the works of Scott Joplin, Jelly Roll Morton, and Louis Moreau Gottschalk.

On his first visit to the United States in the late 1970s, he spoke virtually no English. But at a party at my place in New Orleans in honor of Eubie Blake, he melted the ladies with a dazzling smile, European manners, and general modesty.

Morten was overwhelmed with the excitement of meeting Eubie in person. I told Eubie this nineteen-year-old was a piano shark. Morten was reluctant to demonstrate his abilities before the legendary composer and virtuoso, but we overcame his diffidence, though not without difficulty. He opened with Eubie's challenging "Charleston Rag," which was composed in 1899 with the express motive of "cutting" all his contemporaries in piano competition. Eubie would later say he didn't think he, himself, had ever rendered the piece so flawlessly. With urging, Morten continued to play for most of the afternoon. Eubie never moved, but at last he said, "I been waitin' all day for this kid to make a mistake, but he never did."

Danny Barker

Anytime I get back to New Orleans after having been away for an appreciable time, there are a few people I check in with—first to satisfy myself that they're all right and second to find out what's going on. One of these is my old and valued friend, Danny Barker, one of jazz's great musician-entertainers.

There has been a rumor afloat for years in the jazz world that Danny Barker is an outstanding writer, and I happen to know that's true. I have had the opportunity to read through his unpublished manuscripts, and I can enthusiastically report that he's as good a teller of tales as I've read. Danny turned all that stuff over to me in the hope that I could help him sort it out and put it into the initial stages of preparation for submission to publishers. I have also personally brought the material to two publishers, both of whom were delighted with the material and with Danny's often hilarious literary style. The reason you've never gotten to read any of this material is that nothing ever gets finished.

I spent a lot of time with Danny, explaining the differences between primary and secondary sources. I pointed out to him that he is himself a primary source, as is demonstrated by the frequency with which he is quoted (and sometimes credited) in books by other people. Together we fished out of his pile of writings all of what was written in the first person, with a view toward putting together a volume based entirely on his own personal recollections and experiences. Together we drew up a table of contents. I suggested to him that if he would *finish* each memoir he had begun, he'd wind up with a very publishable book. But it's one of Danny's weaknesses that every yarn reminds him of something else he wants to tell. So he wanders off into delightful and brilliant development of one more unfinished tale. Nobody can write finishes on Danny's yarns because only he knows how they end. I keep hoping that he'll grasp the simple principle involved and go on to produce what will become a gem in the literature of jazz. He also has exceptional skill in writing historical fiction based on the early New Orleans scene, sometimes using characters drawn directly from life. He has clearly mastered the techniques for bringing his people to life. I remain confident that some day he'll bring it off.

Many of his friends don't know that he's also an excellent painter. Unschooled though he is, he has the eye as well as the ear of an artist. Add to all that his well-known abilities as a composer, plus the universally recognized fact that he's one of the swing world's all-time great rhythm guitarists, holds his own as a singer of blues and comedy numbers, and is as spellbinding a monologist as jazz has produced and you have a formidable renaissance man in the Da Vinci mold.

I will not attempt to tell any of Danny's stories. Nobody can tell them as well as he can, and I'm still hoping he will. But I *can* tell you

I've produced Danny on many records, beginning early in the forties, that we've worked together on network TV projects, on radio and films. I've introduced him from many a distinguished concert stage and never seen him fail to hold the audience in the palm of his hand.

Danny's wife, as you know, is no run-of-the-automatic-washer housewife, though that's what she's always aspired to be. A highly successful singer on phonograph records since her 1938 Decca successes, Blue Lu brought something stylistically new to the chanteuse's world, and a host of imitators have borrowed her phrasing ideas. By nature she's not a show-biz person. But being married to Danny for so many years—they must be near a golden wedding anniversary—has forced her to put her delightful vocal skills on display in public.

These days, Danny is a model citizen. He doesn't smoke or drink. He involves himself in developing talent among kids in the hope of generating a new layer of jazz talent for the future. His Fairview Baptist Church Brass Band has already turned out an inordinate number of professionals who have joined the ranks of our jazzmen. He's toured the public school system talking about the music and performing it. The city accepts him as a kind of informal spokesman for the jazz community.

But the very first time I met Danny he hadn't yet become a model citizen. Of course, I *remember* him when I was a kid in the French Quarter. He's several years older than I am, and he used to play in a spasm band in the streets. He performed with a cigar box. He sang and danced a strange little second-line style dance. Anyone could see he was a rhythm man. I didn't meet him then, but I watched him.

Grown up and in college, I read all the jazz publications, which in those days had a lot to say about the New Orleans banjo-guitarist Danny Barker. He was always being nominated for all those hokey awards that *Downbeat* and *Esquire* were always giving out. The press made sure I knew who Danny Barker was. I used to emerge from class right across the street from Nixon's Grand Theater on North Broad Street in Philadelphia. This was a theater that featured black vaudeville. The day Lucky Millender and his Mills Blue Rhythm Orchestra opened there, I went across to say hello to the featured sideman, Henry "Red" Allen, whom I knew and who had already played one concert gig under my auspices. Red and I walked around in the backstage area and came upon a slight figure in a tuxedo, lying on the floor and leaning against a two-by-four. He was snoring loudly, but people just walked around him or stepped over him. It had been twelve years or so and we had both grown up, but I recognized him instantly. The same kid that had played the cigar box and entertained in the streets of the French Quarter.

"I remember him!" I told Red. "What's his name?"

"You got to know him. That's Danny Barker, the guitar player. That's Paul's [Barbarin] nephew. I hope he comes around before show time. He had a hard night, but he made the first show. Don't look too good right now—but we don't go for another hour. Kid drinks too damn much. He'll learn you can't do that and stay in the big time very long."

So I met Danny—though he didn't meet me. Another time I was having dinner in Frank's on 125th Street in Harlem with Jimmy Pemberton, the powerful district leader for that area. There was Danny—again dressed formally, but obviously long out of it.

"That's a musician guy from *your* hometown. You know him?"

I nodded. "Danny Barker," I said. "Great musician." Then I had a recording date with Dan Burley scheduled at Steinway Hall and I needed a guitar player. I asked Dan if he had any suggestions. "Danny Barker," he proposed. "That's the best guitar player I know."

"Do you think you can get him to the hall in shape to play?" I asked, tentatively. "Every time I see him he's so far gone he can't see." Dan guaranteed he'd get him there. And I suppose that's really the first time Danny Barker met *me*.

Over the years we've been to lots of places together—St. Louis, Memphis, New York, Florida, New Orleans, Chicago—and each time he came up with experiences to recount that I'd never heard before. Once when I was driving him to an airport in Memphis he described the ceremony during which he had become a Baptist, and his narrative is one of the great comic monologues of all time. In fact some enterprising record company would do well to issue a record of Danny's tales of the jazzman's life. In 1982 we were both panelists in a scholarly forum with Jelly Roll Morton as the subject. The other distinguished panelists were Fred Ramsey, Alan Lomax, Bill Russell, Richard B. Allen, and Dr. Lawrence Gushee. Danny and Lomax left the rest of us little to do as the two of them extemporized a routine, with Lomax as straight man, that left the audience in Dixon Hall at Tulane University limp with laughter.

George Baquet

In the mid-1940s, after my discharge from the army, I lived in Philadelphia for three years, doing publicity work, mainly theatrical and
musical. I had a house in Quince Street, which is the heart of the
downtown section of the city. Just three blocks away was the Earle
Theater, which featured the top vaudeville acts of the day. In that
time period, the featured attraction was usually a big-name swing
band. As was customary then, theaters of this type always employed a
pit orchestra, too, since the featured traveling band wasn't expected to
supply the music for other acts on the bill.

The Earle orchestra was of exceptionally high quality and important to me because it included New Orleans clarinetist George Baquet,
who had been a member of Jelly Roll Morton's first Red Hot Peppers.
George used to come by my place almost every afternoon for coffee
or, on occasion, a drink. Then we'd sit and talk about music, about
old times in New Orleans, about his father Theogene V. Baquet,
a preacher who also taught music. George told me he thought his
brother Achille, who played in the New Orleans Jazz Band of which
Jimmy Durante was pianist, might go back home to live—things like
that. Sometimes, when a New Orleans fellow was in one of the traveling swing bands, *he'd* come by with George. When Jimmy Lunceford
did his week at the Earle, he had Omer Simeon with him. Millinder
had Red Allen. And, of course, Paul Barbarin and Nicholas were
always either with Luis Russell or Armstrong or somebody else. My
place became a kind of informal headquarters for Crescent City jazzmen away from home—and I enjoyed it. George was in his early sixties at the time, but he looked and moved like a very old man. And in
fact he died in 1949, though he continued to play in the theater and at
Pop Wilson's Bar almost until the very end.

One of the things we talked about at length was the legendary
Bolden cylinder. Jazz collectors know that reasonably reliable testimony has indicated that the Buddy Bolden band, hallowed in the history of jazz, was once actually recorded on a cylinder. Needless to say,
herculean academic efforts have been made to document that event,
not to mention the infinite stratagems that have been employed to
locate the cylinder itself.

I had been told by Bob Lyons, Bolden's sometime bass player who
claimed to have performed on that cylinder, that Baquet had been the

clarinetist. George told me he had indeed played on the recording. He also added further information, that there had been two clarinet players. He didn't remember who the other one was, but suggested it would have been either Big Eye Louie (Nelson Delisle) or Picou. (Thirteen years later, Picou would identify himself as the other clarinetist. *He* recalled Baquet on the session.) George recalled further that they had played "Make Me a Pallet on the Floor" and "Chicken Reel," both on the same cylinder. ("Chicken Reel" wasn't published until 1910, years too late for Bolden. But the tune is nothing but "Turkey in the Straw" in a different key, so it's reasonable that both Baquet and Picou might have called it "Chicken Reel" since it came to be known by that name later in their experience.)

I always enjoyed providing circumstances that made it possible for the original founders of authentic jazz to get together in later life—to play, if possible, and if not, then just to talk. At one time or another, I had the chance to reunite Baquet with Kid Ory, Mutt Carey, Baby Dodds, Paul Barbarin, Zutty Singleton, and John Lindsay. George said such reunions made him feel young again. It was while I was planning to build a jazz concert around him that he had the stroke that eventually led to his death. I suppose there's always some unfinished business in every life.

Louis Armstrong

In 1966, *Life* magazine published a large cover story about Satch. Richard Meryman put the piece together, but it consisted almost entirely of Louis' tape-recorded reminiscences about his career, plus a large number of old photographs, many of which I was able to supply. The editors sent the piece to me for comments before publishing it, and I was very glad they did. Louis frequently had the most colorful and detailed recollections of things that never happened, and their publication could have easily led to unnecessary embarrassment for him. Several months later I happened to be in Macon, Georgia, at the same time Louis and his All-Stars were doing a concert there. I went backstage to see him. Properly, there was an efficient screening process for people wanting to see Louis. It began with Ira Mangel, his band manager. You had to ask for Ira, and if you didn't know that name you just didn't get to see Satch.

"I hope you didn't mind, Louis," I said, "that I made so many changes in the story in *Life*. Some of those things are wrong and you wouldn't want them printed."

Louis said, "People ask me about things happened fifty years ago. I can't remember what happened yesterday." Then he asked, "What did I tell him wrong?"

"That stuff about playing in Storyville. You never played in Storyville," I said.

"Sure I played in Storyville," he insisted. "I played in Henry Ponce's saloon."

I shook my head. "That I know, but Ponce's saloon wasn't in Storyville." I continued, "Do you know where the district actually *was?*"

"Do I know where it was? Sure, I know where it was! I grew up in the district! Perdido Street, South Rampart Street—all in there!"

I sat shaking my head.

"Why you shakin' yo' head? Dat's the district!"

I explained to him where the district actually was and that the neighborhood of his youth wasn't it. He seemed shocked to learn this information. Then he said, "I depend on guys like you to know that kinda stuff. Jeez. I wonder how many people I told dat I was a kid in Storyville?"

Tyree Glenn came into the dressing room and Louis said, "Al jus' told me that where I grew up—what I been tellin' reporters an' magazine people for forty years—well, that ain't Storyville at all."

Tyree said, "Everybody tells me you're ignorant and I tell 'em you ain't—but I guess I'll have to stop that."

It wasn't too long after that the band came to play in New Orleans at the Municipal Auditorium. I didn't plan to attend because it bothered me to hear how the music had deteriorated, to see Louis relying on all his novelty devices and singing so much. I knew it was difficult for him to play the horn, certainly not on the level that had earned him his fame in the jazz world. I just sent him a note of greeting. I did receive an invitation to a party at the Royal Orleans. It was being given for him at the Royal Orleans Hotel, but I didn't plan to go. I never enjoyed these social activities.

I knew lots of people were planning to go out to the airport to welcome Louis home, but again, it's not my kind of scene. I stayed away. Louis wouldn't miss me.

That evening, Allan Jaffe called me on the phone. He told me that Punch Miller had asked to be taken to the airport to watch Louis' arrival. He hadn't seen him in thirty years, and he was proud of his old friend's success. Allan took Punch. When Louis got off the plane, he recognized Punch in the crowd. Being unable to reach him through that mob, he turned to his beautiful wife Lucille and instructed her to stay behind and get hold of Punch, to invite him to the party the New Orleans Jazz Club was giving for him. Lucille did as Louis had asked her, and Allan said Punch went home walking on air.

Allan took Punch, dressed in his good suit, to the Royal Orleans for the party, and the people at the door wouldn't admit him. Allan explained about the invitation direct from Satch, but to no avail. They had then tried to call Louis from the lobby, but whoever answered the phone refused to call him. Allan took a very much disappointed Punch back to his apartment. Then he called me. I'm sure he was at least as distressed as Punch.

"You know Louis," Allan said. "He ought to know about what happened up there. Punch is convinced they wouldn't let him in because he's black."

"I'll get Louis on the phone right away and call you back," I promised. So I called Ira Mangel at his hotel and asked for Satch. Ira said he wouldn't be available for an hour but that he'd call me then.

I had to go out for just a few minutes, but I knew I had plenty of time to get back before Satch returned my call. Well, he called back a minute after I'd left, and Georgia Dabney, who worked for me taking care of my young son Rex, answered the phone. He asked for me and said, "This is Louis Armstrong." And Georgia, that lovely lady, passed out. I was back in about fifteen minutes. When I asked Georgia if there had been any calls, she told me there hadn't but that she'd found the phone off the hook (which obviously happened when she fainted). A few minutes later, Louis called and said, "I just called you and a lady answered but then she didn't talk no mo'. I was worried your phone might not be workin'."

I then related all that Jaffe had told me about his efforts to get Punch admitted to the party. Louis said, "Al, I got to ask you to do somethin' for me. It really means a whole lot to me and I wouldn't ask you to go to no trouble if it wasn't real important. Could you get a hold of Jaffe and Punch and make sure they come to the concert to-morrow night? Tell 'em there'll be tickets with Punch's name at the box office. Then make sure they come backstage at intermission. They can get in because they ain't gonna let nobody else but them back there. I got to let him know I didn't have nothin' to do with that."

So I called Allan and related the conversation. He said Punch was pretty upset but that he'd try to get him there. This is one of the jazz stories that has a happy ending. When Jaffe and Punch arrived at the box office, there was a message for Punch to come right backstage. Allan took him. There was Louis, getting ready to go on. He had a photographer there who took dozens of photographs of Punch and Satch together. There was a table laden with catered delicacies for Punch's enjoyment. He proposed that Punch remain backstage through the whole performance so they could visit. The cash customers got to see very little of Louis that night. He'd blow or sing a chorus, then he'd disappear behind the curtain and talk with Punch. He got the band to extend the ensemble parts, the musicians to take extra solos. Most of the time he and Punch talked over old times.

There was a line of people waiting to get to Louis for autographs during intermission, many of whom had attended the party at the Royal Orleans. Louis just let them wait—never even acknowledged them.

After his final bows he came back to Punch and stuffed several hundred dollar bills into his breast pocket and told him how much he had enjoyed seeing him again. Punch was virtually speechless. He told me later how thrilled he was with what Satch had done for him.

Louis called me later that night and said, "I want to thank you for getting Kid Punch over there tonight. I really appreciate it. I hope I squared everything with him. Them other people never did get backstage and I didn't give no autographs."

I was glad to have had the opportunity to help make things right between these two.

Knocky Parker

Don't let anybody tell you that Knocky Parker isn't one of the all-time jazz greats, because he is. That does not say he isn't a strange one, because he's that, too. He lives in Tampa, Florida, where he teaches various courses at the University of South Florida under the alias of Dr. John W. Parker. And he's never tried to discourage his highly indi-

vidual and charming son Johnny from continually filling the house
with snakes.

Knocky has many talents. One of his best is vanishing. You might
be attending a jazz or ragtime festival with him. Everybody's having a
great time planning the rest of the weekend, catching up on gossip,
going to dinner—all the things you do at a festival besides listen to
music. And then Knocky vanishes. Nobody sees him again until the
next festival, if then. Only recently, Knocky and I were booked to be
interviewed during a festival on the New Orleans public radio station,
WWOZ. He vanished, and I haven't heard from him since.

Anyway, the reasons I say he's one of the all-time jazz greats are
many. One of them is that he knows every tune you or I can think of.
He has that remarkable talent for knowing, as though it were genetic,
what chord to play in any situation. His remarkable, sometimes dazzling ragtime virtuosity is rendered even more amazing when you get
a chance to look at his hands, which are tiny, especially in proportion
to his six-foot frame. Most of all, what he plays is *satisfying*. Now
that's hard to explain—but when Knocky plays something you enjoy
it so much. You have the feeling that you're hearing the tune the way
it's really supposed to be played, for the first time. His novelty act in
which he shows a silent film and supplies the old-style piano accom-
paniment is both ingenious and hilarious. His ability to fit in with
other musicians in virtually any context cannot, I'm sure, be matched
by any other piano player.

Like all true artists, though, he's not without temperament, as I
have had more than one occasion to note. In 1959 I made a session
I'm very proud of, to a great extent because I had the good judgment
to engage Knocky for it. However, as you know, one can only put so
much music on a twelve-inch LP. It was necessary, predictably, for us
to cut down the routines on certain numbers just to try to conform
to our own programming frame. I had originally scheduled a rather
long and elaborate piano introduction to "Trouble in Mind," which I
cut, not failing to consider that I had also called for a full piano solo
in the body of the piece. The band started to play, and it sounded just
fine. I was sitting with the engineer. I had chalked up the blackboard
as a guide to the musicians. "Ensemble chorus, clarinet solo, piano
solo, half-banjo, half-bass" and so on.

After the first run through, I asked to have the number played back. The engineer and I looked at each other and simultaneously said, "Dead mike." He went over to check it out and spent maybe ten minutes making adjustments. Then we tested the microphone and it was obviously all right. The band played another take, with the same result. The piano wasn't coming through. Back went the engineer to check out the mike. I walked around among the musicians, and Sherwood Mangiapane, who was playing bass on the session, said, sotto voce, "Knocky ain't playin'."

"What do you mean, he ain't playin'?" I demanded.

"He ain't *playin'*," Sherwood insisted. "Maybe he's mad or somethin'—but he ain't playin'."

At once I confronted Knocky with this charge and he admitted, somewhat sheepishly, his guilt. Further probing exposed the fact that he was reacting to my having excised the piano introduction to "Trouble in Mind." A little arbitration resolved the matter, and it turned out to be a great, satisfying session.

During the early sixties, Knocky came to stay with me in Key Largo for a month, while he worked on his doctoral dissertation on the history of popular music in America. We spent countless hours discussing the subject. He knew all about it, but his confidence was suffering. He told me how much he wanted that doctorate, just to bring dignity and respect to the music he played. I read along as he wrote and was astonished at the actual amount and thoroughness of his research. Needless to say, the University of Kentucky conferred the degree upon him. He was a proud man.

In 1969, I invited a whole lot of people to my place in Hollywood, Florida, just for fun and possibly some recording—over Christmas week. Unfortunately the key guests, Bobby Hackett and Hoagy Carmichael, who were coming from New York, got snowed in, with all flights canceled. We had a good time anyway, Danny and Blue Lu Barker, Knocky, Johnny Dengler, Bob Greene. And, in fact, willy-nilly we *did* make a session of some truly beautiful things with Blue Lu singing and Danny and Knocky accompanying. I wondered if any singer had ever been more sensitively supported. The session is still in the safe—purely a matter of procrastination.

Hoagy later said to me, "What the hell did you need *me* for? You had some *real* piano players down there."

Anyway, sometime during the week's activities, Knocky vanished.

But he eventually reappeared because he always shows up for his bookings.

There have been any number of newspaper and magazine articles written about Knocky. But the jazz world, I'm sure, would really enjoy reading his autobiography, something he should write, going back to his exciting musical beginnings in his native Palmer, Texas.

My earliest memory of his playing goes back to 1936 and a bar somewhere that had a juke box. The band was weird. I hadn't heard it before. Then I heard the piano, and I knew I was listening to one of the masters. I played many records—maybe a dozen—until I hit that one again to find out what it was. I eventually identified it as a piece performed by the Light Crust Doughboys and entitled—if you're ready for this—"I Wonder Who's Boogiein' My Woogie Now." I went to some trouble to find out that the piano player's name was Knocky Parker. Ever since—and it's not far from fifty years—I've been following his career and his music with great interest and satisfaction.

Johnny Wiggs

It seems a shame that the name of Johnny Wiggs is so little known even to jazz fans, despite his magnificent recorded achievements and his inestimable part in the revival of authentic jazz in the forties and fifties. Wiggs was one of the very few who were able to teach aspiring kids the art of jazz and was responsible for developing George Girard, Jack Delaney, Pete Fountain, Sam Butera, and many other of the stars that generation produced.

It's not that nothing has ever been written about him or that he failed to write autobiographical articles which were published. But two considerations, I think, closed the door to world fame for this superlative artist. First, his personality somehow didn't project well to the public. Second, he deliberately avoided sensational musical devices. For that matter, considerations of showmanship of any kind never entered his head. His clear understanding of jazz as an art form was never approached by any other musician, and he was far and away the finest lead horn that ever performed under *my* auspices in any medium, live or recorded.

The bare bones of his career are these. His real name was John Wigginton Hyman. He changed his name because it was embarrassing

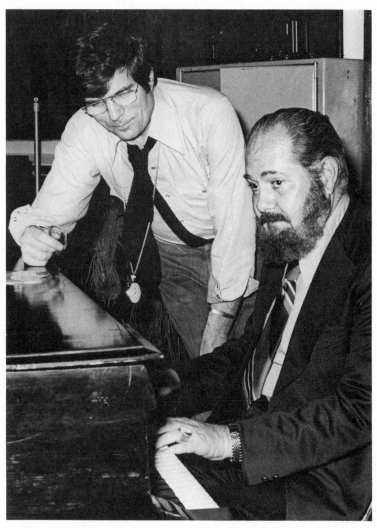

Jean Christophe Averty is the presiding genius of French TV. He used to be a ragtime piano player and insists I must be one, too. This was taken in his Channel 3 studio in Paris. I was translating a great documentary, "New Orleans Bien Aimée," into English. *Photo by Radio France staff photographer.*

This little fellow had the makings of a super hot trumpet, but Red Rodney
cooled off and joined Woody Herman's Herd in 1948. I couldn't stop him.
Photo by Nick Alexakis.

The Dixieland Rhythm Kings do a concert. From left to right are Robin Wettereau, Gene Mayl, Charlie Sonnanstine, Al Rose, Ted Belafield, Bob Hodes, and Jack Vastine. Those are matched Brooks Brothers suits made of Italian silk. Top quality. And that's what these six kids were.   *Photo by John Kuhlman.*

A jazz tribunal examines the life and works of Jelly Roll Morton at the 1983 Tulane Hot Jazz Classic. From left to right are Alan Lomax, Jelly's biographer; Danny Barker, a living jazz legend; Dr. Lawrence Gushee of the University of Illinois, author of the Smithsonian Institution jazz monographs; moderator John Joyce, professor of jazz studies at Tulane; Dr. William Russell, the dean of jazz historians; Richard B. Allen, coauthor of *The Brass Bands*; Fred Ramsay, author of *Jazzmen*; and Al Rose, author of *this* book and others.   *Photo by Joe Marcal.*

When the world was young and Dizzy hadn't yet bent his trumpet. *Photo by Nick Alexakis.*

Oran "Hot Lips" Page, left, never knew the tunes, but whatever he played grabbed you. I don't care what Bud Freeman, right, tells you. *I* think he looks like a musician. *Photo by Nick Alexakis.*

The High Society Jazz Band of Paris. The Napoleon in front is Pierre Merlin
—artist, comedian, cornetist, and bon vivant. Behind him is the leader,
Pierre Atlan, between Diana, rear left, and the lovely piano player, Martine
Morel. This was in Deauville in 1976.   *Photo by Michele Atlan.*

I'm not standing in a hole. I'm six feet one. But Stan Kenton had to be measured in yards.   *Photo by Nick Alexakis.*

Walter "Furry" Lewis, maestro of the bottleneck guitar, with Betty "Washboard" Redelsheimer, rhythm queen of St. Louis. This was in the Peabody Hotel in Memphis in 1970.   *Photo by Harry Godwin.*

Johnny St. Cyr, nerve center of the Louis Armstrong Hot 5, and Doc
Souchon get together on a blues by Al Rose, who tried to keep his cool.
Photo by John Kuhlman.

I told him he had a big future as a clarinet player, but Woody Allen, right,
keeps saying he doesn't have time. In the striped shirt is Dr. Henry Blackburn,
who plays soprano saxophone and built his own hospital in Minnesota. On
the left is Ron Goins, a jazz fan from California. His wife isn't in the picture
so she must have taken it.

Sam Hayakawa is a first-class ragtime piano player. The senate kept interfering, though. Here we exchange our newly published books in the United States Senate office building. *Senate staff photo.*

I'd have fired the photographer if I had been entirely out of this picture with Miff Mole, Pee Wee Russell, and Sidney Bechet. *Photo by Harry Romm.*

Jovial Jack Teagarden liked running a locomotive almost as much as playing the trombone (1939).   *Photo by Nick Alexakis.*

Pete Fountain before either of us wore beards.   *Photo by Mary Mitchell.*

Eddie Condon, seated, and George Brunies. He sang "Everybody Loves My Baby" at Manassas, Virginia, in 1970. *Photo by Harry Godwin.*

Claude Luter, Europe's premiere jazzman, left, and Pierre Atlan, right. I never knew there were that many cabooses in New Orleans railyards. *Photo by Michele Atlan.*

Rudi Blesh, center, ragtime guru, and Edmond Souchon, right, telling me the S.S. *Goldenrod* is sinking. If it had been, they'd already be in the life-boats. This was the St. Louis Ragtime Festival of 1966.   *Photo by Dr. Charles Riley.*

I try to explain to Eddie Miller that a saxophone isn't a genuine musical instrument.   *Photo by Johnny Donnels.*

Buddy Rich played great drums even with a broken arm.

Vaughn Monroe. I arranged for him to take jazz trombone lessons from virtuoso Al Leopold. But the girls only wanted him to sing "Racing with the Moon."

Jimmy McPartland, leader of Chicago's famed Austin High Gang, which included Gene Krupa, Dave Tough, and Jim Lannigan. McPartland became a jazz legend in his own time when he replaced Bix in the Wolverines.

In the fifties, Almerico's Parisian Room was the place to go on a Sunday afternoon in New Orleans. But if you lived in Maine or Oregon you could hear the sounds on your radio. *Photo by Mary Mitchell.*

At sixteen, Sonny Dunham made the hit trumpet chorus on the Casa Loma Orchestra recording of "Memories of You." When I introduced him to the composer, Eubie Blake, in 1940, he turned to me and asked, "Is *he* still alive?" Sonny was embarrassed, but Eubie told him, "I hear that all the time."

Early be-bop. I didn't understand the music then, but I gave it a whirl anyway. After I figured it out, I knew I really hated it. Here, left to right, are vocalist Billy Scott; Jimmy Heath, baritone sax; Al Steele; unknown trumpeter; Percy Heath, later famous as organizer and bassist of the so-called Modern Jazz Quartet; Jimmy Oliver; and unknown drummer. I have fallen out of the picture on the left.   *Photo by Nick Alexakis.*

to his family to have a jazz musician in the family. His grandfather
was chief justice in Louisiana and his uncle wrote, for Alderman
Sidney Story, the ordinance that established Storyville, New Orleans'
notorious legal red-light district.

In 1929 he recorded for Victor under the name of Johnny Hyman's
Bayou Stompers. He founded the New Orleans Jazz Club in 1949.
Born July 25, 1899, he died on October 10, 1977. His musical legacy
is perhaps a dozen LP's and some distinguished original compositions,
including "The Canal Street March" (the official march of the City of
New Orleans), "King Zulu Parade," "The Postman's Lament," "Two
Wing Temple in the Sky," and "Ultra Canal." He assimilated the musical styles of King Oliver and Bix Beiderbecke, blending them into
his own highly personal approach to his cornet. His favorite recording
partners were the trombonists Tom Brown (with whom he was not on
speaking terms for most of their professional careers), Emile Christian, Jack Delaney, and Paul Crawford; clarinetists Harry Shields and
Raymond Burke; pianist Armand Hug; guitarists Snoozer Quinn and
Danny Barker; bassist Sherwood Mangiapane; and drummer Sammy
Penn. Actually, his very favorite drummer was Von Gammon, but he
never recorded with him. I had the great personal privilege of producing, or otherwise contributing to, much of his recording output.

From all of this you might easily conclude that Johnny and I were
also close friends, and indeed we were. I'm sure I spent more time
with him than with any other musician. He would come to my place
in Florida for extended visits, and in New Orleans we explored the
culinary delights of low-class restaurants with much satisfaction. We'd
also listen to records together a lot, which is something most jazzmen
don't do. Sometimes we'd pick up Raymond Burke for an outing.
Together we'd roam New Orleans, always remarking on its unique
charms and congratulating ourselves for having the good fortune and
good judgment to live there. Johnny and I would also go to hear other
jazz musicians perform. We might stop in at Shakey's Pizza Parlor if
Jeff Riddick was playing piano, or go up to the Esplanade Lounge of
the Royal Orleans to spend an entire evening soaking up the sounds of
Armand Hug. We sometimes went long distances together to attend
jazz festivals, just to listen to the live tone of Wingy Mannone or the
subtle ingenuity of Bobby Hackett. Wiggs, on a session, could get
so lost in admiration for a fellow performer's work that he'd forget to
come in on his own chorus.

Wiggs, like no other musician, knew the proper role and function of each instrument in a jazz band. He rated musicians almost entirely on their abilities to improvise collectively in the jazz ensemble. Whatever else they did in the way of solos he felt was secondary. Since I was in complete agreement, it was inevitable that we should work on many things together.

But nobody's perfect.

John's main hang-up, once in the recording studio, was his fear that he was being set up too far from the microphone and that the lead wouldn't be heard. (Of course all this took place in the years before 16-track recording apparatus.) As a result, after I had him seated where I knew the balance would be at its best, he would keep hitching his chair forward, inching closer to the microphone to make sure he'd be heard. Of course, the playback would show—even to him—that the cornet was too close, so I'd move him back and we'd do it again. But the action was subconscious and happened while he was actually concentrating on what he was playing. Eventually I dealt with the problem by driving nails into the floor in front of his chair legs. He'd keep on hitching at it in an effort to move closer to the mike, but of course he stayed put.

I don't think I ever mentioned his sweet, even disposition. That's because he didn't have one. He was irascible, impatient with incompetence, in or out of music, infuriated by colleagues who didn't want to get together for rehearsals to add to their repertoires. (He failed to take note of the fact that the other fellows had to play music for a living and thus had to work most nights and many days.) There were musicians he absolutely refused to play alongside, for real or fancied reasons.

Johnny owned a substantial amount of property—enough to support himself, his wife, and his mother-in-law comfortably. It never got through to him that everyone else was not in the same position. He seemed to regard poverty as a personal idiosyncrasy. However, confronted with *actual* deprivation, he always felt a responsibility to do something about it. He was rabidly anticapitalist and prounion. He was a substantial contributor to any cause endorsed by Martin Luther King, whom he considered the greatest living American, an extraordinary view for a white New Orleans jazz musician.

I wrote an article about him once, entitled "Both of Johnny Wiggs," separating the stern and remorseless music teacher, Professor Hyman, from the fun-loving jazz musician. He called me on the phone when the article came out and insisted I'd used my imagination too freely. Then later in the day, he called again and said his friends had been calling him all day about it. "You bastard!" he said. "They all love it."

Jean Christophe Averty

The word *genius* is, in our time, used much too freely. Even among that rarefied class, the majority aren't necessarily conspicuous. I want to call your attention to one who is in fact a genius—it might not even be inappropriate to employ the cliché "mad genius"—and who *is* conspicuous. He is Jean Christophe Averty. He lives and works in Paris, which he loves, far away from New Orleans, which he also loves. "Paradise," he says, "is to live in Paris and have New Orleans on the other side of the Seine."

Averty began his career as a jazz piano player. He was in the original High Society Jazz Band of Paris (its first pianist), but gravitated into the media to become France's—and maybe the world's—most creative television director. Certainly in dealing with authentic jazz the excellence of his TV treatments has been approached by no one. He has countless classic rags in his head, is one of the major collectors of jazz sheet music and books, and has made enough personal appearances on the tube to make him a familiar face to all Frenchmen. Walking with Averty through the streets of Paris is a unique experience. He carries on a running conversation with the city. It's impossible to go ten steps without someone hailing him from a car or a store front with a comment on his work or some published statement. And he replies—always with good humor, but without ever halting his pace. His personal influence is enormous, and he has had substantial input into his government's communications policies.

Once, when I had come to Paris for just a few days with the intention of looking up information on New Orleans composers in the *bibliothèque nationale*, I was disappointed to learn that I had picked the week when, annually, that distinguished institution closes for inventory. I mentioned my misfortune to Averty, who promptly made telephone calls to arrange for the great library to open for me.

Watching his magnificent series on the Original Dixieland Jazz

Band, four one-hour programs tracing the career of ODJB, with the High Society Jazz Band re-creating the music, I not only marveled at the skill and ingenuity with which the programs were produced, I was also acutely aware of how effectively the jazz form might have been served had there been an American Averty. His series on Eubie Blake and on Bix Beiderbecke need to be shown in this country. I just don't know how to achieve this purpose, but a way must be found.

In New Orleans in 1976, he made two 90-minute documentaries, entitled *New Orleans Bien Aimée,* in which I had the great pleasure of participating. We were brought together by John Shoup, a modern show business impresario who owns the Dukes' Place atop the Monteleone Hotel. I was impressed at once by Averty's enthusiasm and *joie de vivre.* His carefree attitude made me, just for a moment, suspect him of being too frivolous to produce a quality tape. As he said good-bye to his young and beautiful wife, Yvaline, when we started our first day of shooting at the hotel, I watched him counting hundred dollar bills into her hand so that she could shop. He may have been up to fourteen or fifteen when he suddenly stopped, looked doubtful, and then said, "That's enough for a young girl for one morning."

As Averty set up his shots at the various locations, as he yelled confusing instructions to the driver of the car—or later to the pilot of the helicopter—it appeared to me that his approach to this job was anarchic, to say the least. It didn't appear that there was any rhyme or reason to his procedures and methods. Nevertheless, I couldn't fail to notice the loyalty and enthusiasm of his crew. It also became apparent that they were fearful of his wrath should they fail to carry out his instructions in the most precise detail. My experience has taught me, though, that creative people are exceptionally demanding in these matters.

During the fall of that year, Averty engaged me to translate *New Orleans Bien Aimée* into English and to do the voice-over for American consumption. There, in his Paris studio on the rue des Alouettes, I had the opportunity to view the dazzling results of his visit to New Orleans. There had been no way to predict, from the apparent chaos of his activities there, the magnificence of the final product.

While we were watching the finished show in French, Charles Aznavour interrupted us by coming into the studio and explaining to Averty that Channel 3 wanted him for an hour special. He had told them he didn't want to do it unless Averty directed. Jean Christophe tried to tell him tactfully that he had no time available in which to do this, but the diminutive singer wouldn't take no for an answer. The discussion reached a crescendo, with Averty showing symptoms of apoplexy. He seemed on the verge of picking Aznavour up bodily and throwing his tiny figure down the stairs, which would not have represented a difficult physical feat. Initial cordiality vanished and the shouting match ended with Averty having the final word, "Be careful not to pull your socks up or you won't be able to see your way out!"

On an afternoon my wife and I spent with the Avertys in his apartment, he showed me his research files on New Orleans jazz musicians. Carefully stored on index cards is information which, incredibly, traces the day-to-day activities and appearances of hundreds of jazzmen. I saw his extensive correspondence with Nick Larocca and Tom Brown and his newly acquired memorabilia of Josephine Baker, with album after album of fascinating unpublished photographs. We decided that we'd collaborate on a book. Friends had told me that Averty was not dependable, that he developed and abandoned enthusiasms with equal suddenness, that he had so overextended himself that he could no longer be accepted as responsible.

In 1980 at seven o'clock one morning, the phone rang in my New Orleans study. (I am frequently hard at work at the typewriter by that hour.) A voice said, "Al? Al Rose?"

I said I was Al Rose, and the voice continued, "Averty. This is Averty."

I asked him how he was. He asked, "Are you going to be at your phone for the next five minutes?" I told him I had no plan to leave.

He said, "I'm going to call you right back in five minutes. Please stay there." Then he hung up.

That was almost seven years ago, and I haven't heard from him.

Eddie Miller

I never had much professional contact with Eddie Miller, because I have always abjured the use of that deplorable device, the saxophone, in recording or concert work. I understand their function in swing bands, or as replacement parts to be fitted under sinks. But when it comes to music I am convinced the saxophone should revert to the original purpose for which its inventor, Adolph Sax, created it—as a cure for asthma.

Collectors know, though, that Eddie Miller was a superior clarinet player, good enough to help folks overlook his one big vice. They remember him playing "High Society" on that Mound City Blue Blowers record and are aware that on some of those Bob Crosby sides, it's Eddie playing clarinet rather than Fazola or Matty Matlock, both of whom were in that band.

Eddie was in New Orleans for several years during the 1970s, playing in Pete Fountain's band, getting a good press and attracting a lot of cash customers to Pete's Place on Bourbon Street. This was during a period when I had recording commitments to meet and had just lost some of my favorite clarinet players to the Celestial All-Stars. Johnny Wiggs and I were sitting in my studio, suggesting names to each other and realizing how close we were to the bottom of the barrel. Because of this lack, I would close down my jazz recording activities shortly thereafter. But right then I had to produce a record for the state of Louisiana. Suddenly I thought of Eddie Miller.

"My God!" Johnny said. "I don't know if it's fair to ask a man to pick up a clarinet after all these years and expect him to sound decent on such short notice. Anyway, I doubt he'd accept."

"You think he can resist if I tell him who's on the session? You and Jack Delaney and Chink Martin? And Armand Hug, Danny Barker? And with Louis Barbarin on drums? I'll bet he'll give it a shot."

I called and left a message for Eddie to call me when he got home. He returned the call while Johnny was still with me. I outlined the project. He told me he still had his clarinet, but explained that he hadn't touched it in maybe twenty-five years. He said he'd spend a couple of hours with it and if he felt he couldn't cut it he'd call and let me know.

The next day he decided he could handle it, so I called the session for my favorite recording room, the Esplanade Room of the Royal Orleans Hotel. It's really a happy sight to see old friends reunite for another go at their favorite music. The shared affection was so apparent among these hometown kids that I was convinced everything would work out well on the LP.

Eddie and I had never known each other in New Orleans, though we had met and talked in New York, Philadelphia, Chicago, and Los

Angeles. At the session, I think he was surprised to learn that I, too, was a New Orleans kid. That knowledge may have relaxed him.

I told the band the tunes I wanted and included Eddie's own composition, "Lazy Mood," which he'd recorded on tenor sax with Bob Crosby a quarter-century earlier, in 1939. Even Eddie acknowledged it sounded so much better on clarinet. And, of course, Armand Hug's incomparable presence enhanced the piece even further.

Through the session, Eddie's clarinet sounded like he'd never been away from it. That liquid, pervasive tone he'd been developing from the time he won a newsboys' clarinet contest sponsored by the New Orleans *Item* at the age of eleven seemed at the peak of its power and appeal—the essence of the Crescent City sound that reaches its crest in this instrument. I considered the session a personal triumph for him and for me. Needless to say, it was received critically with the highest praise, and the other musicians on the date were ecstatic.

Raymond Burke

Philosophy is a very personal matter and you wouldn't expect to learn it from a jazz musician, but I must admit that my own attitudes toward life and my perspective on people have been discernibly modified by observing at close range Raymond Burke's approaches to life and art. Raymond, as every jazz fan knows, lives in New Orleans, plays the clarinet, and collects things. His formal schooling has been minimal. His accent is the one that is common to New Orleans' pure, easily identifiable working-class culture.

His fabulous wife Catherine babies him, treats him as though he were made of some easily soluble substance that requires watchfulness and exceptional care. "Put your little shoes on, Raymond," she tells him gently before watching him, with great apprehension, go off into the night air to play somewhere. He takes it all for granted, maybe even feeling the need for her solicitousness and management.

Raymond is one of the very few New Orleans jazzmen who has never done anything else for a living but play jazz. He can't imagine anybody doing anything else. One time the two of us were sitting and fishing under the Huey Long Bridge in the Mississippi River's battures (Raymond pronounces it "batches"), silently gaping at the ripples in the water. I say "silently." I mean without speaking. Raymond whistled as he often does—obscure ancient melodies he and I and very few other people know. "Love Dreams," "Peculiar Rag," things like that. I came to understand his unique attitude toward the music when he commented, after perhaps a half-hour of no conversation, "You know, a fella's got to do an awful lot of funny things for a livin' if he don't play."

For several years, in the 1960s, Raymond owned and operated a rabais shop on Bourbon Street, right below St. Ann. I had a long article about this in the *Second Line*. It was widely reprinted around the world. I explained in the article that rabais is not quite junk. It's not necessarily antiques, because the things are not necessarily old. It's just stuff the owner collected because he wanted to. Raymond hadn't especially wanted to run a rabais shop. But Catherine, in the interests of sanitation, had demanded that he clean out his private room. And since the stuff was too valuable to throw out—well, he just rented this tiny store (which had neither window nor electricity, and could thus only operate during bright daylight hours) and moved all his stuff into it. The stuff occupied the entire floor, was totally inaccessible even to him, much less a prospective customer. If somebody came in and asked whether he had, say, a flugelhorn mouthpiece, he'd know if he did or not, but the process of finding it involved moving his entire stock out into the street until he came to it. Of course, if he didn't like the looks of the person making the inquiry, he'd just shake his head and say, "I don't b'leeve."

Sometimes a jazz musician on his way up the street to work or rehearse would stop to talk to him, or maybe sit with him on one of the unsteady chairs he kept on the sidewalk for such visitors. Maybe Santo Pecora or Frank Assunto would tell him to get his clarinet and the two of them would sit for a while and harmonize. I've heard some great music standing in front of Raymond's place.

Always reluctant to leave town for any reason, he has in recent years come to know the joys of travel. I was astonished one evening, watching the CBS evening news, to see Raymond performing in the Soviet Union with the Preservation Hall Jazz Band. When I got back to New Orleans and asked Raymond if he'd enjoyed the trip, he answered, "That's a funny place. Nobody speaks English."

Recording Raymond poses a variety of unusual problems, not the least of which is that he bobs and weaves in all directions—rarely toward the microphone—all the time that he's playing. You can't signal to him, because he always plays with his eyes tightly shut. Trying to follow him around with a hand-held mike is futile, because his twists and turns aren't predictable. And that's not all. No matter what the tune or the circumstance, Raymond never comes in on the first note. If you're looking for your trumpet, trombone, and clarinet to come in with a hard, united attack on that first note, forget it. If you remonstrate with him he'll say, "What is this—a readin' band?"

You just have to recognize the session to accommodate what Raymond will or will not do. If you feel that on a particular piece the effect would be better if the instruments stayed in their conventional ranges with the trumpet in the middle, the trombone on the bottom, and the clarinet on top, you suggest to him that he play this ensemble in the high register. He might do that and he might not. Still his artistry and creativeness are of such a high order that you're sometimes tempted to scrap your own plan and proceed according to Raymond's whims. It might not turn out exactly like you wanted it, but it's still going to be great.

Raymond learned, apparently early in life, that there are a whole lot of things you really just don't have to do. I've seen him sit on a stage as a guest of honor for an out-of-town jazz club, getting ready to play a concert. Raymond's ritual in getting ready includes winding string around the doweling of the parts of his clarinet, arranging rubber bands to compensate for springs that no longer react to the touch, and making infinite adjustments on his reed. So there he sat, watching a person carrying an enormous baritone sax onto the stand. He was followed by another worthy pushing a vibraphone from the wings. As Raymond watched the proceedings with what appeared to be a blank stare, I observed that he was taking his instrument apart and replacing it in the case. When it was properly packed—and while the radio announcer was reviewing his career and extolling his musical achievements, Raymond left the stage and came up the center aisle, signaling to Joe Mares and me that he was ready to go home. We went outside, and he was already seated in the car by the time we got there. We started for home.

Meanwhile, on the car radio, we could hear the announcer continuing to sing Raymond's praises, unaware that the star had left. As we drove toward New Orleans, I commented to Raymond that a lot of people would be disappointed when they discovered he wasn't going to play.

"They asked me to come up there and play some jazz. If they

don't know you can't play jazz on that junk, they ain't ready to listen to *me*."

Raymond and Catherine came to visit me for an extended stay in Key Largo, where Raymond looked forward to keeping his fishing line in the water during every waking hour.

Now, my dock was a fisherman's paradise. The water abounded with snapper, grouper, grunts, sharks, tarpon—about every known variety of southern fish. The first day we sat out there for many hours getting sunburned. I had caught a half-dozen or so nice pan fish—just enough for lunch. But Raymond just kept losing bait and not landing anything. When I examined the way he had rigged his line, it was obvious he had done it in a way that was sure not to catch a fish. He never expressed any curiosity about why *I* was catching 'em and he wasn't. Still, as the hours wore on, I thought I was detecting some signs of frustration in his mien.

At last I told him he wasn't rigged properly and suggested that he might improve his luck by attaching it in accordance with conventional practice for these waters. I explained that these fish didn't act like the tchoupics and sac-à-lait of our native swamps.

He shook his head and told me, "I like to fish like *this*."

Spencer Williams

September was still hot in 1880 New Orleans, though not as bad at Number 3 South Basin Street, because that was a wide, tree-lined boulevard. It was already known for its massive houses of ill-fame such as those presided over by Kate Townsend and Hattie Hamilton. Number 3, though, was a less pretentious structure, flimsily built of clapboard, in a complex of four such buildings. It was just a few steps from Canal Street, the city's main thoroughfare. The railway depot was just on the opposite side of Canal. Therefore the four brothels occupied an ideal location for their economic purposes. Single men, arriving by train, didn't have far to go—just across the street—to be accommodated.

The proprietress of the establishment was a twenty-year-old black chippie whose name was Bessie V. Williams. On this particular fall afternoon, she was depressed because of the heat, because the living room was a mess, and because she was pregnant, a condition not conducive to potential prosperity in her line of work. "My God!" she said to herself, "If Loula hadn't come to New Orleans to help out, there's no telling how all this would resolve itself." Loula and Bessie had had the same mother back in Selma, Alabama, on the plantation where they'd grown up. In those days, where black girls were involved, nobody cared who their father was. Bessie said she couldn't properly remember what slavery was like.

The son she gave birth to the next month, on October 14, to be precise, was Spencer Williams. Loula went on to international notoriety as Lulu White, proprietress of Mahogany Hall and New Orleans' whore queen. Spencer never tried to hide this part of his past, though as an adult he never told the truth if he could help it. When he did, it was hard to separate it from the lies. I knew him slightly in New York, years before he died and before events led me to undertake to write his biography.

When I first met him in 1946, it was in a dressing room normally used by main-event prize fighters in Madison Square Garden. He was on the endless talent list performing for the Pittsburgh Courier Charities annual fund drive, and I was sharing emcee duties with such distinguished colleagues as Manhattan disc jockey Freddie Robbins and Harlem's Symphony Sid. This was a 24-hour marathon function, and our shift was on about two in the morning. I was sitting on a rub-down table with lyricist Andy Razaf ("Memories of You," "Ain't Misbehavin'," "Honeysuckle Rose"). Also present was a thin man I took to be a professional animal trainer, since he had a mean looking monster on a leash. This beast was Billie Holiday's boxer, which went everywhere she went. Billie cared not a tittle for the apprehension of persons into whose environment she had this feral canine herded. Also present were the super ragtime pianist Luckey Roberts and Dan Burley, the piano playing editor of Harlem's *Amsterdam News*. Sissle and Blake had done their turns and gone. Billie was on stage; Herb Jeffries was waiting in the wings. Spencer sat on one of the two leather chairs. He was a huge, well-groomed elderly man of vaguely professorial mien, a type you'd never imagine telling a lie or otherwise compromising his dignity. I had just introduced myself and asked him what he was going to play. He said he'd do a few of his most famous hits. In fifteen minutes we could easily have presented "I Ain't Got Nobody," "Baby Won't You Please Come Home," "Royal Garden Blues," "Everybody Loves My Baby," and "I Found a New Baby." He said if we had time for an encore he'd do "Basin Street Blues."

Billie Holiday never cared about the time. She was into a second encore, and we knew the crowd wouldn't let her get off stage without singing "Strange Fruit." It gave me time to ask Spencer some questions to satisfy my own interest. I asked him where he'd gone to school in New Orleans. He was obviously an educated man and had a polished manner not inconsistent with his having spent so much of his life abroad in London, Paris, and Stockholm. He told me he had attended the Arthur P. Williams School and St. Charles University. I told him I'd gone to St. Aloysius, and he seemed interested to learn that I, too, was a native of New Orleans. Neither of us knew, needless to say, that someday I would undertake to write his biography and in the process learn that New Orleans never had a St. Charles University and that the Arthur P. Williams School came into existence several years after he'd left town. He told me he was born in 1880. (Earlier, he told a Swedish interviewer he'd been born in 1889.)

Having no reason to doubt his veracity, I took this misinformation down in my notebook. He told me he liked living in Europe, that he was going right back, and that in 1936 he'd married an English lass. Meanwhile, Billie finished her set and came back to claim her beast and his handler. I told Spencer to wait while I introduced Jeffries. I told him he'd be next.

When the famed singer had finished, I announced that the celebrated composer, Spencer Williams, was coming out and that he'd play some of his most successful pieces. In fact, he didn't play at all. Someone else I hadn't yet seen appeared from nowhere, sat at the piano, and began to play as Spencer began to sing in his full, clear tenor the "Basin Street Blues." After that he performed a number of pieces I'd never heard, pieces he was "plugging." He did about twelve minutes of unrepresentative tunes, then he walked off stage, saying to me in passing, "We never got to talk much about New Orleans. Let's do that sometime."

As a matter of fact we did do that the following year in the same place, at the same time, under the same auspices. And he told me an entirely different set of lies.

Pierre Atlan

There are always people that you consider lifelong friends, people who seem as though they're part of the family. Even when your communication may be grossly irregular, you never cease to be concerned about and interested in their welfare. For me, Pierre Atlan and his wife Michele are part of my gallery of saints. They have enriched my life, though on at least one occasion, I thought Pierre was about to bring mine to an abrupt halt.

Anyone unfortunate enough to have been driven on one of the French super highways by a Parisian sees his life pass quickly before his eyes many times. I discovered that my own takes thirty-seven seconds, and in the five-hour drive from Paris to Deauville I watched enough reruns to put me in a coma. Atlan likes to cruise at 200 kilometers an hour, and he adds a sporting challenge by carrying on animated conversations with people in the back seat, frequently turning to look them in the eye while pressing harder on the accelerator. Michele, tense and troubled, keeps screaming "attention!" and "regardez!" But Atlan behaves as though these words are synonyms for "faster."

We were headed for the Normandy coast, where Atlan and the High Society Jazz Band were booked to play a college graduation party at the Deauville Casino. Besides the Atlans, there were three passengers: Pierre Merlin, the band's cornetist, about whom this is far too little to say—wait until later; my wife Diana; and someone I had always thought of as Fearless Al Rose. I suppose it was because from time to time a car passed us that I continued to feel I was still clinging to a thread of life. My concern was heightened by Merlin's decision to be let out somewhere, to travel the rest of the way by train. This is not to say there was no relief. Michele had planned well, and we found ourselves leaving the highway and gliding into a driveway that turned out to belong to a chalet in which we were to discover the reason for the world fame of Normandy's cheeses and pâtés.

We arrived intact, incredibly, and had dinner in what appeared to be a private house. We went up to the second floor, where we found the rest of the band waiting. Merlin had made it faster on his own, and we were delighted to see the lovely Martine Morel, who played the piano in the band, as well as Claude Rabanat and the others—I wish I could remember them all.

The evening in the casino was exciting. Claude Bolling and his orchestra had also been booked. This huge, overwhelming organization—I counted twenty-two pieces—was playing arrangements that made Stan Kenton sound like a barbershop quartet. I'd have loved to hear Bolling play some of the rags I knew he could do in his virtuosic extravagance, but the nature of the event precluded that kind of performance.

Michele and Diana, at one point, repaired to the ladies' room, and en route, Diana found a gambling chip. She picked it up, of course, but since games of chance have never played a part in either of our lives, she had to be guided to the roulette table and instructed by Michele in the procedure for breaking the bank. How nice it would be to report that she had parlayed this plastic disc into a huge fortune. Alas, she lost it on the first spin of the wheel. The band, as usual, played superbly.

I had first met Atlan and Merlin when they visited New Orleans, quite a long time ago—I can't date it exactly. I know that from the middle 1950s they had shared an intense interest in railroad trains, along with their confrere, the super-clarinetist Claude Luter. The three of them, working together, had built a train layout in Atlan's huge apartment in the Eighth Arrondissement. The room was 55 × 12. Atlan, an aircraft engineer, was the designer of Air France's *Mercure*, that airline's medium-sized plane. Merlin, a graphic artist of considerable talent, professionally created TV show sets, primarily for Jean Christophe Averty.

By the time these two came to New Orleans, they had already determined that a train layout was not enough. A properly run railroad obviously needed a setting, a depot for the train to end its run in, that sort of thing. What, then, could be more appropriate for two authentic jazz musicians than to have the train run up Basin Street and come to a halt in the Canal Street Station?

It was common knowledge in New Orleans that in the process of preparing my book *Storyville, New Orleans* for publication, I had accumulated many rare photographs and other graphic material. Atlan and Merlin located me to see if I could and would make available to them whatever I had that could abet their project. I did, of course, supply them with a bundle of what they needed, intrigued with the idea. After they got back to Paris I heard from them occasionally, with requests for information and other graphic material. I complied as well as I could, but the whole matter faded from my memory. Diana and I went to Paris twice in 1976. The first time it was just for a week, but the Atlans insisted that despite our busy schedule, we must come to see what they were working on. We were somewhat handicapped by the fact that we had been involved in a plane crash at Kennedy Airport on the flight from New Orleans and had had to leave the plane on one of those inflatable escape chutes. Diana had fractured her heel in the process and was functioning with wheelchair and cane.

But we did make it up to the fourth floor walk-up to this magnificent 16-room apartment. When we were admitted to the room that housed "le layout," I was dumbfounded. There before me, in the smallest commercial scale, lay the entire 1917 city of New Orleans in unbelievable detail. The L & N and the T & P ran on their proper tracks. The Barracks Street ferry came across a real river from Algiers and docked itself in the right dock. I was speechless.

For two years afterward I made a Herculean effort to effect a deal between Merlin and Atlan and the City of New Orleans, to bring the dazzling artifact to what I thought of as its proper permanent home. I got Mayor Moon Landrieu to visit Atlan's apartment to see this work of art. Everybody loved it. In my plan I had it earmarked for Armstrong Park, for which I had been retained by the city to create a use program. That plan never materialized, for various reasons—at least one of which must be the same as what caused the bronze historical plaque in the entrance to display the wrong date for Satch's demise. Anyway, there was a gorgeous TV documentary done on "le layout," which is, alas, still in Paris instead of in New Orleans where it belongs.

The night before we left Paris, Michele gave an unforgettable dinner party for us. At Averty's suggestion, Atlan performed two routines for us which will live forever in our memories among the greatest comedy acts we've ever seen. In one, Atlan does the entire opera "Faust," singing all the parts, doing sound effects, the orchestra, the intermission announcements, and the critical commentary. For an encore he recited the names of every local railroad station on the line from Paris to Bordeaux and return. He did it with expression, rhythm changes, and a variety of intonation. We could never have expected these hidden wells of genius. Averty, who had seen the act hundreds of times, literally rolled on the floor in infantile glee. Michele, not yet inured to this excruciatingly funny performance, made no attempt to restrain her laughter. As for us, we laughed the whole eight thousand miles to home.

Claude Luter

Claude Luter, in the area of authentic jazz, is Europe's foremost musician. His name is a household word in Paris, but unfamiliar, for the most part, to American fans and even collectors. One reason for this is that he has never performed in this country; in fact, he has only been in the United States once in his life.

In 1979 I received a call at my New Orleans home from Time-Life Records. This organization frequently issues record sets centering on our foremost jazz stars—Jelly Roll Morton, Eddie Lang, and others. The lady on the telephone explained that Time-Life was about to produce a Sidney Bechet set of LP's. Since I had cooperated with them before on earlier projects, she had called to ask if I had any data and/ or photographs that might be useful. She also said that they'd been trying for many weeks to locate Luter in Europe, and she wondered if I had any idea where he was.

"This is an unbelievable coincidence," I told her, "but Luter and his new wife are coming to stay with us in New Orleans. They arrive tomorrow, and they'll be here for several days." I didn't mention that Pierre and Michele Atlan would also be with us. The lady asked if I could arrange a telephone interview between Alexandria, Virginia, where the company's offices are, and New Orleans. When I told her that Luter couldn't speak any English at all, she paused for a moment. But I agreed to arrange for competent translation.

And so it happened that on the following day, Luter, Atlan, and I were deployed on three of our telephone extensions, speaking with the interviewer from Time-Life, who was thrilled to have nailed the elusive Luter. (I might mention that in any competition among jazz musicians to induce swooning among members of the fair sex, Luter— tall, handsome, personable—would have been the obvious winner. A sort of combination of Maurice Chevalier and Gary Cooper, he has been celebrated, for forty years, as a devastating charmer. I understand that his appeal also extends to his telephone voice.)

Luter spoke, Atlan translated, and I chipped in an occasional reminder. The discussion went on for about two hours. Our wives pursued *their* business in other parts of the house. Luter told about how I had arranged to bring him and Bechet together in Paris in 1949, how they'd formed a musical alliance that was to last for seven years. He talked of personality quirks, humorous incidents—the things interviewers *like* to talk about—Bechet's influence on his music and such. Eventually, the lady felt that she had plumbed the subject. She expressed her sincere appreciation, and we all said goodbye and hung up.

I must tell you, now, since it's relevant, that I am known to have a phenomenal memory and an apparently uncanny ability to recall facts, details, printed pages, and other information on demand, which, in this case, was fortunate for Time-Life Records. Directly after Claude and Annie Luter and Michele and Pierre Atlan left New Orleans, and while my wife Diana and I were about to leave on an extended trip, I got another call from the Time-Life lady. She began an extended apology which I couldn't make head or tail of until I understood what had happened.

As one traditionally distrustful of modern technology, who has only recently conceded the potential for social advancement inherent in the wheel, I can't say I was astonished to learn that the tape recorder she had used in the long and expensive interview had failed her. The tape yielded not a sound. Luter was gone and would not be accessible again for months. I reached into my memory and repeated the entire interview. She remembered it all as I restated it, and I'm happy to say the set finally came out, incorporating all of the data we had provided in its voluminous notes.

Claude spent virtually all of his time in New Orleans in the company of Atlan and Diana, visiting railroad yards, roundhouses, and terminals, climbing on cabooses and on the ancient Baldwin locomotive in Audubon Park. We had our music exhibit going on at the Louisiana State Museum, which now houses the New Orleans Jazz Museum. There is a soprano saxophone there that belonged to Sidney Bechet, and we prevailed upon Claude to play a solo on it for the television cameras. It proved to be in dreadful condition, but his musicianship is of so high an order that he was able to produce creditable sounds on it. We had proposed some plans, including musical ones, to make the visit of these Parisians satisfying to them. But most everything had to be scrapped because of their zeal to spend every minute in search of exotic boxcars to photograph.

Three years earlier, in Paris, Luter had announced to me his intention to visit New Orleans, stating unhesitatingly that his interest was in seeing railroad-related sites and artifacts. But of course I never assumed that this would be his *only* pursuit in New Orleans—and in the nation, for that matter.

When they left us, I think they were headed toward San Antonio and San Francisco, with the same objectives.

W. C. Handy

The "Father of the Blues" was already a legend forty-five years ago, and most people—even musicians—didn't know he was still alive. He was occupying an office on Broadway opposite the Brill Building, running his music publishing business with what seemed to be moderate success. I tried to make an appointment to talk to him, purely for research reasons, and a very attractive, very officious lady kept telling me he wasn't in and that nobody knew when he'd be in. I explained what I wanted, and she agreed to give him my message and my phone number. The lovely lady was Marion Tyler, widow of a great violinist, Willie Tyler. I would come to know her very well later, after she married Eubie Blake. W. C. never called back, and I was frankly irritated. At twenty-one, we're not always models of patience.

Several months later, I was having lunch with Eubie in the Theresa Hotel in Harlem. I told him I had been thinking of trying to put together an educational tour through the Ivy League schools with Eubie and his lifelong partner Noble Sissle, and with Hall Johnson, W. C. Handy, the black symphonic composer William Grant Still, and two or three more black musical pioneers. Eubie thought he might enjoy that. I confessed I hadn't discussed it with any of them yet and that I'd been unsuccessful in getting to see Handy on other matters.

"The reason you never got to see Handy," he explained, "is that you didn't have any money in your hand. You go up there with money in your hand, he'll talk to you."

I asked Eubie if he thought Handy might be interested in making such a tour. His eyesight hadn't failed completely yet, and moving him from one place to another wasn't as difficult as it would become in later years.

"Shaz," Eubie advised, "don't try to talk any business with Handy if you don't have money in your hand. He'll always listen to any offer. He doesn't want to know about percentages or getting paid at the end of the month. You go with money in your hand, he'll listen."

I thanked Eubie for the advice and as I got ready to leave him, he said, "Remember what I said. In your *hand*. That don't mean in your pocket. He can't see in your pocket. In your hand, see?"

The building where W. C.'s office was was almost exclusively occupied by other blacks in the music business, just as the Brill Building was occupied by whites in the same pursuits. The black music building was referred to in the trade as "Uncle Tom's Cabin." The Pace and Handy Music Publishing Company consisted of a very small, neatly kept suite of offices. When I entered and announced myself to Mrs. Tyler, I could hear a loud voice, speaking in gossiping tones, which I assumed was on the phone. I immediately recognized the fact that the speaker was a compulsive talker. The door to Handy's private office was partially open. Mrs. Tyler said he'd see me in a minute, and she walked into his office without hesitation. I heard her interrupt him in midsentence to tell him I was there. In a matter of seconds a gaunt little figure emerged, saying goodbye to Mrs. Tyler and to me. I met the little man sometime later at Tom Delaney's in Harlem. It was Perry Bradford, who had been responsible for the first blues to be issued on records.

Before going into Handy's office, I took a thousand dollars out of my pocket and held it in my hand, just as Eubie had advised. Eubie had also warned me to go right ahead and talk. "That guy will tell you the history of the world, the troubles Negroes had when they were slaves, how the white folks were claiming they invented the blues. If you don't go ahead and talk, you'll never get a chance to tell him your proposition. You might not anyway. You might look too young. The money in your hand will help that."

In my life, I never went wrong following Eubie's advice.

Around Handy's wall were framed copies of original sheet music— first editions of "St. Louis Blues," "Yellow Dog Rag," "Memphis Blues." I went right ahead and told him what I proposed to do, judiciously putting the ten hundred dollar bills on the desk as I outlined the deal. It called for four weeks at $500 a week. The money on the table was for the first two weeks. I would provide transportation and hotel accommodations.

If you're old enough to remember 1937, I won't need to tell you that this was big money. In the same year I had paid Bechet $300 a week, and he had been on tour with Sissle's orchestra for about half that figure. I paid jazzmen about twice what they'd make on other jobs. Handy complained the money wasn't enough, and then he wanted to talk about billing. He wouldn't appear anywhere unless he got top billing, he said. It had to say, "W. C. Handy, the Father of the Blues." I explained to him that there would be no billing at all, since there wouldn't be any advertising. The function would be closed. All that appeared to him to be nonsense.

I said I'd spoken with Eubie about it and that he was interested. W. C. then told me, "Eubie? You don't talk to Eubie about anything like that. You've got to talk to Sissle about it."

"Okay," I pursued, moving the bills around on his desk a little, "but if Sissle agrees will you go along?" He stared at the desktop where the money was. In the time I was to know him later, this would prove to be the longest uninterrupted stretch of silence I'd ever see him initiate.

Then he said, "Not for that money."

I abandoned the project right there, realizing that whatever made him refuse, it had to be something other than money that made him turn me down. A decade later he'd appear nightly for less money at Billy Rose's Diamond Horseshoe. And 1947 was a year of much greater prosperity, too.

After W. C. had passed on to his reward, my good friend Harry Godwin invited me to come to Memphis for the dedication of the W. C. Handy statue and park the city was inaugurating. I suppose the statue is all right, but nobody could do a real likeness of W. C. Handy unless it talked.

David Thomas Roberts

During my long association with American music, only two musicians have assured me that they were the most important creative artists of their time in their idiom. One was Jelly Roll Morton, who, in 1939, told me, "All these other guys is playin' Jelly Roll. You turn on the radio or play a new record, you're listenin' to Jelly Roll. I made all that up that they're playin'."

About a half-century later a nineteen-year-old explained to me that no other contemporary approached his skill in the composition and execution of classic rags. His name is David Thomas Roberts. What is curious is that both of these men were right.

In Jelly Roll's case, because of the times and the then-higher level of public taste, he was able to build a significantly large following.

Roberts, on the other hand, has come along in an era when only
a handful of musicians and ragtime enthusiasts know about him or
understand what he is bringing into music. This young man came to
visit me at my home in New Orleans, asking me to listen to his work,
frankly in the hope that I could help him further his career. I tend to
be skeptical about such requests. At best somebody merely wants to
demonstrate to me his technical achievements, and I am only an average judge of these. I agreed to listen to him, and it took about three
minutes for me to realize that I was being treated to a performance of
some of the most satisfying original composition I'd heard in fifty
years, played by a dazzlingly virtuosic artist. Needless to say, I got on
the phone while David was still in my living room to alert the people
I thought could do him the most good. This resulted almost immediately in an invitation from Trebor Jay Tichenor to come to St. Louis.

In a matter of five years, David Thomas Roberts has become an
admired and respected leader in the ragtime community. By the time
this reaches the bookstores, he will have premiered his ambitious suite
for piano, "New Orleans Streets." The piece takes an hour and ten
minutes to perform. Its debut at Dixon Hall on the Tulane University
campus on September 20, 1985, the centennial of the birth of Jelly
Roll Morton, was predictably fine. Having been privileged to hear it
informally, I felt confident in proclaiming it, even before its debut,
the most significant contribution to the culture of New Orleans in the
past fifty years.

But nobody's perfect.

As it happens, David Thomas Roberts has an abrasive personality
and frequently conducts himself in the kind of arrogant manner not
likely to endear him to audiences or employers. I have found, though,
that like Jelly Roll, David's apparent eccentricities follow a certain de-
monstrable logic. Generally, if you follow what he's saying, he turns
out to be on sound ground. If the temperature in the auditorium is
a mite too chilly, he gets up from the piano bench. He leaves, convinced that if he's not comfortable, he can't supply the quality of
performance his audience has come to hear. He's inhospitable to programming suggestions from his sponsors and not inclined to cooperate
with dress requirements. But whenever such issues have arisen between us, there's never been a time that his position was not defensible
on other than frivolous bases.

I contracted with him to perform at the 1983 "Fingerbreaker" concert, a part of the Tulane Hot Jazz Classic. I only presented two pianists, David and Dick Wellstood. A week or so before the event, it occurred to me that I had left a stone unturned. I called David, who's never easy to find, and told him that if, as I suspected, he had no tuxedo, I'd be happy to rent one for him. He was silent for a moment, and then he said, "You know, Al, it doesn't say anything in my contract about a tuxedo."

"I know that," I agreed. "But this is a prestigious event and a prestigious appearance for anybody who's on the bill. I'm sure that there'll be many people in the audience who could do you some good. I want for you to make the best possible personal impression."

"Well," he told me, "if it was anybody but you asking me, I'd give him a flat out 'No.' But I know you only have my best interests at heart, so I promise you I'll think it over. I'll let you know."

He called back a couple of days later and told me he had decided against the tuxedo. The prime consideration, he explained, was that for him to give his optimum performance, he had to feel completely comfortable, which he couldn't be so long as he felt he was compromising his integrity.

Not without some dismay, I asked him what he planned to wear.

"I have a very nice red sweater and matching pants," he announced. "I'm sure I'll appear neat and that my clothes won't offend anybody."

I told him I was sorry he saw it that way. I was on the point, I confess, of canceling him, but my own commitment to excellence prevented that. I only replied, "I'm glad you took the time to think it over."

The concert was an unqualified artistic triumph. I had to acknowledge to myself that his unconventional outfit seemed exactly right for him. So, I realize, would a burlap sack have been. I told him so later, but he wasn't in the least bit astonished by my acceptance.

In 1985 I asked him to supply me with a list of the fifteen parts of "New Orleans Streets" because I planned to write an article on it well in advance of the initial performance. In St. Louis he gave me a handwritten list which he asked me to return after I'd copied it. At home, the following week, I made neatly typed copies of the list, one of which I sent to him. Immediately he wrote back, thanking me for the prompt action, but explained that he, in fact, wanted his own handwritten list back. I realized then that he puts a certain value on holographic matter from his own pen, on the assumption that it will all one day be of significant historical value in the same way that anything in Jelly Roll's hand is inestimable today. Initially I was astonished, even amused, by his egotism. Not long ago, in discussing the work of another pianist-composer, John Rummel of Denver, David told me, "He's the most important composer to come along since me!"

I have learned now never to dismiss anything David says or does as nonsensical. He makes sense, and his music makes sense. I never considered it my role in life to play John the Baptist to any musician; but in this case, I feel comfortable in the part.

Chink Martin

His name was Martin Abraham. The music world called him Chink Martin, an unfortunate use of an ethnic slur. But what could he do about it, or who would have wanted to, during the years before the general public began to frown on the use of such nicknames? If you'd used his correct name, nobody would have known who you were talking about.

He was born on June 10, 1886, and he spent a continuous, uninterrupted career as a jazz musician for seventy years. He was the first jazzman I ever knew personally. I was four years old, and he worked in the pit orchestra of my grandfather's Dauphine theater. He was, even then, the most exciting and proficient jazz tuba player in the history of the idiom. The issue of a German father and a Filipino mother, he had neither discernible Oriental coloring nor features, though he was no more than five feet tall, if that. He can be heard playing string bass or tuba on some of the recordings of the New Orleans Rhythm Kings, many of the recordings of Sharkey's Kings of Dixieland, and lots of Southland records of the 1950s. His involvement in the music literally goes back to the very beginnings of jazz.

"Man, we were terrible!" he recalled during supper at the Pontchartrain Hotel while we were making a British ITV series entitled "All You Need Is Love." "It's a good thing those first bands didn't record. Nobody today would want to hear that music we called 'ragtime.' I'd be ashamed to listen to a record from that time if I was on it."

My wife and Terry Waldo, the ragtime virtuoso and scholar, had been speculating about the actual musical content of those bands of the pre-1910 era and had virtually forgotten that Chink was present. After he'd listened for a while to the discussion, he decided to put aside his veal cutlet and remind them. "I was there! I played in them bands. They wasn't no good at all!"

One day in the early fifties I met Chink as we were both going into Joe Mares's warehouse on St. Louis Street. Chink mentioned that Joe had asked him to be sure and drop in that day. When we saw Joe, he explained that he had stopped by and picked up government forms to make it possible for Chink to make his application for social security. Chink said he didn't want any and I, out of curiosity, asked him why not. It turned out that he had no idea what social security was, but was merely afraid of forms and suspicious of anything that had to do with the government. I explained that he had this money coming to him, that he had been paying a percentage of his income since the thirties in order to provide himself with an income after he had reached the age of sixty-five.

He shook his head. "I ain't never paid them people nothin'," he asserted. "They ain't never asked me and I ain't never paid."

"But," I pursued, "I, myself, took money out for social security on every job I ever hired you for—and I'm sure anybody else you worked for did the same thing. Joe, too."

Chink looked at Joe, hurt and suspicious. "You mean," he asked, with a "say-it-ain't-so" plea in his voice, "You mean you guys been holdin' out on my money all these years?"

"Of course!" I told him. "That's the law. We have to make the deductions."

He brightened. "The *dee*-ducts!" he said with relief. "You mean the *dee-ducts!* Why didn't you say so?"

Further discussion elicited the fact that Chink had always thought the people who hired him were able to deduct a certain amount of his pay as a sort of commission for finding him or supplying him with any job. My attempt to explain what this money was for, I could see, was falling on uncomprehending ears. I went on further, to point out to him that on the first of the month, after his papers cleared, he'd receive a check for a couple of hundred dollars from Uncle Sam.

"What I gotta do for it?" he demanded.

I told him he didn't have to do anything, that it was his own money. He looked extremely skeptical. Only his close relationship and past history with Joe and me reassured him.

"If that's for true, what you tellin' me, I'm gonna buy you a box of cigars," he promised. As he spoke further of his forthcoming windfall, I realized that I had neglected a detail in my explanation to him. He didn't yet realize that this wasn't a one-time payment, that he'd receive a check every month for the rest of his life. He was speechless and unbelieving. Many months had to go by, and many checks come in, before he realized that he really didn't have to work anymore. Not that that stopped him. He continued to work in Preservation Hall until his death in 1980 at the age of ninety-four.

And just to put in perspective the extent of his career in jazz, I must report this brief excerpt from an interview I did with him while preparing the publicity handout that would accompany him to Disneyland for Frank Bull's Jazz Jubilee. I asked him when was the very first time he had recorded. This was his reply.

"Well, you know, Al, them first records we did, they wasn't jazz, see. There wasn't even no such word then. It was 1905, just Ropollo and me. We made them *cylinders*, banjo and guitar."

"How were they?" I asked. "Did they ever come out?"

"Oh, yes," he assured me. "They come out. Mr. Edison didn't like 'em at first, but . . . ."

Walter Bowe

During the mid-1940s, I often found myself embarrassed by the incontrovertible fact that no blacks attended my Journeys Into Jazz concerts. It would have seemed as though I had been systematically excluding Negroes, since we found we were playing exclusively to all-white audiences. In historical perspective, I understand now why black society had turned its back on the authentic music it had done so much to create. Blacks were going in droves to Norman Granz's Jazz at the Philharmonic productions to watch his succession of saxophone honkers at work, people like Illinois Jacquet leaping into the air and spinning as he blew his tenor, that sort of thing. But when it came to the real, fundamental jazz form, they just junked it along with the characteristics they considered Uncle Tom—eating watermelon or fried chicken in public, watching Stepinfetchit movies, or mugging on stage. (In the mid-1940s *mugging* didn't mean assaulting in the street for purposes of robbery and/or mayhem. It meant making grotesque faces.) This was a part of their heritage that blacks merely junked. My own reputation as a civil rights activist constituted no redemption in black eyes. I distributed free tickets to black organizations, press, and personal friends to no avail. At least half the musicians I hired were black—and famous, too, for that matter.

It was, therefore, an astonishment to me when, during one intermission, a young black boy of fifteen or sixteen, carrying a trumpet case, approached me and asked very politely if he might have the opportunity to meet the musicians. Needless to say, I was delighted with this obviously well-bred youngster who was interested in authentic jazz. I took him backstage and introduced him around. I don't recall who was being featured that night. I remember I told him that Bunk would be in town in a couple of weeks and was elated to discover that Bunk was the boy's idol. He had tried to model his trumpet playing after Bunk's records. I promised him that I'd invite him to my house to meet Bunk, and he seemed to feel as though the world was his.

At that time, there was a group of youngsters—all white—in his age group which I permitted to play during the intermissions at the concerts, just to give them a chance to perform on stage before a concert audience. The band was better than you might have expected. It included the clarinetist Larry Gushee (now Dr. Lawrence Gushee of the University of Illinois) and Dick Hadlock on soprano sax. (He would become the publisher of *Record Changer* magazine.) I persuaded them to give young Walter Bowe a turn sitting in with the band. He proved to be an unpromising lead horn, but this didn't dampen my enthusiasm. I had a teenage black boy eager to play the real jazz. That was enough. Maybe I could reawaken in a new generation the spirit of its forefathers.

So Bunk, Baby Dodds, and Pops Foster came to visit, and I invited Walter. He was enthralled to be in the presence of these masters. Other black kids—even musicians—wouldn't even have known their names. Each time Bunk came to visit, I'd have Walter over. Bunk would show him some things about playing the horn, and the kid would ask questions. Later, he took to going to New York frequently to sit at the feet of the master at Stuyvesant Casino or the Central Plaza.

Then he'd come home and during the week stop by at my place to talk about his dreams and aspirations—about restoring the musical heritage to his people, about perfecting his technique. He never failed to express to me his deep and sincere appreciation for all I was doing for the music, for his people, and for him personally. If ever I saw a highly motivated kid, it was Walter Bowe.

One day he came and told me he was going to live in New York and try to find work playing jazz. He promised to let me know how he was doing from time to time. We shook hands, and I wished him well. For a couple of years, he'd call me and tell me what he was doing and where he was working. I never had expected him to be able to support himself as a musician at that stage of his career, but he was doing it. Every now and then someone would report to me that they'd heard him and that he was playing pretty well. I was delighted.

Then, one fine morning, I opened the Philadelphia *Inquirer,* and there on the front page was a photograph of Walter Bowe. The accompanying text identified him as a Philadelphia boy who had been placed under arrest, along with a number of other people, because of his involvement in a plot to blow up the Statue of Liberty. I followed the story with considerable interest as you might imagine. In the end he was convicted, along with the others, and sent to prison. I can't tell you any more, because that's all I know.

"Buglin' Sam" Dekemel

"Buglin' Sam the Waffle Man" was a New Orleans institution in the early twenties, when his colorful, horse-drawn wagon would ply the streets of New Orleans selling hot waffles, four for a nickel. You could always tell when he was in the neighborhood, because he heralded his own proximity by playing the blues on a battered army bugle. You might be playing stoop ball or running in Jackson Square when, suddenly, you'd be aware of that raucous and rhythmic sound, and you'd react like a Pavlov dog. Your mouth would water and you could already visualize the four, playing-card size waffles covered with powdered sugar, deployed on a quarter-page of the *Times-Picayune,* ready to eat. Buglin' Sam was a fourth-generation scion of the Dekemel waffle family, but he was certainly not the first of his clan to announce himself with the bugle. When I asked him in 1954 how he had learned to perform in that manner, he told me his grandmother had taught him.

Although I'd often been a customer of his during my growing-up years, I didn't really get to know him until about 1952 when he began to appear as a bugle soloist with Tony Almerico's jazz band. It's not easy, if you haven't heard it, to imagine a role for a bugle in an authentic jazz band. But this one managed an impressive repertoire. Sam had the uninhibited, vulgar comedy style common to a certain class of New Orleans musicians that would be exemplified by Wingy Mannone and George Brunies. Still, he could be funny, and much of his following was based on that fact. Like so many other jazzmen of the city, he had a "day job." He was a juvenile probation officer with headquarters in the courthouse, a half-block from Joe Mares's place. When I interviewed him for a publicity handout when he went to California with other New Orleans luminaries to appear at Disneyland, I asked him for his full name. He blushed and asked me, "Whaddya wanna know *dat* for?"

I explained that to prepare his résumé it was important to know such facts about an artist. He insisted he was no artist, but at last I persuaded him that people would want to know what his full name was. Eventually, I elicited it—Matthew Antoine Desire Dekemel.

Dekemel wasn't one of the town's brighter intellectual lights, and as a result he was frequently the butt of the practical jokery and humor of his musical confreres, who often were a mere half-step above him in cerebral evolution. One day, Johnny Wiggs and I were standing in front of the Austin Inn after a particularly successful seafood gumbo when the drummer Monk Hazel approached us. He told us that if we happened to be near Bayou St. John at the head of St. Philip Street at 11 P.M. we might be witnesses to an amusing spectacle.

That night we drove to the designated location at the time indicated, turned out the lights, and awaited developments. In a very little while a car slowed down and stopped. A veiled figure got out slowly. She was dressed in flowing robes that were impressive in the light of the full moon, for which this event had clearly been timed. Despite the costume, Wiggs and I recognized her instantly as she took the few steps to the bank of the Bayou. You couldn't fail to recognize that walk and those movements; the veiled figure was Lizzie Miles, an early recording star who developed a large following singing Creole songs and popular jazz numbers in Creole patois.

Directly after she took up her position, we saw three figures walking slowly from Dumaine Street along the bank of the bayou. The middle one was a blindfolded Buglin' Sam. Guiding him were Monk and the trombonist Julian "Digger" Laine. All three had obviously been into the sauce. When they had confronted the "priestess," Monk said something in Sam's ear, and Digger removed the blindfold.

Lizzie managed some portentous tones as she pointed her finger into Sam's face and accused him of having masturbated on four successive Sundays. She explained that the voodoo law required that he take off all of his clothes and wade into the bayou playing "Basin Street Blues" on his bugle. He would be required, she explained, in order to avoid eternal damnation which might be scheduled to begin at that very moment, to play four complete choruses. He would then have to take an oath that he would never again masturbate on more than three successive Sundays.

So Sam took all his clothes off, cavilling at removing his jockey shorts, but Lizzie commanded him to take them off, too. Quaking and embarrassed, he followed orders, then marched into the shallow bayou, which wasn't more than three feet deep, and began to play "Basin Street Blues." Almost immediately, a squad car appeared (by pre-arrangement, as we later learned) and arrested him for indecent exposure. As they dragged him off, he was screaming, "Fellas! I still gotta make three-and-a-half more choruses!"

Harry Shields

There's as much technique involved in *listening* to jazz as there is in playing it. Superficial performers attract hordes of superficial listeners. There are so many more of them. As one learns to really hear the jazz, one's interest in the ingeniousness and beauty of ensemble play burgeons as one's response to virtuosic solos ebbs. And as one's emotional and aesthetic satisfaction develop into a genuine understanding and appreciation of the original elements that qualify jazz as an art form, one's favorites are gradually replaced by others. The effect of all of this process, logically, is that the very greatest of the jazzmen are frequently among the least known.

All of that is a prelude to explaining why Harry Shields has always been my personal clarinet choice for most record sessions and concerts. In the matter of improvising complex and satisfying—and hot—harmonies to a great lead horn, he was without equal. He was the clarinet in the best jazz ensembles I ever recorded or listened to. He knew the secrets of where the excitement is hidden in every melody. He understood better than anyone I ever knew that it was the sound of the band that counted. There was no room for stars in his world—not even himself. The roster of clarinetists I've worked with is jazz's Who's Who on that instrument. Nicholas, Pee Wee, Omer Simeon, Baquet, Faz, Ray Burke, Bechet, George Lewis, Edmond Hall were each, in context, superb. But Harry Shields was in a class by himself. His horn was closer to the core of genuine jazz than any other clarinet. I have seen tears well up in the eyes of lead horn players like Sharkey, Alvin Alcorn, Wiggs, even as they played, when Harry's supporting web of harmony raised their own work to greater levels of intensity and beauty. Wiggs always said that "any cornet player is a genius with *that* behind him. I don't need to go to heaven if I've got that guy next to me."

Harry had his problems, but they weren't musical ones. Something about him attracted women of unrestrained passion, and he had a jealous wife. It's true, too, that though he never had much to say and could never have been described as jovial or convivial, a pretty girl could always rivet his attention.

His wife had him thoroughly trained to bring all his pay checks home. Then she'd dole out to him trivial amounts—never enough to keep him in cigars, let alone paramours. So he worked out a deal with me whereby I'd pay him half of his money in cash and give him the rest in the check he'd bring back to Mrs. Shields. So far as I know, she never caught him at this game.

It seemed that every time Harry got through playing a job, there was always a pretty lady with a fancy automobile waiting for him. If it was my job, he'd say to me, "Al, I've got some important business to take care of but I don't want to be carrying a lot of money around. How about giving me twenty when I'm finished and I'll pick up the rest tomorrow."

This meant, obviously, that his young lady was expected to provide the entertainment one way or another, because he always had the same twenty on him the next day when I paid him off. Even today I wonder how he did it. The ladies would be maybe twenty-five or, at the most, thirty years old when Harry was in his sixties. I remember him in his twenties, and even then I can't believe anyone thought he

178 • *I Remember Jazz*

was handsome. He had no wit or personal charisma. If he could have merchandised his secret he'd have made a lot more money than he ever made playing jazz. From time to time I watched ladies in his audiences as he played and I took note of the fact that when he played his solos, many of the girls would get the look in their eyes that I'd seen on the faces of women in the presence of Frank Sinatra. Now that was when Harry was an underweight, elderly gentleman with steel-rimmed utility eyeglasses and white hair. It had to be the music. How he managed to live a relatively normal married life and raise children under these conditions will always remain a mystery to me.

His musically distinguished brothers had already passed on. Eddie had been slated to be the piano player in the Original Dixieland Jazz Band, but died suddenly in his youth. The eldest, Pat, was reported to be an excellent guitar player, but that was in a time when musicians couldn't make a living in New Orleans. Larry, as is well known, was in the ODJB and composed "The Original Dixieland Jazz Band One-Step," "Clarinet Marmalade," and "At the Jazz Band Ball."

With Harry in his advancing years I was saddened by the fact that this particular family tradition had little time to go. Then one day I walked into Joe Mares's studio where there was a youngster of thirteen or so practicing by himself. His tone was of that superior New Orleans timbre, the one all jazz fans recognize. He was playing the old Albert system, just like Harry Shields, and was quite the best youngster I had heard. I asked him his name, and he said he was Harry Shields.

Johnny St. Cyr

I always saved the business cards of jazz musicians. Most of them are now in the Tulane University Jazz Archive Collection. Among New Orleans jazzmen, though, many of the cards advertised their "day jobs" and made no mention of their music. That's how it came to be that I went through my card file to find one that read, "John A. St. Cyr, Plasterer." I called him on the phone, not because I needed a banjo player, but because I needed to install a room partition. Musicians have done my stationery (Tom Brown), painted a house for me (Julian Laine and pianist Emile Guerin), made me a vest (Sidney Bechet), filled a cavity (Dr. Leonard Bechet), tailored a suit (Santo Pecora), termite-proofed my house (Mike Lala, Pete Fountain, Al

Hirt), delivered lumber (Sing Miller) where I was making repairs. It was therefore perfectly logical that I should have called St. Cyr to plaster a wall.

When he arrived he handed me a carton of milk to keep in the refrigerator for him, and I showed him the job. I'd already bought all of the materials. He said the job would take him almost all day and that he'd have to get twenty dollars for it.

"Twenty dollars!" I said, astonished at the low price.

"I'm sorry," he apologized. "I can't do a job like this for any less."

I explained that I'd have reasonably expected to pay a lot more for the job. In fact, I proceeded, I would pay him more.

He shook his head. "I'm not rich, Al. You know that. I know you called me for this job because you're my friend. But you could have called fifty different plasterers, and any one of 'em is gonna do this job for twenty dollars more or less. I'm not gonna take more than that because you're my friend."

I had estimated it would cost me about fifty dollars—but what did I know. Those were bad times in the mid-fifties, for both the music and building trades. I stayed with Johnny while he worked—not to keep an eye on him, but because I wanted to keep him company and talk with him.

Now, just in case you don't know who Johnny St. Cyr was, I might mention that he's the banjo and guitar player of the Louis Armstrong Hot Five, the one who made all the historic recordings. In his later years the Disney organization engaged him to be the regular bandleader on the *Mark Twain*, the replica of the Mississippi River paddlewheeler that plies the lake in Disneyland. His was a name hallowed in jazz history, a byword among record collectors. He was a superior musician even in his advanced years. (He was still employed on the boat when he died in 1966 at the age of seventy-seven.) Unsurpassed as a rhythm man, he was also expert in his single string work, which he used extensively when he performed with his trio from time to time in New Orleans.

We talked about the Hot Five days and he had a word or two to say that I hadn't expected. "That po' li'l gal—don't get me wrong—she was a fine piano player [Lil Hardin Armstrong] but, you see, we were tryin' to play jazz—an' you know, jazz is a workin' man's music and it need to be played by a workin' man. That li'l gal—she was a sweet li'l gal—but she didn't know anything about work, y' see. An' she played hell of a piano, but she get off the rhythm. You got to have that rhythm. So who that leave? That leave me. We didn' have no drum, we didn' have no bass, jus' *me*. Them records could have been better. Now when we made them other things—Jelly Roll, y'see an' th' Red Hot Peppers—now that was different—that was some rhythm. Lindsay, John Lindsay, whoo! That was some rhythm—that was some bass and the li'l French drummer, too [Andre Hillaire], he made nice rhythm, so y'see all that make it easy for me and nacherly, the records, they better."

Somewhere before, I had read an interview with Johnny in which he maintained, "A jazz musician got to be a workin' class of man," and I realized this was a basic part of his musical philosophy.

I reminded him, "Jelly Roll was no working class man. I don't think he ever worked a day in his life."

"Yeah," Johnny agreed, "but *he* was Jelly Roll. Only one like that."

The wall turned out beautifully, and I complimented him.

"You got to do good work," he told me. "If it's plasterin' or pickin', you got to do it right."

Johnny, in his entire illustrious career, only had one record album under his name as leader. I'm proud that the album notes are mine.

Sharkey Bonano

Sharkey really captured the fancy of the Dixieland fans, but not necessarily for the right reasons. A natural showman, his slight figure was never at rest on stage. His brown derby with the little feather in it was one of the best-known trademarks in jazz. His tiny, raspy, almost soprano voice could never be called pleasant, but he'd sing away with all the assurance of a Luciano Pavarotti. All of those things were cute, but they weren't jazz.

What *was* jazz was his hard-driving, flawlessly syncopated lead horn and his beautifully controlled, full trumpet tone. Audiences found him childlike and lovable, but musicians who worked with him saw him in a different light. Sharkey was self-centered and egotistical, characteristics which are never improved by either ignorance or bad judgment. Sharkey had a surplus of all these elements.

It may be that Sharkey was the only jazzman I ever knew with whom I was not on speaking terms. Even so, I hated to see him un-employed because in the late 1940s and early 1950s, we needed all the great jazz horns we could find. I'd give anything to have that horn back today, even if we had to take Sharkey along with it.

I guess it was early in the 1950s when I pulled all the strings I could, used whatever influence I had, to get Sharkey and his band a booking in the Blue Room. (That's one of the big-name spots in New Orleans, in the Roosevelt Hotel.) The band wasn't too enthusiastic, because working with Sharkey didn't represent any jazzman's garden of Eden. The Blue Room's management always did everything in good taste. It was a real class establishment—and still is, for that matter. When the band arrived to open its engagement, the men saw a well-designed advertising card at the entrance of the room. Stanley Men-delson walked over to try out the piano, and the manager was being pleasant, greeting the musicians. The advertising card had a large photograph of Sharkey in the center and, spaced around it, smaller photos of the members of the band—all top names in Dixieland.

When Sharkey came in and saw the card, he accosted the man-ager. "What the hell is this?" he demanded angrily, pointing to the card. All the musicians were standing around observing the scene. Stanley sat at the piano. "This card stinks!" he charged. "Why the hell do you need pictures of all these guys on it? People come in this place to see *me*, Sharkey, see! These guys don't make no difference! I could play this job with five Chinamen!"

A moment of silence ensued and then Stanley, to ease the ten-sion, idly played "Chinatown, My Chinatown" on the piano—where-upon Sharkey fired the band. I need not go into the details of the attendant chaos in the Blue Room, in the Musicians Mutual Protec-tive Association, and among the musicians. Because the bandsmen were as good as they were, they had no difficulty at all getting other jobs. Little Chink and Harry Shields went to the Dukes of Dixieland, Jack Delaney joined Tony Almerico, and so on. I was distressed, be-cause I'd gone to all that trouble to get Sharkey that choice oppor-tunity for exposure only to see him blow it.

After that, months went by when Sharkey didn't have any work. Needless to say, the Chinatown story quickly passed into legend on Bourbon Street, and Sharkey's attempts to put a decent band together proved fruitless. And Sharkey knew a good band when he heard one. His musical ear wasn't one of the many things that were wrong with him.

In any case, I was sitting and talking with Joe Mares, as I did on many afternoons, and he told me Sharkey had come in, crying the blues. He didn't have any work and he was depressed. The whole world, he charged, had turned against him. That same night—it was in 1954—I talked with Sid Davila who operated the Mardi Gras Lounge on Bourbon Street and persuaded him to abandon his entertainment policy (strip tease, continuous, 9 P.M. to 3 A.M.) in favor of a genuine, quality jazz band with Sharkey at the helm.

Davila, himself a super clarinet artist, asked me, quite sensibly, "Who in the hell is going to play with Sharkey? He can't get a band together."

I assured Davila I could assemble a band for Sharkey.

It wasn't easy. I didn't make any points with the Dukes for retrieving Little Chink and Shields, though I made it up to them by finding them replacements even more suited to their style. Almerico was livid when I came for Delaney. And as for the musicians, you can imagine it wasn't easy to get Mendelson to resume working under Sharkey's leadership. I was selling the idea of putting the best possible music on Bourbon Street. That, I constantly assured everybody, would provide long-term security for everyone. And so I prevailed and Sharkey had a job and a band.

For Davila, the change in policy represented a substantial investment. He had scrapped a sure-fire, proven format, which was bringing in a substantial profit, purely for principle—that is, because he felt that good jazz was noble and worthwhile whereas strippers and B-drinkers represented a sleazy way to make a living. The musicians had given up good jobs for the chance only to play a higher order of music. I had put in a lot of time, but of course, there was no way for me to benefit financially, since I was not a booking agent or an entrepreneur. I was just trying to contribute to the quality of the environment.

Davila organized a big grand opening party, inviting the press and other important folk, most of whom showed up with their engraved invitations. The place was packed for the opening—naturally, since everything was on the house. Sid and I sat at a table and watched the show together. First Lizzie Miles sang her little Creole things, accompanied by Joe Robichaux at the piano. Then Smilin' Joe (Pleasant Joseph), with his guitar and trolley car conductor's cap, did his monologue, singing his blues and convulsing the crowd with his comedy. Sharkey and the band were last, and there was no better band in the city. When the set was over there was tumultuous applause.

Sharkey came off the stage and joined us at the table. This is exactly what he said. I guarantee it's verbatim. "Man, you guys got the life. We stand up there and blow our asses off and you sit down here and rake in all that money."

Sid got up and left the table. And I never said another word to Sharkey as long as he lived.

Armand Hug

There are many kinds of piano players. Among the most numerous is the kind that can dazzle you with their sheer brilliance. Even among them there is a hierarchy of the super-brilliant, and if you've sat in an audience being overwhelmed with the consummate skills of a Johnny Guarnieri or a John Arpin you know how that is. Then there are the good-time boys. You go to see them, and they make a holiday of any ordinary day. I come away from listening to Max Morath or Knocky Parker just feeling good. These are people that bring their ambience with them. I tell Max how good he is and he looks at me in amazement, certain that I've heard a hundred better piano players—but I haven't. Knocky just shrugs and says, "How nice of you to say so." But he feels like he's just putting one over; after all, he reasons, he makes so many mistakes and he doesn't practice, doesn't even have a piano in his own house. Then there have been a very few who sit down at the keyboard and hit those chords that grab your internal organs and drag you through a tour of your own unexplored emotions. Some of those keyboards—Joe Sullivan, Art Hodes—preach to you, telling you, showing you how it is, how it ought to be, what it all means.

And then there was Armand Hug. Armand's conceptions were huge, sometimes involved tapestries of elaborate and compelling fantasies weaving together sunny nostalgia and primal urges, calling upon the rich, colorful cultural threads of which he himself was made. Armand, more than any other pianist, could enthrall me.

The first time I met him I was seven and he was fifteen. I had discovered that if you stood on Iberville Street opposite what we called the Budweiser (because of the advertising sign in the window), which was really the Fern Dance Hall Number Two, you could hear the wonderful band that played in the taxi dance ballroom on the second floor (dime a dance). I know now that Harry Shields was the star, but the bandleaders varied. When individual musicians came out for five-minute breaks (one at a time, because the music wasn't permitted to stop for eleven consecutive hours), I could tell they were musicians because they wore tuxedos. One of them was obviously a young lad, obviously too young to be playing in a dance band. He'd come outside, light a cigarette, and stand there.

After a few nights I spoke to him, commenting that he seemed too young to be a musician. He confessed his age, showed me that he didn't smoke, but just held the cigarette so people would think he was older. He said he played piano in the band. After that I tried to listen for the piano, but I could never hear it very well. However, I went by there many a night and always stopped to talk with Armand. We got to know each other very well. When I got to be old enough to go into saloons, I'd find Armand playing in the poshest bars in New Orleans. He discovered that I knew thousands of tunes, and often he'd play melodies he liked but didn't know the names of so that I could tell him the titles and he could go to Werlein's to get copies.

One day I met him on Canal Street when he was perhaps eighteen. I was going to McCrory's dime store where Jeannette Kimball was the demonstrator in the music department. I met Armand on the way in and learned that he went there often just to hear Jeannette play. I suspected he also came just to *look* at her, because she was—and still is—the prettiest lady in town. Of course, that didn't count with me yet. I was only ten.

The day came when I would occasionally need to engage a few musicians to play for some function, and I'd hire Armand if there was a piano. Then one day a friend in Biloxi asked me if I could bring a band to play for his sister's wedding. That was the first time I discovered that Armand would never leave New Orleans, not even for a few hours. I think he had a superstitious belief that he would die if he stepped on unfamiliar soil, but he'd never give me his real reason. He'd tell me his wife's health was bad, or that he was expecting to have to close a mortgage on his house, or anything to keep from leaving town. Once I called him from Chicago where I was doing a concert in partnership with Dave Garroway at the Chicago Civic Opera House. I offered him $500 and transportation for one night. (This was, at that time, more than twice what big name jazz attractions were getting.) He was apologetic but he refused. Then I offered him a thousand.

"Gee, that's nice of you, Al—but I can't leave here," he told me.

Then, just to establish a principle, I offered him $2000. No go. I tried $5000 ("You don't make that much in a *year!*" I reminded him). Nothing.

So we left it at that. He never did leave town, except once when he played with a band on the *Mississippi Queen* for one trip to Memphis and back. The other musicians told me, though, that during the few free hours they had in Memphis, Armand had chosen to stay aboard the boat, so he never set foot in Tennessee. His lovely wife Linda conspired with me to get him away somewhere just once, and I think we were making some progress just at the time he died.

Like so many New Orleans musicians, Armand overate consistently. By St. Joseph's Day of 1977 (St. Joseph's Day is an Italian festival in the city during which overeating is part of the fun), when he went to visit one of his friends who had a holiday shrine laden with great New Orleans food, Armand overdid it and expired on the spot. That same night my wife Diana and I, along with Bob Greene, went down to the Royal Orleans Hotel where Armand worked regularly in the Esplanade Lounge. Normally, we dropped in on him there once or twice a week. The maitre d' told us what had happened. Only weeks before I had recorded a solo session with him playing the pieces identified with Bix. I'm glad we weren't too late.

Earl "Fatha" Hines

Anybody who *knew* him didn't call him "Fatha." That was PR stuff. His friends and other musicians called him Earl, though he, himself, called his own close associates by various nicknames, many of which he made up. He called Louis Armstrong "Homey" because, he alleged, Satch was so naive and ill-equipped to deal with the phenomena of the nonmusical world. He teased Louis about his tastes ("I keep tellin' him they don't serve red beans and rice in the Waldorf"), his uncertainty about the social graces ("Tell him he doesn't have to take his hat off in the men's room"), and his speech ("I played with him for years before I realized it's no act. Homey really talks like that").

It's true that by contrast with Satch, whom Earl really thought should have been president of the United States, Hines was an urbane, witty man-of-the-world who exuded genuine confidence. His confidence never failed him, except when he was called upon to play an unaccompanied piano. Everybody else in the jazz world recognized him from the beginning as a consummate master of piano playing techniques, but Earl always felt he was pulling the wool over their eyes and misleading the public with a musical trickery that had little to do with the art of piano. He was constantly concerned that he might be called upon to perform before an audience that would see through his legerdemain.

Collectors, of course, have his early recorded piano solos, and his talent and taste in the twenties and early thirties are not controversial. There are those people who seem, from the outset, to fuse their own consciousness with the principles of music, and it all seems so simple to them that they find it hard to grasp the fact that not everybody can play. Earl was one of those who could never understand why anybody would come to hear him.

During the mid-1940s, I persuaded Frank Palumbo to book Earl into Ciro's in Philadelphia as a solo act. I thought his name would be big enough to draw customers, and I personally would have enjoyed spending the week listening to him. You never could really get to hear all of Earl Hines so long as his sound was going to be complicated by bass, guitar, and drums. If he could have them, he wanted saxophones, too. The more the better. He always felt that the bigger the band the less his deficiencies would show up.

The plan was all right with Palumbo. The money was exceptionally good for the time, too. I seem to remember that it was something like $1800 for the week. Anyway I called Joe Glazer, who booked Earl, as well as Satch (this was before the All-Stars), and told him what we wanted.

"Yeah," Joe agreed, "but Earl, you know how he is. He won't want to be on by himself—but I'll ask him."

I explained to Joe that it wasn't a matter of money. It wasn't that we'd have to pay extra for accompanying musicians. I had hundreds of people who would have patronized the place to hear him playing solo, people who wouldn't have been interested if anyone else was on the stand with him.

Despite this explanation, Joe called me back and told me Earl would hire a bass and guitar out of his own pocket for the gig. I asked Joe whether he'd mind if I talked the situation over directly with Hines, and Joe said, "I don't care. I know you're not going to try to cut me out of anything."

So I called Earl to press my case.

"Come on, man," he insisted. "You know people don't want to hear me by myself. What am I going to play?"

"How about 'Sheltering Palms' for instance?" I asked, selecting an early recorded piano solo, "or 'Glad Rag Doll'?"

"Where you been, man?" he demanded. "Music has come a long way since that stuff. They'd laugh at me."

I tried to assure him there were still countless fans out there who wanted to hear only that. I had him persuaded for a moment, and he agreed to do it. Then he called me back, maybe two minutes later, to rescind his acceptance.

"I can't take a chance like that, man. I could blow my reputation in a minute." The upshot of it all was that he never accepted the booking.

Ten years later, I was sitting with him in San Francisco in the Hangover Club where he was working in a band that included Darnell Howard, Pops Foster, Baby Dodds, and Henry Goodwin. And he told me, "I'm gonna play one just for you!"

When he got back on the stand, he said a few words to the other musicians and then sat on the piano bench and played the first sixteen of "Down Among the Sheltering Palms." Then the band blared in, in unison, as he laughed his trademarked laugh.

A quarter-century later, Eubie and I sat watching his act for the New Orleans Jazz and Heritage Festival. By this time, he had surrounded himself with certain modern virtuosi of no genuine jazz interest. At one stage, he pointed to me and played eight of "Sheltering Palms," then he gave his group their cue and they did something else very uninterestingly. The saxophonist went through endless meaningless choruses to the delight of the rabble shouting "Go! Go!" and other musical terms of encouragement.

It was George Wein's concert and I asked him if he'd had any luck

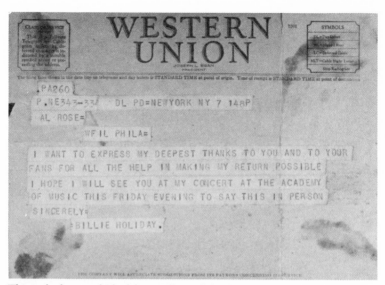

This is the last word I had from Billie Holiday before the police got her on drug charges.

The front line of my last record session for the state of Louisiana. From left to right are Preston Jackson, Louis Cottrell, and Alvin Alcorn.   *Photo courtesy Louisiana Department of Commerce and Industry.*

I couldn't find room for all my photographs so I persuaded Dick Allen, then curator of the jazz archives, and Dr. Herbert E. Longenecker, then president of Tulane (and a pretty good hot clarinet man), to take the jazz and Storyville pictures off my hands. *Photo by Tulane University Staff.*

Signing the first contract ever by a black musician to host his own radio show. Sammy Price was the star. (That's me in the horn rims.) I had to move mountains to make this possible in 1947, persuading the station to break with racist tradition, finding a sponsor. Then came the second week, and he didn't show up. That's the last I ever saw of him. *Photo by Henry McCrary.*

Sweet Emma Barrett had no idea what "public domain" meant. *Photo by Grauman Marks.*

George H. Buck, with the aid of his wife Eleanor, right, carefully built a virtual monopoly by buying up nearly every authentic jazz record company in America. I was honored to have some of my sessions on his labels. Diana and Eleanor were close friends until Eleanor's passing in 1982.   *Photo by Grauman Marks.*

A scene to remember! The High Society Jazz Band and thirteen other hot groups, including Alvin Alcorn's Imperial Brass Band of New Orleans, parade on the Champs Elysées in celebration of Louisiana Week in Paris, 1976. So why isn't Al Rose in this picture? Because he's *leading* the parade in a jeep.   *Photo by Diana Rose.*

Chris Burke doesn't look like this anymore since he left Nottingham and Sherwood Forest. The seventeen-year-old girl is Kelly Edmiston, who had just won a fellowship to the Royal Academy theater. When she was an infant she used to ride my shoulder to Mardi Gras parades.   *Photo by Diana Rose.*

Jimmy McPartland and I compare acquired girth since our previous meeting, as Johnny Wiggs offers to bring out the tape measure.   *Photo by Diana Rose.*

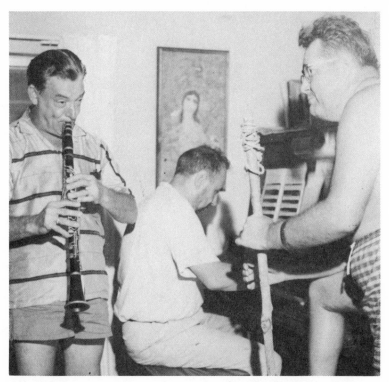

You can find jazz everywhere—even in Key Largo. Raymond Burke, left, Knocky Parker on piano, and a tub-a-phone player scare the fish away from my dock in 1961.   *Photo by Mary Mitchell.*

The incomparable Art Hodes offers me a flower as drummer Hillard Brown and trombone whiz Jim Beebe wonder if it's my birthday.   *Photo by Diana Rose.*

Australia's ranking jazz star, Graeme Bell, looks over my shoulder as I draw a caricature of somebody.   *Photo by Diana Rose.*

The statue destined for the new Armstrong Park in New Orleans is delivered on Decatur Street with a broken arm. Sculptress Lynn Emery made the repairs. Lucille (Mrs. Louis) Armstrong unveiled it at the dedication, while Louis Alter played his "Do You Know What It Means to Miss New Orleans" on the piano through the ceremony.   *Photo by Rex Rose.*

The dynamic Dick Zimmerman holds still while I draw him at the Scott Joplin Festival in Sedalia, Missouri, in 1976. He's a toy designer, a magician, and one of the best ragtime piano players in the country. *Photo by Diana Rose.*

This is the product—Rose's caricature of Zimmerman.

Preston Jackson, the celebrated trombone star of the Louis Armstrong Orchestra, was a great source of information about early Chicago jazzmen.

Pee Wee Russell as I saw him in 1946.

Greeting late-arriving James P. Johnson, who's just missed the first half of a
Journeys Into Jazz concert in which he was to be featured. Way over on the
right you can see his replacement, George Wein, making his concert debut.
(Later Wein went into the festival business.) Between James P. and me is
Freddie "Gatemouth" Moore.   *Photo by Nick Alexakis.*

This is May Fisher in 1901,
who may have been the
first ragtime piano player I
ever heard. She was still
playing to accompany silent
films at the Penny Won-
derland Theater on Canal
Street in 1922.

Spencer Williams wrote more hits than any other black composer. Even in 1985 "I Ain't Got Nobody" was on the charts.

Gene Krupa said, "You've got a couple of smart kids here. They're gonna grow up to be college professors." And so they did. That's Frank on the left and Pancho on the right.   *Photo by Harry Romm.*

"No, sir," said Earl "Fatha" Hines, left. "I'm not gonna play a piano solo in front of *this* man!"—Eubie Blake, center. Al, right, failed to persuade him.   *Photo by Jules Cahn.*

Ian Whitcomb became a rock star in the sixties and then reformed. With his ukelele, he now shows us how the razz-ma-tazz sounded in the twenties. *Photo by Diana Rose.*

Even if he says so himself, David Thomas Roberts is the most important living ragtime composer. *Photo by Diana Rose.*

On stage with scat singer Jo Jo Carter at Town Hall in Philadelphia. Behind him is Bud Freeman, and that's Dan Burley clapping his hands and "Hot Lips" Page on the snare drum.   *Photo by Nick Alexakis.*

"Buglin' Sam" Dekemel played hot jazz on an army bugle. He said his grandmother taught him how.   *Photo by Mary Mitchell.*

getting Earl to play the way he *could* play, and he confessed that he'd tried with no success. Afterward, Hines came down to sit with Eubie and me, and Jules Cahn took our picture together. Hines said, "I'd have played that solo for you this time—but not in front of *this* guy!"

I had brought along a photograph of Satch, Earl, Bigard, Arvel Shaw, and me that was taken thirty-five years earlier. I got a copy for him. He was very appreciative and promised, "Next time I see you, I'll play that tune!"

He died in 1983. So if I want to hear it again, it'll have to be on the record player.

Gene Krupa

After 1935, Gene Krupa was all the rage. Before that hardly anybody had ever heard of him, though I had been dimly aware of him, I suppose, from hearing musicians talk. I can't really remember when I met him, but I'm almost sure it was while the Goodman band and the Berigan band were both in New York at the same time—maybe early 1938. I remember going out into the street with him from some drinking place and noting that the sun was up. We were both wearing tuxedos. There were a large number of young ladies with us, and I told him his face was covered with lipstick. He said mine was too and also that I had some on my collar. I had very little recollection of what had taken place earlier in the evening—or rather on the previous night—and he said he didn't have to go to work until late in the afternoon. We were ignoring the rest of the company. It turned out that none of the young ladies was known to either of us, and we didn't have a clear idea of how they happened to be with us.

With an expertise patently the result of extensive experience, he disposed of our following, with a slight and less-enthusiastic assist from me, after which we went to a nearby kosher-style restaurant for breakfast. I really don't remember whether we'd chosen the place beforehand or not. But it seems to me he just directed the cab to stop, we got out and paid the bill, and then we went into the nearest restaurant. He said he was going to have to stop doing this stuff except on his day off. I had no recollection of whom I'd been with, but Krupa appeared to be more in possession of himself.

Coffee seemed to change the color and contour of the planet.

Neither of us seemed to be too far out of it to eat. I still remember the smoked sturgeon and boiled eggs, the inevitable bagel and cream cheese.

"Weren't any of those young ladies yours?" he asked me.

I disclaimed proprietorship and told him I was quite sure I hadn't had a girl with me, because it wasn't like me to ignore that sort of responsibility. Nevertheless, I was racking my brain trying to figure out how and why I'd been there, but with no success.

Finally, he said, "You know something; I'm tired of this routine. Working and drinking and playing with these girls. Man, I can't wait until I can find me a nice girl and get married, with a house in the country and kids around."

"I'll bet a few years ago you wouldn't have said that," I suggested. "Most any stud in the United States would sell his soul to change places with you."

"The kids, maybe," he acknowledged, "but I'm almost twenty-eight years old. Any guy my age that would want to change places with me is stupid. Say a guy is married and he's got a couple of nice children. You think he's gonna want to give all that up? I'm not rich. I work hard at least six nights a week, besides rehearsals, and I've got no future. I'm just a drummer—not even a chance to ever be a band-leader! Drummers don't get to be bandleaders. So when this fad is over, I'll still be a drummer. These girls that are always tryin' to jump in bed with me—they won't even remember my name."

We finished our substantial breakfast, and he asked me if I had any gum. I gave him my pack. I didn't chew gum, but I always kept some for purposes Berigan had taught me. I told that story to Krupa, who thought it was funny and also a great idea to jam juke boxes with chewing gum. He told me his reason for wanting it was so that liquor wouldn't be too obvious on his breath.

A decade later we were guests together on a Philadelphia radio program called "Juke Box Jury," hosted by the ebullient Ed Hurst. By that time I was married and had two sons who were about six and four years old. They liked to watch me doing radio, either my own show or guest shots on somebody else's. (This was just when TV was coming in, and I don't think I'd been on it yet at that time.) I sometimes brought them to the studios so they could watch. They always behaved like gentlemen.

"I see you did it," Krupa commented. "You're lucky."

I asked him if he found himself any closer to his goals, and he shook his head. I reminded him that he had told me drummers didn't get to be bandleaders. His band was now among the most popular in the nation. He acknowledged that he had achieved some financial stability, but denied that the quality of life had improved for him. He gathered my kids, Pancho and Frank, together with him and motioned to my photographer to take their picture. Then he scribbled an address on a note pad and handed it to me.

"I hope you'll send me a print of this," he said.

I did, of course.

The Exterminators: Pete Fountain and Al Hirt

Things were hard for jazzmen in the fifties—especially the early fifties—and most especially in New Orleans. Bourbon Street was still a year or so away from full bloom, and the Dixieland bands that were to proliferate hadn't yet secured their jobs. There were places like La Lune, a dance spot where Mike Lala and his band held forth, playing Mickey Mouse music—rhumbas, slow fox-trots, and businessmen's bounce a la Lester Lanin. But even Mike, though employed, couldn't make ends meet on the low pay of that time. He took a job during the daytime working for the Orkin Exterminating Company. During the day he'd go around making home termite inspections and bug-proofing houses. But Mike wasn't the only musician that needed money, and Joe Mares and I used to talk frequently about the plight of the music and the difficulties performers were having to confront. There were two of the younger ones we were especially concerned about, and I suggested we might find out from Lala whether there were any openings where he worked. He said he'd see. I think one of his relatives was part of the firm. The building, by the way, is the original "Halfway House," a historic jazz spot of the twenties. It was fitting that though there was no music, the place was still employing jazzmen.

It all ended with the young men getting the jobs. I will always remember how they looked in their yellow jump suits with the Orkin logo on them as they dropped in on Joe during their lunch hour, looking for all the world like Laurel and Hardy in one of those two-reelers. Al Hirt, in those days, had no beard, but he was even heftier than he is now, and Pete Fountain was a skinny kid, ill-adapted to anything other than playing his clarinet. I'd have given anything for the chance to watch them on the job. It must have been one of the all-time great comedy acts.

Fortunately for the music world, neither of them had to stay with that occupation long enough to become expert at it. I suppose you could say that they began to attract attention in about 1955 when they worked at Dan's International, at Bourbon and Toulouse streets, with a scary trombone player named Bob Havens who is now the hot sliphorn man in the Lawrence Welk band.

We were concerned about Pete, anyway, in the exterminating job. He had a long history of respiratory problems (which actually had led to his taking up the clarinet), and he was generally frail. Al, however, had to do all the work he could with his enormous family (a wife and eleven children). He had been so thoroughly trained in music, having occupied a trumpet chair for a long time in the New Orleans Symphony under the direction of Alexander Hillsberg, that he showed all the signs of disillusionment at having to go outside his music to earn the kind of living he needed.

Joe and I sat at a table in the club listening to this hair-raising band, and Al and Pete came to sit with us during a break. I said to Al, "How long can you keep up that pace? Your lip probably feels like it's turning to stone."

Pete said, "This sonofabitch never gets tired. My God! Playin' with him is like a track meet."

"This guy," Joe predicted, "in a year or two is gonna be a super-star. He's goin' to Vegas and when they hear him out there, that'll be *it*."

Afterward, I was standing outside the club with Al and I told him what Joe had said. He told me, "Joe's got more confidence about all that than I do."

Later, I told Joe I didn't think Al would ever get to be a significant factor in the music business. "He really doesn't play jazz," I explained. "But anyway he'll blow himself out. Nobody can play with that power for so long night after night and stay healthy. He'll be burned out in six months."

Now, after the intervening twenty years, I don't mind eating my prophecy at all, and Joe has been generous enough not to say "I told you so."

As for Pete Fountain, Johnny Wiggs, his teacher, had explained that he'd told Pete to give up the music. "I told him," Johnny said, "that he'd never be able to play jazz. It's too bad. He loves it and he's got a nice tone, but he'll never be a jazz musician."

Several years later, Wiggs and I were sitting in my living room watching Pete on the television as he performed on a network show. And Johnny said, "I told you he'd never be a jazz musician."

Dizzy Gillespie

In a book about the real jazz you wouldn't reasonably expect to find anything about Dizzy Gillespie, but I've included him to make a point. The point could be of interest to people who feel that the music began to decline roughly around the time it began to be recorded. It's only fair to confess, though, that I lost interest in the movies when they started to talk.

In Philadelphia in 1940 or 1941—just before I got drafted, anyway—I had a concert going on in the Academy of Music. I don't remember who was playing, but it must have been an authentic New Orleans jazz band, with maybe a Chicagoan or two thrown in. I'm sure Joe Sullivan was on piano. A local entrepreneur named Nat Segal, who owned a club called the Downbeat in South Philadelphia, asked me if I would, as a favor to him, permit a young trumpet player and a girl singer to participate. In those days there weren't any major music controversies going on in the business. We were still saying, in our sublime ignorance, "It's all jazz." So I agreed to have Nat's people on stage briefly, to give them an opportunity to be exposed to the concert audience. The skinny little girl singer, whom I judged to be about sixteen, told me her name was Sarah Vaughan. And the trumpeter, whom I had met before in Minton's in New York where he had seemed to be only fooling around with the other musicians on the stand, Thelonius Monk and Charlie Parker and, I think, Slim Gaillard (it's hard to remember for sure—after all, it was more than forty years ago), was Dizzy Gillespie.

So, anyway, he played in one or two sets at the Academy, and he *still* seemed to be just fooling around. I talked to him for a while back-stage, and it struck me that he was far more personable and intelligent than most of the musicians I had been associated with in the world of authentic jazz. On reflection, I admitted to myself that most of these younger musicians playing that strange music they were calling "be-bop" were superior folks, generally better educated, more civilized. Their manners were better, they were more polite, more considerate of each other. I found what they were playing very boring, and the more I heard it and understood it, the less I liked it. I said all that to young Dizzy, and he said, "Everything moves along, man. It's not a question of whether it's better or worse, it just keeps movin'. There's no reason musicians, especially young ones, shouldn't experiment with the instruments—find out how far they can go."

A few years later, I'd go far enough into it to actually produce a Lenny Tristano concert, featuring such newcomers as Fats Navarro and Eddie "Lockjaw" Davis. I made a record session with Percy Heath (long before the "Modern Jazz Quartet"). And at last I confronted the fact that while I enjoyed working with these really very nice people, I just couldn't stand what they were playing. That was what got me off on the whole complex business of jazz theory, about which I've written at length. All of my predictions about the music business—like how the public would never go for long playing records, how Stan Kenton was too complex ever to be a commercial success, and how the public would be sick of the Beatles in two months—didn't work out. But I was right about be-bop. It was a musical deadend. I hoped when it was over that some of the excellent musicians it produced would turn their attentions to genuine jazz, but that never happened.

Five or six years later, Dizzy and a group were booked into one of Frank Palumbo's places. In order to publicize his appearance I took him around for radio interviews on various disc jockey shows and then up to a school called "The Twentieth Century Institute of Music," which was run by some friends of mine, Bernie Lowenthal and Art Singer. Naturally, all the students, mostly studying on the G. I. Bill, were so impressed by Dizzy's friendly, gentle manner that they flocked down to the place to see him perform.

I remember saying to him, "Well, you're still doin' it."

He smiled and said, "If you're not doin' it, you're not doin' anything." After that I'd see him from time to time in Felix Valdera's Para-

mount Record Shop or at a benefit where I might be doing some
emceeing or at a jazz festival.

But I heard him play jazz one time, which I'll always remember.
It was in 1980 and I had just published my biography of Eubie Blake.
B. Dalton and Company gave a closed autographing party for the
benefit of the New York Public Library in their Fifth Avenue store.
Eubie and I were there to autograph the book, and Dizzy had just
written his own autobiography. The place was alive with author-
celebrities—Leroy Neimann, caricaturist Al Hirshfeld, Rona Jaffe.
There were also a lot of very rich folks, donors to the library, and so
on. I was surprised to see Larry Adler, who lives in London now.
Eubie, of course, never could get away from any place without performing, and he asked Dizzy if he had his horn with him so they
could play together. Dizzy said he didn't live too far away and that he'd
be back in a few minutes with his horn. When he returned, he and
Eubie began to play "Memories of You." To our surprise, Larry Adler
produced a harmonica, which I swear didn't measure more than an
inch and a half in length, and joined in. Well, it was jazz. Genuine,
hot, and authentic. Gillespie did all the things a great jazz trumpeter
is supposed to do. The crowd, aware that what was going on was an
unusual event, responded with uncontrolled enthusiasm. Eubie, at
ninety-seven, was in his usual euphoric condition while playing his
own music, and the idea of playing in public with Dizzy and Larry
tickled him. I told Dizzy afterwards that it was nice of him to have
gone and gotten his horn. He said he wouldn't have missed the honor
of sitting in with Eubie.

Miff Mole

There used to be a little middle-Eastern restaurant on Fourteenth
Street in New York. It was called The Kafkaz, and many evenings
when I planned to go to Nick's to listen to some music, I'd go in there
for some shashlik and kasha. I was on my way in one night when I
encountered Eddie Condon on the corner, and I invited him to have
dinner with me.

"The aftertaste of foreign food," he demurred, "spoils the clean,
pure flavor of gin for hours."

Nevertheless, I persuaded him to join me, since it was still too early for music. Inside the restaurant we found Pee Wee Russell and Miff Mole, both of whom were slated to play on Nick Rongetti's bandstand with Phil Napoleon some hours thence. Miff had all the charisma of tepid ovaltine; without his legendary trombone skills he might have become the most anonymous individual in history. He rarely had much to say, and when he did speak his conversation was homiletic and cliché-laden. But Miff, a true boy scout at heart, was reliable, sober, responsible, and charitable. This was before World War II and he had undertaken the responsibility of acting *in loco parentis* to Pee Wee toward whom he behaved like a mother with a retarded child. When Condon and I entered, Miff was explaining to Pee Wee that the glass of *kvass* he had ordered for him would satisfy his insatiable craving for the mixture of gin and milk on which he lived. *Kvass*, he explained, was not without alcohol since it was fermented from honey and, I think, wheat. Not only that, but it was far more healthful and nutritious, as proven by the fact that it was well-known that natives of the Caucasus lived longer than any other people in the world. (*Kafkaz* means *Caucasus* in Russian.)

"This stuff's got no alcohol in it!" Pee Wee protested. "Gin is medicine to me. You think I drink it to get drunk. I need it, see?" Then, turning to Condon, "You know what I mean, Ed."

Condon shook his head solemnly. "Miff is right, you know. This whaddyacallit is much better for you." He picked the glass up and took a sip. "Got a real kick, too!" he reported earnestly.

Pee Wee had an unfocussed look of one who has been betrayed by a close friend. Miff, grateful for the support, assured Pee Wee that by the time the night was over he'd realize how much better he felt. Pee Wee squirmed in his seat, picked at his pilaf without enthusiasm, and kept saying, "Aw, c'mon, Miff! When can I have a real drink?"

Miff promised him a gin and milk at the midnight break.

Condon went off into a monologue on sadism, the Inquisition, Cain and Abel, and other accusatory comments about Miff's fundamental cruelty. But Pee Wee's eyes were wandering around the room. He never had a long attention span.

Later that night, during the break at Nick's, I was over at Julius' Bar across the street when Miff and a shaky Pee Wee came in. Miff was really concerned about him. Pee Wee was sweating so that it was dripping off the ends of his moustache, and it wasn't even hot. They sat at the bar and Miff instructed the bartender about the proper mix of milk and gin. Pee Wee asked if he could have an extra slug of gin and Miff told him he couldn't. The bartender was new. He said they didn't have any milk, but Miff explained that Julius always kept milk just for Pee Wee and told him where to look for it. The drink pulled Pee Wee together enough so he could go back for the next set. Miff said he was making arrangements for Pee Wee to go to a sanitarium.

Miff had so little personality that I never even thought of him when I was hiring trombone players. It's true that his style didn't add much to the kind of music I produced. But if you listened to him for two minutes, you'd know you were in the presence of one of the great masters of sliphorn. I used him when I hired Pee Wee because, for one thing, they played so well together, and, for another thing, it was the only way I could be sure Pee Wee would get there.

I was talking to Red Nichols in California the day after he'd signed the contract to have a movie made of his life, with Danny Kaye as himself. Red was elated because he said the deal, at last, provided for an honest and authentic film on a jazz theme. "They have to *finish* every tune they start!" he exulted. "No breaking away to something else in the middle of something good!"

I don't know what happened to that deal. They never finished a single number. The picture brought in a hokey scene presenting a relationship between Red and Louis Armstrong that never existed. Red, in fact, said he'd only met Armstrong once. But worst of all, the film never mentioned or portrayed Miff Mole, who worked as closely with Nichols as Sissle did with Blake. Nothing about "Red and Miff's Stompers" or the "Cotton Pickers," those early groups that drove the jazz collectors wild. Miff and Red were like ham and eggs. I can't tell you how embarrassed Nichols was over the movie in general and this omission in particular.

In New York, I mentioned to Miff that I'd talked with Nichols and told him how badly Red felt about it all.

"That's a funny thing," Miff said, without apparent rancor. "I've always been easy to forget. Every time I shave, I look in the mirror and I see somebody there and I always come out on photographs."

One time I asked Phil Napoleon to try to reassemble the Original Memphis Five for a concert and possibly a recording session, but he wrote me that he couldn't get them together. I think Jack Roth, the drummer, had died, but Signorelli and Jimmy Lytell were all right.

Miff was ailing, he said, and I'm ashamed to say my first thought was how that was going to affect Pee Wee. But then I remembered that I ought to be worrying about Miff.

Johnny Wiggs went to New York for a while in the mid-1950s. He stayed in the same hotel as Miff and played a few jobs with him. Miff's decline, he wrote, was quick and horrible. His ailments cost him a leg, among other things. He tried to go on playing till the end, and I had the feeling that nobody noticed.

Clarence Williams

I didn't get to know Clarence Williams until the late forties. He wasn't playing music anymore, having made his pile out of his music pub-lishing business and other hustles he seemed to generate consistently. I had always wanted to talk to him, and when I found out from Jimmy Pemberton, who was then the Harlem District Leader, that he was operating a shop on 125th Street in Harlem, I made my way over there one weekday afternoon.

Wearing a plaid lumberjack shirt and leather boots, he was sitting outside the store with his chair tilted back against the building. He was in his fifties, still looking fit and vigorous. The shop was a kind of junk shop, it appeared to me, and I have no idea who his customers could have been. Williams, however, didn't look like a junk man. He was neat and crisp, and he looked like somebody who spent time every day in the gymnasium.

I introduced myself and asked him if he might still be interested in appearing in an occasional concert. He said he wasn't. "Don't need to do any o' that any more," he explained.

I asked him questions about his composing and publishing career, his playing days with Bessie Smith and other blues and jazz stars.

"Wait just a minute, man! It's pretty near closing time, and it's gonna take a long time for me to tell you all the things you want to know. Can you come back tomorrow?"

I was committed for the rest of the week until noon Friday. I asked him about the weekend.

"Not this weekend," he said. "This weekend I'm gonna do a little huntin' up in the mountains. I'm gonna meet some friends and we're gonna try to find us some deer."

It would be a long time before I'd get another chance to talk with him since I was starting on a concert tour the following Tuesday. "Have you got room for one more?" I asked, innocently.

He tilted his chair down so all four legs were on the sidewalk. "Well, you know, we'll be in the Catskills and we got to stay someplace. The place we stay is just for colored, you understand."

"You think I could pass?" I suggested.

He thought that was pretty funny. "Hell, I guess it would be all right with them if it's all right with you. The place is called the Notch." He didn't think they actually had a policy against ofays. It amused him. The idea of bringing a southern white to the place seemed a little *outré*.

He asked me about my gear, since he knew I'd come in from out of town. I told him I could be ready with everything but a gun, and he generously volunteered to supply me with one. He seemed to have lots of them. What he didn't ask me was whether I'd ever hunted before. I'd have had to confess that I hadn't.

The next morning I went to an Army-Navy Surplus Store and bought cut-rate fatigues and boots, after describing my intentions to the storekeeper. I also bought some extras. A red bandana, dark glasses, a metal box to keep matches dry. (I smoked in those days.) And I bought one of those knives with all kinds of tools that popped out like blades. Ready for the kill.

I didn't know whether I had the kind of emotional makeup that would permit me to go out and assassinate Bambi, but I wasn't about to miss the chance to spend the time with the illustrious Clarence Williams.

Our party, on the way up, consisted of Clarence, me, and an attractive young lady whose name I don't remember. By their behavior I would have had to assume she was something more than a secretary. She was quick, literate, relaxed. Her color was dark gold; her hair short and dyed blonde. She could have been a model. I'm sure she was under thirty. Clarence drove. I pay so little attention to cars that I can't say what make or color the car was, but I remember that it rode more comfortably than most cars. The lady was looking forward to playing tennis with other ladies she knew who frequented the Notch. I gathered she wasn't planning to join us in the high grass or swamps or wherever the hell you went to look for deer.

The trip wasn't as long as I expected it to be. By the time we reached the Notch, the sun was still up, and we were in time for a great dinner. Since the girl had maintained a continuous monologue for the entire drive, I had had no chance to talk with Clarence. Dinner proved to be a culinary triumph. The lodge catered to well-to-do folks, and there was a real opulence about the fare. They served a great deal of butter and genuine heavy cream with things. There was roast chicken, fried chicken, baked apples, fresh corn on the cob. By the time we were through, Clarence's friends had arrived. They were New York musicians I didn't know and hadn't heard of. I noticed they were wet when they came in, and that was the first time I realized that it had begun to rain.

For the rest of the weekend, St. Swithin was in charge. Going outdoors was out of the question, much less hunting. I was full of gratitude to the deities for this untoward weather. We spent two delightful days in the parlor around the piano, listening to Clarence play and tell stories in answer to my questions. Just as the nimrods had been foiled, so had the "racqueteers." The young ladies stayed with us, and the one who had come up with us proved to be a very talented singer who knew, apparently, hundreds of Clarence's songs.

I brought him up to date on Armand Piron's last days and recalled with him the scenes of his youth. He almost wept when I told him they were about to tear down the Big 25, which he had managed in New Orleans. And we talked of river shrimp, buster crabs, and lost bread. In answer to one of my questions, I got an answer I must pass on to you.

"No, man. I didn't really write that. The only tune I ever really wrote was 'The Sugar Blues,' and I did that because I needed it in a hurry for Oliver. You see I already had told him I had this tune dedicated to him, because, you know, he always ate those sugar sandwiches. Po' boy bread spread all over with butter and then as much sugar as he could get on it. So I needed it in a hurry and I didn't have anybody to do the tune, so I did it myself. But you understand I never stole anything. That was the way the music business worked in those days. If you couldn't get a piece of the copyright, it didn't pay to publish it. Songwriters understood that putting the publisher's name on it, along with his own, was part of the original deal. Of course I published a lot of big hits."

He told me of Bessie Smith's first recording session, "The Gulf Coast Blues," and how he'd had to explain to her what the microphone was for, that she'd have to sing into it. He said how difficult it was for her to get started with no audience before her. He told me how she was dressed in calico and how she demanded that a spittoon be brought into the studio before she began. "I just gave her a water glass full of gin and she was fine," he recalled.

He didn't drop me off in Harlem, but took me all the way into town to the Algonquin Hotel where I was staying. (The rain continued to come down torrentially.) He asked me if I was planning to write a magazine article, and I told him I expected sometime to use our conversation in a book. This is the book.

The Dixieland Rhythm Kings

This is about six youngsters from Dayton, Ohio—at least that's where they'd been playing in their short careers and the leader, Gene Mayl, was from there. He performed expertly on a four-valve tuba. All of them were enamored with early New Orleans jazz and most particularly with King Oliver. They had been affected by the sounds being generated in California by the Lu Watters Orchestra. But by the time I encountered them in New Orleans in 1954, they had developed something genuine of their own that was rooted firmly in the original jazz form. The band had no drummer, for the simple reason that they couldn't find a competent one who would add anything to their ensemble. Today's leaders will empathize.

The trumpet player, Bob Hodes, a slight, intense, straightforward young man, played a hard-driving, no-frills lead that was the answer to a real jazz fan's prayer. The trombonist, a sandy-haired kid with Kaiser Wilhelm mustachios, was an intellectual—not only a brilliant tailgater but a polished artist and writer; his name was Charlie Sonnanstine, and the last I heard of him he was hand-crafting harpsichords. Jack Vastine, a banjoist who also sang, supplied much of the beat. And a fascinating pianist, Robin Wetterau, had, at the age of nineteen or so, already begun participating in a ragtime revival that would not come to fruition for another decade. The clarinetist, Ted Belafield, would die while still in his twenties.

This band came to New Orleans to fulfill an ill-advised booking in the Dream Room on Bourbon Street, an upholstered sewer run by characters that shouldn't have had a license. Many native jazz bands were working the street in those years, but they'd become stereotyped and lazy, playing a handful of tired tunes too fast and too loud, mainly following the dictates of proprietors who were (and are) convinced that this kind of jazzoid music will bring the customers in off the street. I am offended by the fact that they're probably right.

I had the opportunity to listen to these kids informally before their engagement opened, and they were so good that I booked them to play for the New Orleans Jazz Club's annual function at the municipal auditorium. This booking was to follow their "Dream Room" stint. During that week, at least, they were the best band in New Orleans.

The night they opened at the club, I was there for the first set. I found their performance fascinating, exciting, and extremely professional. The management, however, had a different view. They were disturbed because this band was playing unfamiliar tunes. They didn't do the standard Bourbon Street book, but had gone to the trouble of learning and developing lesser-known items of early jazz as played by the old masters. Club owners were under the illusion that such tin-pan-alley favorites as "The Birth of the Blues" were typical New Orleans melodies. The band didn't do "Basin Street Blues" or "Bourbon Street Parade"—that sort of thing. They did, though, play Oliver and Morton things beautifully, and in the correct tempos.

Outside the club I talked with the business agent of the union who was hostile to the appearance of any out-of-town band. I asked him how he liked the music and he answered, "It's okay if you like that authentic stuff."

The club owners fired the band without notice on the second night. They didn't care about the union rules. They threatened bodily harm to the band if they decided to make an issue of it; and the union, to its extreme discredit, took no action against the proprietors of the room. I must hasten to add that this failure to act was certainly not typical of the great New Orleans local of the musicians' union.

Needless to say, the band was disheartened by this turn of events, and I tried to do what I could to organize their stay in New Orleans— until the jazz club concert—in a way that would alleviate their disappointment. We had gotten together the Papa Celestin Orchestra, Sharkey and his band, and a couple of other attractions for the event. I went on stage to introduce the performers, knowing in my heart that despite the stars on the bill, the kids from Dayton were going to steal the show. I'm sure I was motivated to do my very best emceeing to prepare the crowd for their act.

The Dixieland Rhythm Kings took New Orleans jazz fans by

storm. They stopped the show. I don't know how many encores there were, but they captured the hearts of maybe two thousand jazz lovers. The newspapers the next day sealed their claim to being the best band in the concert, in the city, and maybe in the country. I don't need to tell you they were all smiles before they took their leave of us that week— especially when I relayed to them the messages that two Bourbon Street club owners, plus the ones who had just fired them, wanted to offer them bookings. Gene Mayl asked me to refuse the two owners with thanks. And he gave me a special message for the Dream Room owners, which is too indelicate to print in this context but which I did repeat faithfully to the parties concerned.

Anyway, I like seeing the good guys finish first.

The Brunies

George was the most famous Brunies. I think he's the best jazz trombonist I ever heard, but I finally had to stop using him on concerts because he was incorrigible. I can't talk about the characters of Richie and Henny, who played with Papa Laine, though the old man had a lot to say about them. Abbie, the leader of the legendary Halfway House Orchestra, was a solid lead horn who was built like a fire plug and never got tired. In his old age he looked exactly like Colonel Sanders. Merrit, who recorded as the leader of the Friars' Society Orchestra in the twenties, was a typical southern redneck who even became a Mississippi sheriff, if you can believe that. He played beautiful cornet and valve trombone. All five were brothers, and together they certainly constituted one of the great families of New Orleans jazz. There was also Little Abbie, an excellent drummer who was the son of Henny.

I remember the Halfway House, so-called because it marked the halfway point of the trip from downtown New Orleans to Old Spanish Fort on Lake Pontchartrain. Here people would stop to refresh themselves en route, and many would take the opportunity for a dance or two to Abbie's music. Ropollo and Charlie Cordilla had played in that band, as had the almost mythical Emile "Stalebread" Lacoume. The food was good, too; I doubt whether there's a better stuffed flounder in the world than the ones you could get for lunch there on the bayou. Abbie played all the latest songs from New York, as well as the work of local composers like Tom Brown, Irwin Leclere, and Nick Clesi.

The times I talked with Merrit, whom I didn't know well, he was always more interested in programs to clamp down on drunken drivers, "who were mostly niggers," he explained, "because everybody knew that niggers couldn't hold their liquor." Whites, presumably, could. I also discovered, through my brief discussion with him, that "niggers invented jazz but didn't know what to do with it" and that white musicians "improved" it to make it what it was at its best. For illustration he cited the music of Shep Fields and his Rippling Rhythm.

Little Abbie was a good drummer and a real gentleman whom I knew well. He had little education and no concept of the world outside of New Orleans, though he'd made a trip or two to the northern metropolises. He had become enamored of Jewish food in Chicago, and I sometimes thought he married his lovely wife Jerri largely because she could cook it.

But George was something else again. He was rude, crude, and obnoxious. Time after time I flagged him down in his inclination to perform his belly dance on stage or to invite a very large person from the audience to come up on stage and stand on his chest while he lay flat on his back and played his chorus of "Tin Roof Blues." I never condoned that kind of clowning in the presentation of authentic jazz, since I'm satisfied that great music is cheapened by such conduct. What ultimately caused me to close the lid on his shenanigans as far as Journeys Into Jazz was concerned happened one night during a concert in the Academy of Music in Philadelphia. I had a regular Friday night audience, many of whom had been driven there in their chauffeured limousines. Rolls Royces were parked all around the place on those nights, and the aficionados were a conservative lot that included the likes of Lessing Rosenwald, Russel Sage, Leopold Stokowski, and, once, Nelson Rockefeller. Generally speaking, outside of its interest in authentic jazz, it was a very square crowd.

During intermission, George wandered out on stage, trailed by Wingy Mannone and the piano player, Frank Signorelli, and began to sing an obscene song about Eddie Condon to the tune of "M-O-T-H-E-R." As soon as I was alerted to this jollity, I ran out and escorted him off the stage. The audience didn't fail to note that we carried on the second half of the concert without a trombone. Never again did I hire him to perform under my auspices. Oddly, we remained friends, and I often saw and spoke with him at various fes-

tivals and a record session or two. Once at the Cotton Carnival in
Memphis, I came into the coffee shop of the headquarters hotel and
found George having brunch with other musicians and fans. I heard
him say, "Watch your language. Here comes Al Rose."

Still, there were things I approved of about George besides his
musical artistry. I approved of the fact that he was color blind on
racial matters. He always said, "We learned everything we knew about
jazz from black musicians." I doubt that that was true, but he believed
it. I certainly am aware of the fact that he was deeply influenced by
Roy Palmer, an early black trombonist. But, as I have written before,
that music is a product not of a race but of a place and all the people
in it. George demonstrated, however, that bigotry doesn't necessarily
run in families.

In matters like building fires under the chairs of his fellow musicians while they were performing, however, or stuffing limburger
cheese into the horns of unsuspecting tuba players or switching banjo
strings on people and otherwise comporting himself in sophomoric
ways in public, he was intolerable. In combination with a Wild Bill
Davison or a Wingy Mannone, he could be a catastrophe. Muggsy
Spanier could control him pretty well, but Muggsy could deviate
from genteel behavior on occasion himself.

I saw the taciturn bassist Steve Brown slug George in the stomach
in an elevator one time—hard enough to bring him to his knees. I
had no idea what the controversy had been about, but I would have
been ready to bet it was something George had initiated.

Paul Barbarin

Paul Barbarin was one of the finest gentlemen in jazz—and a good
friend besides. He rarely appeared to react to the stupidity and crass-
ness of others. But when ugliness became so blatant that even he felt
compelled to respond, he could be withering.

In 1958 the morning TV show "Wide Wide World" decided to
cover the tenth anniversary celebration of the New Orleans Jazz Club
aboard the steamer *President*. The vessel was alive with jazz stars,
including Paul's band, Sharkey's band, Wiggs's band with Edmond
Souchon, Lizzie Miles, Joe Robichaux, and Fats Pichon playing the
calliope on the top deck. Dave Garroway, the show's host with whom
I'd worked on concerts in earlier days, called me a few days before-

hand and asked if I'd do him the favor of keeping an eye on things. I'm not sure he knew what he wanted me to keep an eye on, but I was there.

The production people knew absolutely nothing about the music, and they kept asking for retake after retake until Lizzie's voice was about gone and the musicians were getting irked. Barbarin was playing the "Basin Street Blues." It was a great band and the rendition was superb, even though they'd done it a dozen times that day. A young assistant director approached him and said, "Paul, can't you play that a little *dirtier?*"

Paul asked, "Where you from, young fella?"

"Iowa," the kid said.

"An' how old are you?" Paul pursued.

"Twenty-two," was the answer.

Paul fixed him with a glare worthy of one of Macbeth's witches. Then this jazz pioneer who had played behind King Oliver, Freddie Keppard, Louis Armstrong, and Kid Ory said, "Young fella, you're from Iowa, you're twenty-two years old, and you are tellin' *me* how to play the blues?"

Maybe ten years before that I was sitting in Childs's Paramount Restaurant in New York, watching Paul's band as he was completing an engagement there. When the set was over, Paul and the renowned clarinetist Willie Humphrey joined me at the table. We talked a few minutes and Paul said, "I got a tune we're gonna play for you. You're a big man with words, would you try to write me some words to this? I was thinkin' of somethin' about Bourbon Street. Like Bourbon Street Parade—you know, like South Rampart Street Parade."

I promised I would if I could think of something. So the band played a couple of choruses and I wrote down on the menu, "Let's drive down or fly down to Bourbon Street . . . etc."

Paul had already had at least one successful number; it was "Come Back Sweet Papa." Louis recorded it a couple of times.

Paul said, "I'll try this out and if it goes, I'll put you down for the lyrics."

"No," I told him, "I don't want any of your copyright. Hell, it only took me five minutes and I don't think the words are that great."

I still don't but the number was a big hit anyway. I hope Paul made a bundle on it. Willie Humphrey was the only witness to the affair.

Paul died on February 17, 1969, right in the middle of Mardi Gras. He was playing the snare drums in the Onward Brass Band and parading as he'd always done. I was standing on a gallery overlooking Royal Street with drummer Leonard Ferguson, whose apartment it was. Maskers were throwing beads and doubloons at us. Leonard is a superior drummer, coleader of the beautiful Crawford-Ferguson Night Owls, which produced one of the great LP's of the jazz revival. There were lots of other guests, too. These were the days when the carnival parades still came through the French Quarter and came up Royal Street right past where we were standing. A musician—I think it was Brother Cornbread Thomas—called up to us to tell us that Paul had fallen out a short time before. By the time I called Charity Hospital he was dead.

The wake was attended by most every jazzman in town, besides a host of other distinguished citizens. The funeral next day, in the pouring rain, attracted one of the great mobs in New Orleans funeral history. Pete Fountain played "A Closer Walk With Thee," and the various bands played many of Paul's tunes. I was doing a recording session the following week and I had dialed halfway through his phone number before I remembered he wouldn't make this session.

Neighborhoods

Somewhere there's a doctoral dissertation yet to be done on the seeming coincidence of certain neighborhoods producing a disproportionate share of jazzmen. I've known everybody in the so-called "Austin High Gang" of Chicago. It included Krupa, Bud Freeman, Jimmy and Dick McPartland, and, I think, Dave Tough, and the bassist Jim Lannigan. I talked with Jimmy McPartland at a concert at St. Joseph's Academy in Covington, Louisiana, during the late 1970s. He said he thought everybody was trying to play jazz in those days—not just the Austin High kids. Art Hodes was the bandleader that day. He's from Chicago, too, but he pointed out that the Austin gang was younger, and he had no idea what was going on with them. Krupa never saw anything extraordinary about it. As for Dave Tough, it was always difficult to get him to concentrate on a question for more than a few seconds.

The Scarsdale High School troupe of the forties was another of

these phenomena. Nominally, Bob Wilber headed the band. Each of
its members seemed to have his own role model. Wilber, of course,
got some pointers personally from Bechet while I watched. Trumpeter
Johnny Glazel was clearly a copy of Wild Bill Davison, and Jerry
Blumberg, another trumpet man, was a shade of Bunk. The band,
with Dick Wellstood on piano, had a very convincing sound in its earliest days. Wilber seemed to feel, not without justification, that he,
himself, was the catalyst that pulled it all together.

There were sections of New Orleans that spawned whole bands,
too. Between 1915 and 1925 there was an area in the Faubourg St. John
that spawned early Dixieland stars like Johnny Bayersdorffer, Lester
Bouchon, Jules and Ray Bauduc, the drummer Roland "Dutch"
Flick, and later Pete Fountain. I lived there for a while, too; but, of
course, I never attempted to play with these guys. Bayersdorffer, an
early recording star, once said, "It was nice and cool in the evenings
under the trees in the neutral ground. In those days there was no
television—hell, there was no *radio*. And when I started out there was
no jazz on phonograph records, either. If you wanted that music, you
just had to play it yourself."

When an Orleanian says "down*town*" he means the French Quarter and its immediate environs. When he says *down*town, he's talking
about an area roughly back of Elysian Fields Avenue. Part of it is the
Faubourg Marigny, and the rest is spread all the way back to the Indus-
trial Canal toward Chalmette. Here, the three Christians—Frank,
Charlie, and Emile—grew up, along with Willie Guitar, the Baquets,
the Bechets, and dozens of others. Uptown, the section known as the
"Irish Channel" brought together the Brunies, Tom and Steve Brown,
Nick Larocca, Yellow Nunez, and the components of the Original
Dixieland Jazz Band, as well as the Loyacanos, Armand Hug, and
another twenty or so. They were all centered on Jackson and Magazine. Also uptown, Joe Oliver, Kid Ory, and the Dutreys lived within
a two-block radius. Buddy Bolden, Charlie Galloway, and Wallace
Collins all lived in the section around First Street and Simon Bolivar.
They played music together almost from childhood. The Shields family lived in the same block as Bolden.

The section known as Treme is now mostly gone and has been
replaced by Armstrong Park. Back in there lived Picou, Kid Rena, Big
Eye Louis Nelson, Sam, Isaiah, Andrew, and Albert Morgan, the

Keppards, Jim Robinson, George Lewis, and the composer of "When the Saints Go Marchin' In," Edward Boatner. Jim Robinson had no explanation for this concentration. "It seemed like everybody played music when I come up from the country. I started out on guitar before the war [World War II], and music was just somethin' you had to do," he said.

Joe Robichaux once told me, "When I put together my big swing band, I didn't have to go out of the neighborhood to get my men. And they were musicians! Those two great trombones, 'Frog' [Joseph] and Clement Tervalon. Guys like Turk and Kildee lived right near me, and Freddie Kohlman. I don't remember where [Guy] Kelly lived, but he was the only one didn't live close."

Jelly Roll and Piron lived in what we always called the "Creole Section," roughly bounded by Esplanade, Elysian Fields, Claiborne Avenue, and North Broad Avenue. The Nicholases, Albert and Wooden Joe, John Lindsay, and Buddy Petit were from around there. And a few came up from the slums. The area around Perdido and South Rampart was the roughest area of the city at the turn of the century. Louis Armstrong, Johnny and Baby Dodds, Kid Shots Madison, Punch Miller, and most of their early musical associates developed right around there.

The various neighborhoods of New York City didn't follow this rule. It seemed as though each of the jazzmen that city produced came out of isolation into the jazz world. Harlem didn't become the black musical center until too late. Before the late twenties, its ethnic composition was entirely different. It was a largely Jewish community, much of it Orthodox—not the kind of culture that produced jazz.

I hope someday someone will do the research on the connection between jazz and the various neighborhoods. Maybe Trebor Tichenor is trying to find out why so much ragtime was generated in Missouri, of all places. And maybe Harry Godwin knows why the blues got so much impetus out of Memphis and the barren hell of the Mississippi Delta country.

Lagniappe

Four Bar Breaks

One of the world's great jazz bass players is Sherwood Mangiapane of New Orleans. He's retired from his "day job" now as an officer of the Whitney National Bank. He's one of my best friends among jazz-men I've known, and he has a number of talents besides slapping a bull fiddle, which he plays backwards because he's left-handed. (He doesn't restring the instrument—he just plays it backwards, but right.) One of his other talents is that he sings in the time-honored Crescent City tradition of Armstrong, Wingy, Prima. Not only that, but he's the best hot whistler of them all. The problem is that he finds it impossible to whistle in front of an audience, so you'll very likely never get to see him do it live. On recording sessions if you want him to whistle, you've got to let him turn his back to the musicians so that nobody can look at him. He's known among his contemporaries for his uncanny musical ear. If something trivial goes wrong in a chord, he stops playing and says, "That's wrong!" He doesn't know music so he can't tell you what's wrong, but he can surely tell you where it's wrong. By now nobody questions his ukase. When he says, "That's wrong!" we all get to going over what happened until we find it. (The rest of us usually can't read either.)

• • •

I've had the chance to work with some great drummers. Baby Dodds was always ready to lecture aspiring youngsters about the absolute necessity of practice. People who asked him how he had developed his phenomenal skills all got a one-word reply: "PRACTICE!"

There were several weekends in the summer of 1947 when you could have sailed up the river on the Hudson River Day Line for a jazz cruise and huddled in the bow of the ship to get as close as possible to the performers. The band included Bechet, Marty Marsala, Sam Price, Pops Foster, and Baby. On one such evening, I sat between Baby and a tweedy spectator who was smoking a cigarette and had become so intent on the intricacies of Baby's magic with the sticks that he had permitted a large, glowing ember to drop off his cigarette onto the knee of his obviously expensive trousers. Baby, without missing a beat, flicked the tip of his drumstick and removed the potentially destructive fire so adroitly that the smoker was never aware of anything. Baby winked at me and whispered, "Practice!"

• • •

Big Sid Catlett was a great drummer and a great showman. I always thought he could also have been a great stand-up comedian. He was the original drummer in the Louis Armstrong All-Stars. He told me,

"I might not be the best drummer in the world, but I'm big enough to slug any drummer who says I ain't."

• • •

George "Silver" Wettling, whenever he was working for me, always brought along a sketch pad full of drawings and color sketches for paintings. (I don't know if I ever mentioned that art is *my* profession. It's what made everything else possible.) I would criticize his work and try to give him helpful hints about improving it. I never took his things seriously because he didn't seem to show much promise. But hell, everybody needs a hobby. Before he died, his things were bringing high prices and I suspect they're worth even more now.

• • •

We had Buddy Rich working in the Click in 1947 with his left arm in a cast. That's not easy for a drummer. But broken wing and all, he maintained his hectic pace through every set and remained ready to make the rounds with me on all the promotional activities I had planned. I asked him if it was a strain on him, and he said everything he'd ever done was a strain—even sex.

• • •

I got involved with helping a group of very eccentric folks produce a recording session in the mid-1970s. It was a stupid concept they'd started with. The leader, a guitar player of negligible ability, wanted to play with the best possible New Orleans jazz band behind him. I got Wiggs and Raymond Burke, Jack Delaney and Chester Zardis, and for a drummer none other than Louis Barbarin, who at that time was the best living jazz drummer.

This gang—one of those now-notorious California "families"—decided they couldn't use Louis because he was born under the wrong sign. I had to pay Louis off and try to explain the problem to him. (They hadn't even heard him play!) He said, "I already met some crazy people in the music business. At least these guys pay off."

• • •

Arthur "Monk" Hazel spent a large part of his life on the road. He was clearly in the big time, especially during the years when he supported Gene Austin along with Candy and Coco. He played his drums with a strong feeling of the burlesque house and played on many occasions with Bix. Monk was an alcoholic, and I can't believe he lived to be sixty-five years old in his condition. He can't have had much liver left. He was back in New Orleans and working in Santo Pecora's band at the Famous Door once when I actually saw him fall off the bandstand. I picked him up, carried him outside to my car, and drove him to his house on Arabella Street where he lived with his sister. Then I went back and saw Santo, who was extremely embarrassed to have had one of his musicians pass out from drinking in front of a full house. He was finishing the evening without a drummer.

"Whatya gonna do?" he asked. "I been playin' with him all my life—and when he's sober he's the best drummer I know. He ain't bad when he's drunk, either. I hope the boss lets me keep him on."

I had a talk with Hyp Guinle, the proprietor, expecting to have to make a plea for Monk's job. He said, "If you're somebody's friend, you're his friend when he's drunk, too."

Checking on Monk the next day I found him bright and cheerful and ready to work. He thanked me for bringing him home again. His sister had told him. He explained, "I gotta stop drinkin' that scotch and go back to gin. Scotch'll make a drunk out of a man."

He gave me a mute that had belonged to Emmet Hardy. I still have it.

• • •

I never knew the king of the brass band bass drummers, Ernest "Ninesse" Trepagnier, even though he lived until 1968. But there's a photograph, well-known to all jazz fans, of him with a band that included Clarence Williams, A. J. Piron, Kid Ory, and Oscar Celestin. Visible in the picture is an unusual, one-of-a-kind, hand-made snare drum, which, after his death, came into the possession of yet another outstanding drummer, Alfred Williams. Young Barrie Martyn, an English kid who would later organize his own band, "The Legends of Jazz," to tour the world with great success, coveted that drum. But Barrie was in no financial position to pay the twenty-five dollars Alfred wanted for it, so I bought the drum for him with the understanding that he would pay me when he got the money. It took him quite a long time, but I got my money back. More years later, I heard, to my dismay, that he'd sold this historic treasure. I didn't recognize him the next time I saw him, because he was approximately a hundred pounds heavier than the skinny kid I'd bought the drum for. I had worked myself up to tell him off for disposing of Ninesse's drum. But it turned out he hadn't sold it at all. Someone had stolen it. He was even more distressed than I was. Take a good look at the famous photo and observe the snare drum. If you ever see another drummer using it, you'll know how he got it.

• • •

Ray McKinley was one of the demon drummers of the swing era—according to many, the best in the world. This tall, skinny, bespectacled Texan took over the Glenn Miller Orchestra after its famous leader was lost on a flight during World War II. But by 1947 he was the leader of his own band, and I sat with him as he rehearsed it in preparation for a recording session of the first Sauter-Finnegan arrangements. They were entitled "Borderline" and "Sandstorm" and would come out on the Majestic label. I didn't have much I needed to do besides move his drums back fifteen feet or so and try out the mike on Lou Stein's piano. I asked Ray how he felt and he said, "I'd feel better if I knew what I was doin'."

The record was acclaimed by the "experts," but I had the feeling Ray's enthusiasm was limited. When he came to Philadelphia, he appeared on my radio show at the WFIL studio and talked about how much more fun it was to play with a real jazz band where you weren't restricted by arrangements.

• • •

Wiggs had a job for his band in the St. Charles Hotel in the late forties. His drummer was Ray Bauduc, who had been sitting pretty a decade earlier when he gained fame as one of Bob Crosby's celebrated Bob Cats. Wiggs didn't hold the job long—though the short engagement was not because the music wasn't outstanding. I spent quite a few evenings there because I knew it wouldn't last, and I talked with Ray during many of the breaks. He once said, "I *love* this band! But when you've been up there at the top of show business it gets in your blood—New York, Hollywood, all that. You'd have thought I could save some money, but I didn't. I've gotta have a go at it again, though."

Ray and Nappy Lamare organized their "Riverboat Dandies" and made it to the big time for a last hurrah.

I talked to him in Fort Lauderdale in the fifties and he told me, "Ten years from now, I think the real music we play will be all gone. The kids comin' up are doin' something else. I'm not saying it's no good—it just isn't our kind of music." Nappy nodded along in agreement.

• • •

I don't remember any time in my life when I didn't know Albert Francis. Before I was aware of him, he was employed as the drummer in the trio that performed nightly in Tom Anderson's legendary saloon in the Storyville district. It was here that the Prince of Wales (later Edward VIII) walked in one night with his entourage for a spot of amusement. The prince politely asked Albert if he might borrow his sticks. He then sat down on the stool and played for an hour with the group. Albert told me the prince's performance was creditable. But he added, "Sure, it sounded good to me! If he's playin', that means I ain't playin' and after eight, ten hours a man got enough playin'."

I was happy to sit and talk with him at the Tulane Hot Jazz Classic series of events in May, 1983. The vigorous nonagenarian greeted me with, "I didn't know youngsters like you was allowed out after dark."

I showed him my medicare card.

• • •

Zutty Singleton was showing me how he made his press roll on the snare drum. He slowly counted out eight rhythmic beats as he played them, then repeated that slightly faster, then sixteen, even faster, but still not too fast to count the beats. Then he said, "Now you turn your tape recorder on and I'll do you a couple of thirty-twos and then a couple of sixty-fours. Then you play it back at a speed where you can count 'em and you'll see there's exactly the right number in each set."

He played three sets of beats in what sounded like approximately the same time. Then he did three more sets in what seemed like half the time. Of course, as a *roll*, it was an apparently continuous sound, since it was too fast to distinguish an individual drumbeat.

"Now you slow that tape down and see what you got."

But slowing it to the slowest speed the beats were still too fast to count, so I rerecorded it later to make it come in even slower. At last I got it slow enough and was able to establish that the first sets had all been exactly thirty-two beats and the last ones twice that speed.

On a later occasion I had some questions to ask Zutty, like "I know you can't count that fast! How do you get it to come out right on the money?"

"When I first started out I counted. But after I got really good at it, I didn't have to count any more and it would just come out right. Today's young kids can't even play a roll that doesn't count out right. I s'pose it's just a gift."

Zutty's delightful wife Margie said, "He can't tell how he does any of that. I've seen him show a lot of people, but I guess you can't explain a gift."

If You Pick It It Won't Get Better

That's what Edmond Souchon used to tell other banjo and guitar players: "If you pick it, it won't get better." Jazz bands that had to operate on short budgets in the old days would try to get by with the minimum number of musicians. They eventually settled, informally, on five as a minimum number of components for a jazz band. Of these five, three had to be the front line horns—trumpet or cornet, trombone, and clarinet. A proper seven-piece band also included piano and drums, plus guitar (banjo) and bass. Expediency eventually dictated that the way you cut a seven-piece band down was first to drop the banjo/guitar player, then the bass. This fact created a clear-cut defensive attitude among guitar and banjo players. Lonnie Johnson, famed for his work with Armstrong and his recorded duets with Eddie Lang, explained it to me like this:

"So you got a job in this seven-piece outfit, see, and you workin' steady, say in a club or a dance hall. Then the band gets popular and they send for 'em to come out of town somewhere. The telegram says 'five pieces,' maybe 'six pieces.' It don't *never* say seven pieces. So the band goes, the guitar player stays home. A guitar player got to learn to do a single or he don't work much. That means sing, too."

Elmer Snowden's version went like this: "A banjo player wants to play for a livin', full time, he's got to put together his own band. Got to be the leader. Of course I did that when I first started out in Washington. I had this band, and I hired me a piano player [Duke Ellington] and he stole my band [The Washingtonians] and my job!"

• • •

Emanuel Sayles is an accomplished banjoist and guitarist. He plays regularly in Preservation Hall, and his musical credits include having played in the history-making recording session issued under the name of the Jones-Collins Astoria Hot Eight. This was the first racially mixed session in the South. We had an argument one time, about 1958, when he handed me his card advertising the Three Chocolate Bars. I objected that he shouldn't be identifying his group racially at all—that designations such as the Ink Spots, the Black and Tan Orchestra, and the Black Eagles had become socially retrogressive.

Sayles' view was that he was proud to be a Negro and wanted everyone to know it.

He was the teacher of Danny Barker, and it has been my great pleasure to have had both of them, at various times, making record sessions. (I really prefer Danny on guitar, Sayles on banjo.) Several years ago, a young and talented free-lance television producer, Stevenson Palfi, sought my counsel in the development of a documentary based on a New Orleans jazzman's career. I talked over with him a number of possible personalities he might use. Among the names that came up were Danny, Narvin Kimball, and Percy Humphrey. At last Palfi and his associates came up with the choice of Sayles, and I was happy to be asked to help with and appear on the show.

It was entitled "This Cat Can Play Anything," and it won the Leigh Whipper Award for the best musical biography of the year on television. Since it was shown on a network, it earned national recognition for its subject. When Sayles played in the Soviet Union during a Preservation Hall European tour, he was astonished to find there were many Russian jazz fans who were familiar with his name and his work. "They never even saw the TV show, either," he commented.

• • •

Within even the narrow scope of New Orleans jazz banjo, specialties develop that become unique to certain individuals. Narvin Kimball, for instance, is a true virtuoso in the matter of single-string picking on the plectrum, and he also has a style of singing standard gospel songs that captures the hearts and wrings the emotions of his audiences.

Kimball is a fine, cultured gentleman. He's one of the few New Orleans jazzmen that have never worked with me on anything. He let me know he was aware of that, too, and I just couldn't bring myself to explain to him that what he does best doesn't fit the context of what I produce. I have a principle objection to religious music of any kind, and never do any in any medium. But that doesn't mean that I don't enjoy listening to him or that we don't greet each other when we meet.

• • •

Creole George Guesnon was a pretty good banjo player who recorded as a soloist for Decca. He was also a kind of jazz historian, and since he grew up at the source of the subject, he had an expert's knowledge of his own environment. When our first edition of *New Orleans Jazz: A Family Album* was published, Bill Russell brought him a copy to

look at. Guesnon, a cynic who was convinced the world had conspired to keep him out of the spotlight, found an error in the text.
(There were several.) He was quick to point it out to Bill, who said
he'd pass the information on to me so that the error might be changed
in future printings.

George said, "Don't you do that, now! That's down in the book
now! That's *hist'ry!* You can't change *hist'ry!*"

• • •

Lawrence Marrero gained most of his fame as the banjo player in the
bands of George Lewis and Bunk Johnson. Even most of his many
fans had no idea he was once a professional boxer, too, or that he
often played bass drum in street parades. I was following one of these
parades one day in 1954 when a tall young man, respectably dressed
and carrying a camera, attempted to grab Lawrence's wire beater as the
band stood at rest. I saw Marrero grab the young man's arm with one
hand and hit him in the abdomen with the other. As the aspiring thief
doubled over, Marrero, a quiet man if ever there was one, shouted,
"Somebody call an ambulance." The policemen assigned to provide
security for the parade were on the spot in an instant. The band struck
up and marched away. I followed the band but looked back to notice
that the cops had stood the offender on his feet and one of them hit
him on the head with a billy club. I walked alongside Lawrence and
told him what was happening, and he said, "If they hit him too hard
he'll forget how much his stomach hurts. I got him a good one."

It had obviously made his day.

• • •

There was a period during the thirties when Joe Capraro's Orchestra
was the only outfit in town with steady work. He's a genuine master of
jazz guitar, a beautiful musician whom I've known for years. There
was something about his face, though, that haunted me. I was sure I
knew somebody who looked exactly like him. I told him he had a
double in town, but I couldn't remember who it was.

"Yeah?" he said. "There can't be another face like this."

But I had this face in my head—and in a uniform. Policeman?
No. Postman? No. I couldn't get it off my mind whenever I was
around Joe.

I frequently have business around City Hall, and one day I was in
a group of people leaving the building. A limousine was waiting, and
the chauffeur jumped out to open the door. The driver, fully liveried

from billed cap to leather puttees, was Joe Capraro. He showed no sign of recognition.

The next afternoon I saw him at Joe Mares's studio. I couldn't wait to tell him who his double was—the mayor's chauffeur.

He told me. "That wasn't no double. That was me. That's my day job."

I asked him why he never spoke to me. He told me, "I ain't allowed, but I thought you *knew* it was me."

Some Piano Sharks

It's always been hard to find a piano player that can fit into a genuine jazz band. Most of them think like soloists and can never grasp the instrument's basic percussive function. Getting a pianist to limit himself to keeping rhythm and making the chord changes is now almost impossible. Some of them can't do it and some of them won't, but it isn't easily established which is which. In the past there were some great band piano men. Sammy Price, Joe Sullivan, Art Hodes, Gene Schroeder, Armand Hug, Stanley Mendelson, Jess Stacy, and Hank Duncan were outstanding. Price, Stacy, and Mendelson survive, though Stacy doesn't play anymore. Knocky Parker still performs frequently, if not regularly, with bands, and he's hard to beat.

Don Ewell, who was Bunk Johnson's favorite, has a place in my gallery of great people. He stayed at my house for an extended visit once, while he was working at the Royal Orleans Hotel. He was an intellectual with a scholar's grasp of the humanities, and he had one major vice, chess. His lovely wife Mary gave him a Christmas present of an electronic, computerized chess opponent while he was at my place, and I think we never discussed anything after that. He kept competing with this box every waking moment. His health was failing at the time, and his physician established the fact that he needed a heart by-pass desperately. Don was shocked by this news, reluctant to take the necessary steps to get himself repaired. I spent lots of time giving him pep talks and convincing him to follow the doctor's orders. I finally persuaded him to let me drive him to the Ochsner Clinic for the surgery. He improved dramatically after that, moved back to his home in Pompano Beach, Florida. I'm such an unreliable correspondent that I didn't keep in touch with him for too long. He stayed on my list of things to do until he died. Now he's gone and I feel guilty.

Dick Wellstood, whom I had the chance to present at the 1982

Tulane Hot Jazz Classic, is another chess freak—one of those who carries on international competition by mail. He played piano behind Bechet frequently. I remember him when he was just a youngster and I had brought Bechet and some other musicians to Boston for a do at Symphony Hall where he performed brilliantly. One of the numbers he played at the concert this year was James P. Johnson's "Old Fashioned Love," which Wellstood defined as "love before herpes."

• • •

Frank Amacker was an old man by the time I met him. He had been, in the period from 1907 to 1913, a piano-playing professor in the bordellos of Storyville, and I set about finding him for an interview while researching my book on that subject. He proved to be a mine of information and color background. I'd find him in the carriageway of Preservation Hall occasionally, and it became my custom to shake hands with him and leave a dollar or two in his palm as a kind of gratuity. One evening I discovered I'd left my wallet in my apartment and I told him I was going back to get it and that I'd have a little something for him. He said, "That's all right, Mr. Al. Your credit's good with me."

• • •

Professor Manuel Manetta lived across the river from New Orleans in Algiers. He started many an aspiring jazzman on his career, including many of his relatives. The family included pianist Dolly (Douroux) Adams and her illustrious sons—bass player Placide, guitarist Justin, and drummer Gerald. He, too, played piano in the district but was competent on all other instruments. Sometimes, when Buddy Bolden had a job for an expanded orchestra, which he sometimes did, he'd hire Manetta just to wave the baton.

Manetta told me an exciting story of how he'd been leading his orchestra on the bandstand of the Tuxedo Dance Hall on the fateful Easter night of 1913 when the altercation took place that left the owner of the place, Harry Parker, and his rival from across the street, Billy Phillips, owner of the 101 Ranch, dead. Manetta described all of the action. He told how he and his musicians had dropped to the floor and taken refuge behind chairs, how they'd escaped from the place through a trapdoor in the ceiling. I duly made notes of the gory details, which all made for some fast-moving melodrama. Being, however, the compulsive researcher that I am, it wasn't long before I discovered that since it *was* Easter night, there couldn't have been any orchestra in there because music wasn't allowed in dance halls on Sunday. Besides, the police blotter showed that only one musician, drummer Abbey "Chinee" Foster, had been present, and he was only there to see about a job for the following week.

• • •

Joe Sullivan, the great Chicago piano player, and I looked very much alike in the forties. Jazz fans coming backstage would frequently ask me for my autograph on the assumption that I was Joe. I was considerably taller and ten years younger, but audiences don't get the proper perspective seeing people on stage. I was coming out of a stage door with Eddie Condon one night, and a girl came up to us with an autograph book. She asked for our signatures. I said, "Young lady, I'm not Joe Sullivan. He should be out in a minute or two."

Condon signed his name and handed the book back. He said, "Sure, he's Sullivan. Whenever he doesn't want people to recognize him he doesn't carry a piano."

• • •

In 1965 a junket left New Orleans aboard the private plane of Mrs. Winthrop Rockefeller. Our purpose was to participate in the dedication of the John Reid Jazz Wing of the Arkansas Cultural Center. Allan Jaffe was aboard, with musicians from Preservation Hall including Kid Thomas, George Lewis, and the piano player Charlie Hamilton. Hamilton hadn't been hired for the job originally. On the Wednesday before this particular weekend, Jaffe had engaged Joe Robichaux. On the following day, January 17, Robichaux died in New Orleans, a grievous loss for all followers of the real jazz.

But the show must go on. Jaffe immediately phoned Lester "Blackie" Santiago, an illustrious piano artist from Celestin's band. Santiago accepted and then died on the following day, January 18. It's understandable that Charlie Hamilton was reluctant to accept the job.

On our arrival in Arkansas, after checking into the hotel, we were informed that late the previous night, Papa John Joseph, ninety-two years old, had been playing "When the Saints Go Marchin' In" in Preservation Hall, had turned to the other musicians at the conclusion of the piece and said, "That about took everything out of me." He then collapsed and died on the spot. Larry Borenstein, who was with us, immediately flew back to New Orleans, missing the ceremonies, to settle the chaos that had resulted from Papa John's death.

Despite Mrs. Rockefeller's generous hospitality, that proved to be one weekend none of us were anxious to relive.

. . .

It is time honored custom in New Orleans for Rex's Mardi Gras float to be followed by an old fashioned circus wagon atop which a real jazz band holds forth during the entire parade. This marathon effect is achieved by having a full rhythm section going all the time and two front lines, one on either side of the wagon, which alternate. It was my function as director to control these shifts and to call the tunes, besides constantly regulating the amplifying system's volume according to the width of the streets we went through. Each Mardi Gras provides unpredictable events for the musicians, and in each case, one way or another, it all works out all right. Of course, you must remember to carry empty fruit juice cans for the older and less continent performers, you must monitor the distribution of alcoholic beverages that are all too generously supplied by Rex, the King of Carnival, and you must keep the two front lines from playing simultaneously from the beginning of the parade because, if they *do*, the music won't last from 8 A.M. to 3 P.M. as it must.

In 1966, we had a breakdown ahead of us, and the bandwagon was stalled at Lee Circle, where thousands were gathered to watch the parade and grab for the beads and doubloons the maskers throw. The band is too busy playing to throw anything and that makes the street throngs restive.

Stanley Mendelson was doing the piano chores that day, and he began to play "Alley Cat" right after I had flagged both front lines down for a break. Now, Mendelson's rhythm is irresistible. It has that subtle, compelling drive to which nobody is immune. The predictable result was that that enormous mass of humanity began to rock to that subtle, syncopated beat. Since there was no square inch unoccupied, I hesitate to describe what was taking place as dancing. From atop the bandwagon it looked like the ocean getting increasingly turbid. Stanley worked that mob up to a feverish heat and held them in his sway for over a half-hour until we got the signal from up ahead to resume our progress. Stanley brought the number to a halt and you could see that entire populace sag. I hope they enjoyed the rest of the parade.

As we approached the gallery of the Boston Club, where Rex and the governor of Louisiana toast each other, we knew to look for the honored guests, Lynda Bird Johnson, daughter of the President, and her swain of that time, actor George Hamilton. Directly behind us was a marine drill squad going through their dazzlingly complex maneuvers. I had my eye on the gallery and the happy couple as the drill squad concluded its routine by firing its rifles simultaneously. Lynda Bird vanished before my very eyes, her escort bewildered by her disappearance. She had been trained well by the secret service, and she knew that if she heard a shot she must drop to the floor. She did it reflexively. I'm sure she must have taken some moments to explain her bizarre action to her distinguished neighbors on the gallery.

It was the following year that the bandwagon stood in front of Gallier Hall, the old city hall, waiting for the king to exchange toasts with the mayor. I was supposed to cue the band when those two smashed their glasses, and the band's assignment was to play "If Ever I Cease To Love," which is the Rex theme. I had my ten good men and true ready to hit it at the instant the glasses were thrown. The musicians, sitting down, couldn't see the action taking place.

Unknown to me, right around the corner was the United States Navy Band, eighty pieces strong, which had been instructed to take *its* cue from me. I had no idea they were there. The only person in their outfit I could see was their drum major, and I saw him with upraised arm in the same stance I had taken. I wondered why he was staring at me. In due course the king and the mayor hurled their champagne glasses to the pavement, I gave the downbeat, expecting my jazz band to respond on cue. Whether they did or not I'll never know, because the response I got was the blast of that eighty-piece Navy band, which very nearly caused me to fall off the wagon in shock. I'm not sure I recovered during the rest of the parade. Our trombonist Paul Crawford said, "Don't we get a nice, full sound?"

• • •

Bud Freeman wrote a book a few years back entitled *You Don't Look Like a Musician*, a sort of autobiographical work full of short anecdotes that involved himself through his career. Of course, I don't care what he says, he does look like a musician, as you can tell from looking at his picture in *this* book. But Doc Evans didn't look like a musician or talk like one either for that matter. When he started on his cornet or trumpet, though, the result left no doubt in your mind about his profession. I sat with him for many hours in Chicago's Jazz Limited, in the mid-1940s, trying to get him to go on tour with me. He wasn't steadily employed; and even though the charming hosts of the place, Bill and Renee Reinhardt, were as generous as they could be, he wasn't going to augment his bank account much playing that job. He refused because he said he didn't like to travel. It made him feel too much like a professional musician, and when you were a professional musician you didn't get to play the way *you* wanted to. I offered him more than twice what he was getting. He'd have had a chance to play with the very best jazzmen. He found every excuse. He didn't want to go to the west coast. He got car sick riding in Greyhound buses. He had to lay off for a while because something was going wrong with his lip. I understood that for reasons of his own, whatever they were, he wasn't going to become a part of Journeys Into Jazz. Just then, it was about one in the morning, a pretty little girl with blonde ringlets, about half his age, maybe less, approached the table where we were sitting and asked him, "Will I see you again tonight, honey?" Then, of course, I understood.

• • •

It was well into the seventies when Jabbo Smith decided to come out of the long retirement that had made all but the most dedicated jazz collectors forget him, and he came to New Orleans to find work. As long as there's a Preservation Hall, musicians with his credentials will not remain unemployed and Allan Jaffe found room for him.

"I got to get my lip up," he explained to me. "You know, that takes some time if you're a trumpet player. Then I'm gonna go to New York. That's where the big action, the big *money* is. New York! Man, that's the place!"

In 1980, Jabbo was playing at the Village Gate, and I went down to see the show that featured him, "One Mo' Time," which starred the show's writer and producer, Vernel Bagneris. I had seen the show four times before in New Orleans, but it was new and exciting every time, in no small part because of the jazz band that accompanied it. It included the phenomenal Swedes, Lars Edegran and Orange Kellin; but it was Jabbo who overwhelmed the crowd in his two specialty numbers. I went back to the band room to greet my friends, and Jabbo was sitting dejectedly at a make-up table.

"Well, Jabbo," I began, "I see you made it up here to New York. It didn't take you too long either. Congratulations."

Jabbo said, "I got to get out of this damn place."

Pee Wee Erwin was another trumpet player who never seemed to be satisfied with his lot. He certainly achieved success in his career, both in the big bands, notably with Tommy Dorsey, and with small Dixieland combinations at Nick's or Condon's. He came to Boston one night to play for me as a substitute for Muggsy, who had fallen ill. I commented that he looked very unhappy and asked if he felt all right.

"Oh, yeah," he reassured me. "It's just that I hate music."

• • •

Billy Butterfield was still with Bob Crosby's Band the first time I met him. He looked like a very large kewpie doll with his chubby cheeks and big eyes. That illusion vanished the instant he began to blow his horn. I had another trumpet player, Sterling Bose, with me, and we dropped in to see Fazola, Eddie Miller, Nappy, and Ray Bauduc backstage at the Oriental Theater in Chicago. Bose listened awhile as we stood in the wings watching Butterfield on stage doing a solo. Then he said, "I used to stay up all day practicing Bix choruses, and now *this*."

Years later, Butterfield and I were on a radio show called "Juke Box Jury" together, and I recalled the incident and Bose's comment. Billy said, "I'm sure there are trumpet players around copying Bose's choruses."

• • •

Thomas Valentine, known to the Preservation Hall world as Kid Thomas, was born in 1896 in Reserve, Louisiana. As of 1985, he was still taking his turn two or three times a week with his band and going on the Hall's scheduled tours. But Thomas had a life before Preservation Hall. I began to be aware of him in the mid-1940s and by the mid-1950s he was playing with a distinguished band of his own every Friday night at the Westwego Fireman's Hall. Larry Borenstein and I used to go over the river every single Friday to hear him with Louis Nelson on trombone, Joe James playing piano, and Sammy Penn on his drums. As big an attraction as the music was, there was a couple that always joined the dancers and commanded at least as much attention as did the band. This pair had brought the art of jazz ballroom dancing to its very peak, and the other couples always tended to drift off the floor to give them room and to admire their extraordinary grace and rapport. It looked like a union made in heaven and their performance brought out the romantic sighs from the ladies in the house.

This couple turned up every place Thomas played. They were a true delight to watch.

Larry and I never stayed until closing time, but no matter how late we left, those same dancers would still be on the floor, still exhibiting their matchless grace and dexterity. Then one night, we *did* stay through the final set. Those two superb terpsichoreans were obviously saddened by the fact that they'd have to terminate their activities for that night. Not many people were left in the house and Thomas came over and introduced us. I don't remember their names, but I remember that we also met her husband and his wife.

The S.S. Capitol

The Strekfus steamship line, whose boats plied the Mississippi River until late in this century, was well-known to jazz fans around the world. The fascinating photographs published in jazz histories show the Fate Marable band with Louis Armstrong, Baby Dodds, Johnny St. Cyr, and Pops Foster clearly in evidence in about 1919. I almost missed it all; but in 1932 I had the opportunity to attend a dance on board, along with a large number of my classmates from St. Aloysius High School. The orchestra on duty that night was led by Sidney Desvigne, and there was a kind of pick-up band playing, too. It seemed to be under the direction of the saxophone player, who I later learned was David Jones.

I had a chance to talk with some of the band members. The drummer I came to know much better later. His name was Sidney Montegue. But most interesting was the tall, dissipated looking trombone player with a Shanghai face, who told me, in a boastful and unconvincing manner, that he had been the regular trombone player in Charles "Buddy" Bolden's band. He boasted of the musicians he'd beat out for the job. Having heard him play, I would have had to assume that there was a shortage of quality musicians available back then. This fellow's name was Frankie Duson, and I was not to hear of him again until Jelly Roll recorded his "Buddy Bolden's Blues" and sang these lines:

> I thought I heard Frankie Duson say,
> Gimme that money. . . .

I learned from Jelly Roll that Duson had indeed been a regular with Bolden and with Edouárd Clem. It turned out that most of what he had told me was true. Jelly said, "Pimpin' was his main line of work. He just played music to stay close to the action."

• • •

During the filming of "The Cincinnati Kid" in New Orleans I looked at the "dailies" after every day's shooting. ("Dailies" are the raw footage shot during the day. The director checks his results and makes decisions on preliminary cutting and other changes.) Sweet Emma, "The Bell Gal," well into her eighties at the time, was on the movieola screen playing in Preservation Hall. The piece she was playing was Clarence Williams' "Nobody Knows the Trouble I've Seen," to which Clarence held the copyright. The rights belonged to ABC-Paramount. During the day an assistant director had approached Emma and asked her to "play some public domain blues." Emma, having no idea in the world what "public domain" meant, had played Clarence's piece.

When I explained that what she was playing was copyrighted, general consternation followed. It appeared that they had left themselves the choice of either reshooting the sequence or paying ABC-Paramount $35,000 for the rights. Shooting costs being what they are, they bought the rights. I teased Sweet Emma about how free she was with other people's money, and she said, "Pshaw! If they come out an' say what they *want*, I'd a played it for 'em."

• • •

Back in 1918, jazz in New Orleans was still a lower-class diversion. Uptown folks wouldn't have been caught dead listening to what they called, unself-consciously and inaccurately, "nigger music," despite the fact that whites and blacks alike had been playing it, sometimes together, for more than a quarter-century. In any case, the form had no acceptance among the local bourgeoisie at all.

Then one of their favorite restaurants, Kolb's on St. Charles Street, hired a real jazz band, led by Johnny Dedroit, to play for dancing every night. This decision, once and for all, eliminated the class distinctions surrounding the art form. The Dedroit band was an instant success and stayed on for several years.

When I was in charge of production for the 1983 Tulane University Hot Jazz Classic, one of my better ideas was to persuade the management of Kolb's to recreate a night in 1918 by once more featuring an authentic jazz band and having it conducted by none other than Johnny Dedroit, now ninety-two years old. The diners that night (it was the hottest ticket in town) danced to Fred Starr's Louisiana Repertory Jazz Ensemble, conducted by Johnny Dedroit, and they were surprised and delighted by the grace and agility this nonagenarian displayed in joining his wife for dance after dance.

"Tired?" he laughed. "I haven't had so much fun in fifty years!"

• • •

I was just in town briefly (New Orleans, of course) en route to Mexico City in the early summer of 1938, and there were a pair of old-time jazzmen I was determined to talk with. I wasn't planning to write or produce anything right then. These were just two gentlemen I'd never seen or heard. They were getting on in years, and I wanted to have some impression of them in my head before they passed on. One of them was Manuel Perez and the other, Emile "Stalebread" Lacoume.

Perez, renowned as a cornetist in a period before I was even aware of the music, proved to be a gentle, slightly cynical gentleman of sixty, who felt that the musicians of 1938 needed to go back to fundamentals to ever play the music properly.

"These young fellas nowadays," he assured me, "can't hardly read a note. They can't learn no new tunes and they don't know nothin' about tempo or harmony."

Louis Armstrong?

"He got a lip like iron. Strong as a bull!—But he got a lot to learn. When he was a kid around here he never wanted to learn nothin'."

White musicians?

"They makin' the best music now. Used to be we made the best music. 'Course we still got some people playin' good right here in New Orleans, but our people don't take that music serious enough. The good ones, they tryin' to play opera."

His favorites?

"Guy Lombardo! I always wanted my bands to sound like that! And you ever hear this Casa Loma? That's real music!"

• • •

Stalebread Lacoume was younger than Perez—only 53. But he was blind and generally incapacitated. Many had claimed for him the honor of having been the originator of jazz, but he was not among his own claque.

"Me? Not me! We had this little spasm band—you know—most

all homemade instruments. We were really lousy but we had good rhythm—just kids, you know. I guess I was ten, twelve years old. We played around in the district and people used to throw us money. Even them whores. Sarah Bernhardt—you know—the French actress—she come by an' give us a dime. The whores tipped better than that.

"There was plenty kids before us done that. We copied off somebody, I don't remember who. We didn't make up all the dirty songs, neither. We heard 'em in the streets an' we sang 'em in the streets. Now they say we invented jazz. Ain't nobody invented that music.

"Later on I really became a musician. Played for a livin'! I never knew no music, but I worked playin' the guitar. Good bands, too! Charlie Fishbein, Max Fink. Good bands. I was the onliest one couldn't read in them bands. 'Course at the Halfway House, that was all fakin'. None o' them guys could read. Mickey Marcour, Red Long—maybe Roppolo could read a little bit. Not Brunies or Hook [Loyacano] or none o' them."

Would he still be playing if he were able?

"Not no more. These new guys are sharks. They playin' stuff we never even thought about. You hear Snoozer [Quinn] or some o' these dagoes in the hotel bands. They mus' spend all their time playin' or practicin'. We played for fun, y'see."

• • •

Larry Borenstein owned the Associated Artists Gallery, which was right where Preservation Hall is now. I spent many an afternoon during the fifties hanging out with him on his premises, talking about the innumerable subjects he was able to discuss with sometimes-startling competence. Now and then Lemon Nash would drop by for a glass of water or to use the rest room. He'd put his ukelele down, satisfy his immediate need, and then, to repay Larry's hospitality, he'd play and sing a tune. Lemon knew hundreds of pop tunes of the twenties— "June Night," "Linger Awhile," "Swingin' Down the Lane." Not jazz pieces, just melodic pop tunes. If customers were in the gallery, it didn't make any difference; he'd just go right into his number, and anybody that was around would usually tip him afterward. His regular occupation was playing in the street or wandering around the tables in night spots that permitted him to, doing the troubador thing.

Apparently the art gallery patrons and Larry's friends were more generous than the world outside, so Nash took to playing longer there.

Pretty soon he started to bring friends along, other musicians. Harrison Verret, Sam Rankins, Kid Thomas, Noon Johnson, and others began to show up regularly, and lots of people with no interest in paintings began to come around in the hope of hearing some of this spontaneous, good-natured jazz. They encouraged the performers with really generous gratuities. And Larry, whose expertise in business surpassed even his mastery of art and collectibles, noted that the entertainers were taking in more than the art was.

So Larry determined to improve the use of his space by moving the paintings out and the music in. That's how Preservation Hall was born. During the middle sixties I was standing outside the Hall one night with Lemon, watching the long line of people waiting to get in. He said, "Nobody knows but you and me how all this started."

• • •

Lawrence Duhé was a very early jazz clarinetist from Lafayette, Louisiana, who toured in vaudeville with King Oliver's band in the early 1920s. I had a long talk with him at his home in Lafayette, in the late 1950s. I think it was 1957. I never heard him play, to my knowledge, but among his contemporaries he had an excellent musical reputation.

Came the time when *National Geographic Magazine*, to which I have often served as a consultant on themes relating to New Orleans and its music, decided to go into the phonograph record business. To this end they prepared an LP entitled "Dixieland," as inept and unmusical an abortion as ever was pressed. Then they arrived at the point where it became necessary to produce album notes. They sent me a paste-up dummy that was one of the most ill-conceived, incompetently researched documents it had been my misfortune to deal with. Its four pages included over a hundred gross errors; one of the most minor was the misspelling of the name Duhé, which their researcher wrote as "Dewey."

Now the lady who took my report over the phone seemed to have little patience with my nit-picking and challenged virtually every correction I offered. When we came to Duhé, she asked, "How can you really know how his name was spelled? At least we know we've got it phonetically correct. Do you have any genuine authority for how he spelled his name." (She thought, I guess, that he'd died in the last century.)

"Yes, ma'am," I told her. "I have genuine authority. That's what it says on his doorbell."

• • •

Little Gussie Mueller has been forgotten by all but the most scholarly of jazz followers, largely because his recorded output was negligible. He was a member of Tom Brown's Band from Dixieland and was already playing jazz in Chicago in 1915. Later he worked in big bands led by Gus Arnheim, Irving Aaronson, and Abe Lyman. He was also a member of the early Paul Whiteman Orchestra and is the composer of record of "Wang Wang Blues."

"That's a strange title," I commented. "How did you happen to decide on it?"

"Hawaiian was big in 1922," he explained. "In fact anything oriental. Henry Busse the trumpet player suggested 'Wang.' He said that was oriental. Well, blues was hot at that time, too. My god, you could sell anything if you called it blues. So we decided, me and Buster [Johnson, a sax player] and Busse, that we'd call it 'Wang Blues.' Busse said he'd arrange it for the orchestra. Mr. Whiteman thought the name was too short, and he said, 'How about "Wang Wang Blues"?' That was okay with us, so we called it 'Wang Wang Blues.' It was really a big hit."

• • •

Everybody thinks of the song "Up a Lazy River" as a Hoagy Carmichael composition, but that was a melody he wasn't responsible for. Hoagy wrote the words, but the music came from the pen of one of New Orleans' better clarinetists, Sidney Arodin. As Sidney explained the circumstances, Hoagy had come into the Famous Door on 52nd Street in New York to hear Wingy Mannone's band in which Arodin occupied the clarinet chair. They played the tune, and Wingy sang it; but, of course, it wasn't yet called "Up a Lazy River." The title and words were Arodin's, too. He called it "Just a Lazy Nigger." Of course, in our time, such a title would be an atrocity. Even then it was in pretty bad taste—but Arodin didn't have a scintilla of prejudice in him. He had, in fact, been a party to the first mixed record session in the South (The Jones-Collins Astoria Hot Eight). He had, moreover, been the only white musician in the ensemble. Later I asked Hoagy how much cleaning up he'd had to do with the piece, and he said other than the lyric he'd had to make only a minor change in the chording of the verse.

• • •

Santo Pecora was the composer of the jazz standard, "She's Cryin' for Me." I asked him about the words, since I'd never heard it sung or seen printed lyrics.

"It's got no words," he assured me. "I never wrote words to it."

I said, "With that kind of a title you'd think it did have words. How come you gave it that title?"

He told me, "I was workin' with Arodin on a job and I says, 'I got a new tune I want to try out. You wanna figure out some harmony?' Then I played him the lead on my horn. He says, 'That's a nice tune. What's the title?' I said it didn't have no title. Sidney said, 'How about "She's Cryin' For Me"?' I said that was okay, so that's the name I gave it."

Arodin's been gone for thirty-five years now, so I can't ask him what he had in mind. Pecora died in 1985. I'm sure he never thought about titles or lyrics, though, just where the tailgate licks come in.

Afterword

I knew from the very start that I'd never get it all into a single volume that would be small enough to handle. I never even mentioned some of my best friends—some of the people I was and am fondest of. Nothing about Edmond Hall, Isidore Barbarin, Don Albert, Ricard Alexis, Emile and Polo Barnes, Bob Lyons (who played bass for Bolden), Lester Bouchon, Louis Dumaine, Ed Garland, Happy Goldston, and Tony Fougerat. Every single one of them is gone now. Fats Houston, Dave Oxley—they were at my wedding reception, and I haven't told about them, or about Cagnolatti, Albert Artigues. There seems to have been no end of people I could have talked about. I haven't told about Lil Armstrong giving me her scrapbook, or about eighteen-year-old Howard Rumsey just learning what the musician's life was like by playing bass for the touring Johnny "Scat" Davis band. In a little Philadelphia jazz joint called the Jam Session, operated by an outstanding clarinetist named Billy Kretchmer, Rumsey told me what it was like, and I heard his hopes and aspirations for the future. Not a word about Australia's pride, Graeme Bell, trekking with us around Sedalia, Missouri, during a Joplin festival, wearing baggy Bermuda shorts of the down-under variety and that indescribable hat.

And, of course, my ragtime friends! Max Morath, Terry Waldo, Dick Zimmerman, Ian Whitcomb, Dave Jasen, Trebor Tichenor, or the young prodigy David Boeddinghaus. I guess I'll leave them for another book.

Index

Aaronson, Irving, 243
ABC-Paramount, 239
Abraham, Martin, 81, 89, 91, 93, 97, 153, 170–72
Abraham, Martin, Jr., 14, 81, 181, 182
Adams, Dolly Douroux, 232
Adams, Gerald, 232
Adams, Justin, 232
Adams, Placide, 232
Adler, Larry, 208
Adrian's Tap Room Gang, 55
"Ain't Misbehavin'," 158
"Air Conditioned Nightmare," 11
Albert, Don, 244
Albright, William, 105
Alcorn, Alvin, 38, 52, 75, 76, 77, 177, 188, 191
Alexis, Ricard, 244
Algonquin Hotel (New York), 214
Allen, Henry "Red," 124, 126, 189
Allen, Richard B., 125, 136
Allen, Woody, 140
"Alley Cat," 234
"All You Need Is Love," 170
Almerico, Tony, 120, 121, 175, 181
Alter, Louis, 77, 194
Amacker, Frank, 232
American Music Records, 16
Ammons, 5, 47
Amsterdam News, 47, 48, 158
Anderson, Eddie "Rochester," 2
Anderson, Tom, 227
Andrus, Merwyn "Dutch," 97
Apex Club Orchestra, The, 49
Archey, Jimmy, 40, 47, 61, 62, 92, 114
Arkansas Cultural Center, The, 233
Armstrong All-Stars, Louis, 127, 186
Armstrong, Lil Hardin, 179, 244
Armstrong, Louis, 86, 96, 99, 110, 114, 126, 127–30, 185, 194, 196, 202, 219, 222, 223, 228, 238, 240

Armstrong, Lucille, 129, 184
Armstrong Park, 162, 194, 221
Arnheim, Gus, 243
Arodin, Sidney, 243, 244
Arpin, John, 183
Artigues, Albert, 244
Associated Artists Gallery, 241
Assunto, Frank, 44, 45, 155
Atlan, Michele, 160, 161, 162, 163, 164
Atlan, Pierre, 138, 143, 159–62, 163, 164
"At the Jazz Band Ball," 178
Augustin, Billy Price, 112
"Aunt Hagar's Blues," 111
Austin, Gene, 224
"Austin High Gang, The," 220
Averty, Jean Christophe, 76, 134, 150–52, 161, 162
Averty, Yvaline, 151
Avery, Joseph "Kid," 97
Ayres, Mitchell, 92
Aznavour, Charles, 151, 152

"Baby Won't You Please Come Home," 158
Bachman, Jack, 83
Bagneris, Vernel, 236
Baker, Josephine, 152
Baquet, Achille, 15, 126
Baquet, George, 116, 126, 127, 177
Baquet, Theogene V., 126
Baquets, The, 221
Barbarin, Isidore, 244
Barbarin, Louis, 108, 153, 224
Barbarin, Paul, 14, 125, 126, 127, 218–20
Barker, Blue Lu, 89, 108, 124, 132
Barker, Danny, 47, 61, 77, 81, 92, 97, 108, 122–25, 132, 136, 148, 153, 229
Barkley, Alben W., 100
Barnes, Emile, 244
Barnes, Paul "Polo," 38, 244

Barrett, "Sweet Emma," 190, 239
Basie, Count, 41
"Basin Street Blues, The," 158, 159, 176, 215, 219
Basin Street Six, The, 66
Bauduc, Jules, 221
Bauduc, Ray, 221, 226, 237
Bayersdorffer, Johnny, 221
Bayou Stompers, Johnny Hyman's, 148
Beatles, The, 56
Bechet, Dr. Leonard V., 31, 114, 178
Bechet, Sidney, 17, 60–65, 94, 101, 114, 141, 163, 164, 166, 177, 221, 222, 232
Bechets, The, 22
Beebe, Jim, 193
Beiderbecke, Bix, 55, 57, 147, 148, 151, 237
Belafield, Ted, 136, 214
Bell, Graeme, 194, 244, 245
Belmont Race Track, 42
Berigan, Bunny, 19, 20, 66, 73–75, 202, 203
Bernard, Al, 112
Bigard, Barney, 71, 86, 202
Big 25, The (New Orleans), 213
"Birth of the Blues," 215
Blackburn, Dr. Henry, 140
Blair House (Washington, D.C.), 98
Blair, Lee, 61, 99
Blake, Avis, 103, 104
Blake, Eubie, 3, 17, 18, 29, 47, 68, 87, 103–106, 122, 147, 151, 165, 166, 167, 199, 202, 208, 210
Blake, Marion, 103, 104, 165
Blanchin, George, 67
Blesh, Rudi, 47, 105, 144
"Blue-Eyed Sally," 112
Blue Room (New Orleans), 98, 181
Blue, Walter, 21
Blumberg, Jerry, 221
Boatner, Edward, 222
Bob Cats, Bob Crosby's, 23, 96, 226
Bocage, Peter, 109, 110, 111
Boeddinghaus, David, 245
Bojangles (Bill Robinson), 50
Bolcom, Joanie Morris, 105
Bolcom, William, 105
Bolden, Buddy, 15, 126, 127, 221, 232, 238, 244

Bolling, Claude, 160
Bonano, Sharkey, 14, 66, 81, 96, 177, 181–83, 215, 218
Booker, Beryl, 27
"Borderline," 226
Borenstein, Larry, 51, 233, 237, 238, 241, 242
Bornemann, Charlie, 45
Bose, Sterling, 101, 237
Bouchon, Lester, 221, 244
Boudrier, Mme. Jacqueline, 76
"Bourbon Street Parade," 215, 219
Bowe, Walter, 172–74
Bradford, Perry, 166
Brodsky, George, 25, 40
Brown, Hillard, 193
Brown, Steve, 95, 218, 221
Brown, Tom, 63–64, 65, 89, 97, 148, 152, 176, 216, 221
Brown's Band From Dixieland, 64, 243
Brown's Ice Cream Parlor (New Orleans), 112
Brunies, Abbie, 14, 216, 241
Brunies, "Li'l Abbie," 14, 81, 98, 216, 217
Brunies, George, 14, 79, 94, 95, 143, 175, 216–18
Brunies, Henny, 216
Brunies, Jerri, 98, 217
Brunies, Merrit, 14, 30, 216, 217
Brunies, Richie, 14, 216
Brunies, The, 216–18, 221
Buck, Eleanor, 191
Buck, George, 45, 191
Budweiser, The (New Orleans), 184
Burke, Catherine, 154, 155, 157
Burke, Chris, 70, 71, 72, 192
Burke, Raymond, 37, 64, 81, 83, 91, 96, 97, 148, 154–57, 177, 193, 224
Burley, Dan, xiii, 27, 40, 46–50, 92, 125, 158, 201
Busse, Henry, 243
Butera, Sam, 133
Butterfield, Billy, 237

Cagnolatti, Ernie, 244
Cahn, Jules, 202
California Ramblers, 55
Calloway, Cab, 47

Campbell, Pops, 45
"Canal Street March, The," 148
"Candy and Coco," 224
Capraro, Joe, 230–31
Carey, Mutt, 127
Carlisle, Una Mae, 49, 50, 83
Carmichael, Hoagy, 132, 243–44
Carrazo, Castro, 65
Carter, Jo Jo, 101
Casa Loma, 240
Casbarian, Archie, 77
Casimir, John, 6–10
Catlett, Sidney, 223–24
CBS, 117, 118, 155
Celestin, Oscar "Papa," 7, 21, 77, 97, 215, 225
Centobie, Boogie, 64
Central Plaza, The (New York), 173
"Charleston Rag," 122
Chase, Bill, 50
Chicago Civic Opera House, The, 185
Chicago *Daily Defender*, 47
"Chicken Reel," 127
Childs Paramount Restaurant (New York), 219
Christian, Charlie, 221
Christian, Emile, 108, 109, 148, 221
Christian, Frank, 221
"Cincinnati Kid, The," 239
Ciro's (Philadelphia), 186
"Clarinet Marmalade," 178
Clem, Edouard, 239
Clesi, Nick, 216
Click, The, 52, 54, 224
Clooney, Rosemary, 98
"Closer Walk With Thee, A," 220
Coleman, Bill, 17
Collins, Lee, 66
Collins, Ralph, 22
Collins, Wallace, 221
"Come Back Sweet Papa," 219
Commanders Palace (New Orleans), 13, 77, 118
Condon, Eddie, 72–73, 79, 118, 143, 208, 209, 217, 233
Condon, Phyllis, 73
Condon's (New York), 237
Conger, Larry, 45
Connie's Cafe, 12

Cordilla, Charlie, 216
Cotton Carnival (Memphis), 218
Cotton Club (Philadelphia), 25, 40
Cotton Pickers, The, 210
Cottrell, Louis, 188
Cottrell, Louis, Sr., 109
Crawford-Ferguson Night Owls, 220
Crawford, Paul, 37, 83, 148, 235
Crosby, Bob, 23, 153, 237
Crosby, Octave, 14
Cvetkovich, George, 58, 59, 60

Dabney, Georgia, 129
Dan Burley's Handbook of Harlem Jive, 47
Daniels, Billy, 48
Dan's International (New Orleans), 215
Dauphine Theater (New Orleans), 170
"Davenport Blues," 41
Davila, Sid, 14, 182
Davis, Eddie "Lockjaw," 90, 207
Davis, Johnny "Scat," 75, 244
Davison, "Wild Bill," 83–95, 114, 116, 218, 221
Dedroit, Johnny, 239
Dekemel, "Buglin' Sam," 174–76, 201
Delaney, Beauford, 11
Delaney, Jack, 81, 83, 120, 133, 148, 153, 181, 224
Delaney's, Tom, 70, 166
Delauney, Charles, 57
Dengler, Johnny, 132
De Paris, Sidney, 101
Desvigne, Sidney, 238
Deville, George, 81
Diamond Horseshoe, Billy Rose's, 167
Disneyland, 175
Dixieland Rhythm Kings, The, 136, 214–16
Dixon Hall (Tulane University), 125, 166
Dodds, Johnny, 222
Dodds, Warren "Baby," 40, 49, 61, 93, 94, 99, 100, 101, 115, 116, 127, 173, 187, 222, 223, 238
Donnels, Johnny, 58, 85
Dorsey, Tommy, 73, 75, 111, 237
Dorseys, The, 101
Douglass Hotel (Philadelphia), 2
"Down Among the Sheltering Palms," 187

Downbeat, The (Philadelphia), 206
Doyle, Bob, 32, 121
"Do You Know What It Means to Miss
    New Orleans," 77, 144
Dream Room (New Orleans), 102, 214,
    215, 216
"Dreamy Blues, The," 109
Duhé, Lawrence, 242
Dukes of Dixieland, The, 14, 45, 181
Dukes' Place, The (New Orleans), 151
Dumaine, Louis, 244
Dunham, Sonny, 147
"Dupree Blues," 2
Dupree, Reese, 2
Duson, Frankie, 238, 239
Dutreys, The, 221

Earle Theater (Philadelphia), 126
Eberle, Ray, 80
Edegran, Lars, 237
Edmiston, Kelly, 192
Edwards, Eddie, 106
Edwards, Ralph, 117
Ellington, Duke, 2, 228
Erwin, Pee Wee, 237
Esplanade Lounge (New Orleans), 148,
    185
Esplanade Room (New Orleans), 38, 153
Eugene, Wendell, 38, 77
Eureka Brass Band, 9, 28
Eustis, Sister Elizabeth, 97
Evans, Doc, xiii, 235, 236
"Everybody Loves My Baby," 73, 158
Ewell, Don, 116, 231

Fairview Brass Band, 124
Famous Door (New Orleans), 14, 45, 225
Fazola, Irving, 23–25, 96, 101, 121, 153,
    237
Ferguson, Leonard, 83, 220
Fern Dance Hall No. 2 (New Orleans),
    184
"Fingerbreaker" Concert, 169
Fink, Max, 241
Finola, George, 83
Fishbein Orchestra, Charlie, 241
Fisher, May, 197
Flick, Roland "Dutch," 221

Foster, Abbey, 233
Foster, George "Pops," 47, 48, 61, 92, 94,
    99, 115, 173, 187, 223, 238
Fougerat, Tony, 244
Fountain, Pete, 25, 66, 97, 133, 142, 153,
    178, 204–206, 220, 221
Francis, Albert, 227
Franklin, Joe, 34
Frazier, Josiah "Cié," 77
Freeman, Bud, 137, 201, 220, 235
Friars Society Orchestra, 216

Gaillard, Slim, 206
Galloway, Charlie, 221
Gammon, Von, 148
Garland, Ed "Montudie," 244
Garroway, Dave, 185, 218
Gazebo, The (New Orleans), 72
Gee, Lottie, 103
Gillespie, Dizzy, 137, 206–208
"Gimme a Pigfoot," 10
Girard, George, 14, 29, 65–68, 96, 133
Girard, "Turk," 222
"Glad Rag Doll," 187
Glapion, Raymond, 7
Glasgow, Vaughn L., 76
Glazel, Johnny, 221
Glazer, Joe, 186, 187
Glenn, Tyree, 12, 128
Godwin, Harry, 222
Goins, Ron, 140
Goldkette, Jean, 57
Goldston, "Happy," 244
Goodman, Benny, 101, 111, 202
Goodwin, Henry, 187
Gottschalk, Louis Moreau, 30, 122
Gowans, Brad, 69, 99
Gower, Walt, 61
Grappelle, Stephane, 57–58, 80
Greater Holcamp Carnival Shows, 113
Greene, Bob, 72, 73, 79, 85, 132, 185
Guarnieri, Johnny, 183
Guerin, Emile, 178
Guesnon, "Creole George," 229–30
Guinle, Hyp, 225
Guitar, Willie, 221
"Gulf Coast Blues, The," 213
Gushee, Dr. Lawrence, 125, 136, 173

Hackett, Bobby, 19–20, 132, 148
Hadlock, Dick, 173
"Hail to the Chief," 99
Halfway House Orchestra, 13, 204
Hall, Edmond, 63, 177, 244
Hamilton, Charlie, 233
Hamilton, George, 235
Hammond, John, 80
Hampton, Lionel, 47
Handy, W. C., 165–67
Hangover Club (San Francisco), 187
Hardee, John, 92
Hardy, Emmet, 225
Havens, Bob, 205
Hayakawa, Senator S. I., 141
Hazel, Monk, 88, 91, 96, 176, 224–25
Heath, Jimmy, 147
Heath, Percy, 147, 207
Henderson, Fletcher, 3
Herman, Woody, 135
"He's Just a Cousin of Mine," 112
"He Was a Nice Boy," 112
"High Society," 20, 22, 153, 160
High Society Jazz Band, 138, 150, 151, 191
Hillaire, Andre, 180
Hines, Earl "Fatha," 86, 185–87, 199, 202
Hirshfeld, Al, 208
Hirt, Al, 97, 120, 178, 179, 204–206
Hodes, Art, 41, 183, 193, 220, 231
Hodes, Bob, 136, 214
Holiday, Billie, 158, 159, 188
Holloway, "Kildee," 222
"Honeysuckle Rose," 158
Hot Clubs of France, 57
"Hot Discography," 57
Houston, Matthew "Fats," 244
Howard, Darnell, 187
Hug, Armand, 38, 61, 81, 96, 112, 148, 153, 154, 183–85, 221, 231
Humphrey, Percy, 28, 229
Humphrey, Willie, 84, 219
Humphries, Bill, 82
Huntington, Bill, 93
Hyman, John Wigginton, 150

"I Ain't Got Nobody," 158, 198
"I Can't Get Started," 75

"If Ever I Cease To Love," 235
"I Found a New Baby," 158
"I'm Just Wild About Harry," 103
Imperial Brass Band, 76, 191
"I Wish I Could Shimmy Like My Sister Kate," 110
"I Wonder Who's Boogiein' My Woogie Now," 133

Jackson, Milton, 50
Jackson, "New Orleans Willie," 112
Jackson, Preston, 188, 196
Jacobs Candy Man, 111, 112
Jacobs, Phoebe, 195
Jacquet, Illinois, 172
Jaeger, Alfred L., 108
Jaffe, Allan, 50, 51, 52, 90, 128, 129, 130, 233
Jaffe, Rona, 208
Jaffe, Sandra, 51
James, Joe, 237
Jam Session, The (Philadelphia), 244
Jasen, David, 245
"Jazz at the Philharmonic," 172
Jazz Jubilee, Frank Bull's, 172
Jazz, Ltd. (Chicago), 236
Jefferson, Thomas, 9
Jeffries, Herb, 158
"Jelly Roll Morton Revisited," 85
Jimmy's Chicken Shack (Harlem), 47
Johnny's Po' Boys (New Orleans), 96
Johnson, Bunk, 7, 16, 93, 113–17, 173, 221, 230, 231
Johnson, Buster, 243
Johnson, Hall, 165
Johnson, Harold "Shorty," 83
Johnson, James P., 68–70, 99, 100, 197, 232
Johnson, Lonnie, 228
Johnson, Lynda Bird, 235
Johnson, Noone, 242
Johnson, Pete, 5, 47
Johnson, Phil, 76
Jones, David, 238
Jones-Collins Astoria Hot Eight, 228, 243
Joplin, Scott, 30, 122, 195, 245
Joseph, Papa John, 233
Joseph, Pleasant "Smilin Joe," 183
Joseph, Waldron "Frog," 222

Journeys Into Jazz, 25, 40, 41, 52, 61, 93, 197, 217, 236
"Juke Box Jury," 92, 203
Julius' Bar (New York), 210
"June Night," 241
Jungle Club, The, 4
"Just a Lazy Nigger," 243

Kafkaz, The (New York), 208
Kaminsky, Max, 41, 69, 70
Kansas City Kitty, 99
Kaye, Sammy, 34, 74
Kellin, Orange, 237
Kelly, Guy, 222
Kennedy Center (Washington, D.C.), 76
Kenton, Stan, 139, 161
Keppard, Freddie, 219
Keppards, The, 222
Kimball, Jeannette, 97, 108, 184
Kimball, Narvin, 229
Kimball, Robert, 105
King Jazz Records, 18
"King Zulu Parade," 148
Kinson, Maggie, 71
Kittrell, Jeannie, 108
Kmen, Dr. Henry A. "Hank," 83
Koch, Mayor Edward, 105
Kohlman, Freddie, 222
Kolb's Restaurant, 239
Kramer, Karl, 88, 117, 118
Kretchmer, Billy, 244
Krupa, Gene, 75, 146, 199, 202–204, 220
Kullick, Teddy, 71

Lacoume, Emile "Stalebread," 216, 240, 241
Laine, Jack "Papa," 13, 14–17, 26, 178, 216
Laine, Julian "Digger," 176
Lala, Mike, 97, 178, 204
La Lune (New Orleans), 204
Lamare, Nappy, 226, 237
Lambert, Don, 68
Lamb's Cafe (Chicago), 64
Landrieu, Moon, 81, 162
Lang, Eddie, 57, 228
Lannigan, Jim, 146, 220
La Rocca, Nick, 15, 106, 108, 152, 221

Larsen, Morten Gunnar, 29–30, 84, 122
Laveau, Marie, 7
Lawton, Bob, 38
Laylan, "Preacher Rollo," 44
"Lazy Mood," 154
Leclere, Irwin, 216
Lee, Canada, 11
Legends of Jazz, 72, 225
Le Jazz Hot, 57
Leroy, Wilbur, 112
Lewis, George, 7, 116, 177, 222, 230, 233
Lewis, Meade Lux, 5, 47
Lewis, Steve, 109, 110, 112
Lewis, Walter "Furry," 115–16, 139
"Liebestraum," 111
Life magazine, 127
Light Crust Doughboys, 133
"Li'l Liza Jane," 77
Lindsay, John, 127, 180, 222
"Linger Awhile," 241
"Live and Let Die," 26
Lofton, "Cripple Clarence," 47
Lomax, Alan, 6, 91, 125, 136
Lombardo, Guy, 240
Long, Glyn Lea "Red," 241
Longenecker, Dr. Herbert E., 189
Lonzo, Freddie, 84
Louisiana Repertory Jazz Ensemble, 240
Louisiana State Museum, 76, 164
"Love Dreams," 155
Lowenthal, Bernie, 207
Loyacano, Arnold "Deacon," 121
Loyacano, Joseph "Hook," 121, 241
Lunceford, Jimmy, 126
Luter, Annie, 164
Luter, Claude, 143, 161, 163–65
Lyman, Abe, 243
Lyons, Bob, 244
Lytell, Jimmy, 210

McCree, Johnson "Fat Cat," 72, 79
McGhee, Brownie, 47
McKinley, Ray, 226
McPartland, Dick, 220
McPartland, Jimmy, 146, 192, 220
Madison, "Kid Shots," 222
Madison Square Garden, 12, 158
Mahogany Hall, 158

"Make Me a Pallet on the Floor," 127
Maltz, Bob, 114
Manetta, Manuel, 232
Mangel, Ira, 127, 129
Mangiapane, Sherwood, 38, 82, 83, 89, 97, 132, 148, 222
Mannone, "Wingy," 55, 66, 75, 148, 175, 217, 218, 223
Marable Orchestra, Fate, 238
Marcour, Mickey, 241
Mardi Gras Lounge, 141, 182
Mares, Helen, 98
Mares, Joe, 81, 89, 95–98, 116, 156, 171, 175, 178, 182, 204, 205, 206, 231
Mares, Paul, 95, 96, 116
Mark Twain (Disneyland), 179
Marquis, Don, 32
Marrero, Johnny, 109
Marrero, Lawrence, 230
Marsala, Marty, 223
Marshall, Art, 37
Martin "Chink," 170–72
Martyn, Barrie, 71, 225
Matlock, Matty, 153
Matthews, Emmett, 63
Mayl, Gene, 136, 214, 216
Meadowbrook, Frank Dailey's, 53
"Memories of You," 103, 147, 158, 208
"Memphis Blues," 166
Mendelson, Stanley, 81, 83, 96, 121, 181, 182, 231, 234
Mercantile Hall (Philadelphia), 101
Merlin, Pierre, 138, 160, 161
Mezzrow, Mezz, 17–19
"Mike the Tailor," 2
Miles, Lizzie, 176, 182, 218, 219
Millender, Lucky, 47, 124, 126
Miller, Eddie, 152, 154, 237
Miller, Ernest "Kid Punch," 52, 129, 130, 222
Miller, Glenn, 101, 226
Miller, Henry, 10, 78
Miller, Mitch, 98
Miller, Sing, 179
Mills Brothers, 47
Milneburg Joys, 4, 5
"Mindin' Your Business Blues," 119
Minton's (New York), 206
Mississippi Queen, 185

"Missouri Waltz, The," 100
Mitchell, Herman, 92
Modern Jazz Quartet, 147, 207
Mole, Milford "Miff," 141, 208–11
Monk, Thelonius, 206
Monroe Club, 50
Monroe, Vaughn, 145
Montegue, Sidney, 238
"Mood Indigo," 109
Moore, Freddie "Gatemouth," 197
Morath, Max, 87, 105, 183, 245
Morath, Norma, 105
Morel, Martine, 138, 160
Morgan, Albert, 221
Morgan, Andrew, 221
Morgan, Isaiah, 221
Morgan, Sam, 221
Morrison, DeLesseps S. "Chep," 21
Morton, Jelly Roll, 1, 2–6, 16, 30, 72, 88, 122, 125, 126, 136, 167, 168, 170, 180, 215, 222, 238, 239
Moten, Bennie, 41
Mothers Boys Jazz Band, 61
Mound City Blue Blowers, 153
Mueller, Gussie, 243
Municipal Auditorium (New Orleans), 128
Music Corporation of America, 88, 117
Musicians Union, 181
"Muskrat Ramble," 117

Napoleon, Phil, 12, 209, 210
Napoleon, Teddy, 12
Nash, Lemon, 241, 242
National Geographic, 63, 242
Navarro, Fats, 207
Neimann, Leroy, 208
Nelson, Louis, 237
Nelson, Louis Delisle "Big Eye Louis," 127, 221
"New Leviathan Oriental Fox-Trot Orchestra," 35
"New Orleans Bien Aimee," 134, 151
New Orleans Five, The, 14, 66
New Orleans Jazz, A Family Album, 88, 118, 120, 229
New Orleans Jazz Band, 126
New Orleans Jazz Club, 64, 66, 129, 148, 215, 218

New Orleans Jazz Museum, 38, 164
New Orleans Ragtime Orchestra, 16
New Orleans Rhythm Kings, 5, 13, 95, 170
New Orleans Streets, 168, 169
Newton, Frankie, 10–13
Nicholas, Albert, 49, 65, 93, 114–16, 126, 176, 222
Nicholas, "Wooden Joe," 222
Nichols, Loring "Red," 55, 210
Nick's (New York), 208, 237
Nixon, Richard M., 100
Nixon's Grand Theater (Philadelphia), 124
"Nobody Knows the Trouble I've Seen," 239
Noone, Jimmie, 49
Nunez, Alcide "Yellow," 221

Ochsner, Dr. Alton B., 77
Ochsner Clinic, 77, 231
"Of All the Wrongs You've Done to Me," 97
Old Spanish Fort (New Orleans), 112
Oliver, Jimmy, 147
Oliver, Joseph "King," 88, 148, 213–15, 219, 221
"One Mo' Time," 236
101 Ranch, 232
Onward Brass Band, 220
Oriental Theater (Chicago), 237
Original Dixieland Jazz Band, 13–15, 106–109, 112, 178, 221
"Original Dixieland Jazz Band One-Step, The," 151, 178
Orpheum Theater (New Orleans), 108
Ory, Edward "Kid," 127, 219, 221, 225
Oxley, Dave, 244

Pace and Handy Music Publishers, 166
Paddock, The (New Orleans), 14, 21
Page, Oran "Hot Lips," 25, 40–41, 49, 137, 201
Pajaud, Willie, 10
Palfi, Stevenson, 39, 229
Palmer, Roy, 217
Palumbo, Frank, 52, 53, 186, 207
"Panama," 117
Panassie, Hugues, 57
Paquay, Jean, 23

Parenti, Tony, 41–46, 81, 98, 121
Parisian Room, 120, 146
Parker, Charlie, 206
Parker, John W. "Knocky," 45, 46, 130–33, 183, 193, 231
Pavageau, Alcide "Slow Drag," 7
Pearl Theater (Philadelphia), 1
Pecora, Santo, 96, 155, 178, 225, 244
"Peculiar Rag," 155
Pemberton, Jimmy, 211
Penn, Sammy, 148, 237
Penny Wonderland Theater (New Orleans), 197
Perez, Manuel, 240
Perkins, Dave, 15
Perry, Don, 33, 66
Pete's Place (New Orleans), 153
Petit, Buddy, xii, 222
Petrillo, James Caesar, 54
Philadelphia Academy of Music, 25, 62, 68, 114, 206, 217
Philadelphia Eagles, 34
Philadelphia Phillies, 53
"Piano Players Rarely Get to Play Together," 39
Picadilly Hotel (New York), 24, 78
Pichon, Walter "Fats," 218
Picou, Alphonse, 10, 21–23, 127, 221
Piron, Armand J., 109–11, 213, 222, 225
Piron's Orchestra, 112
Pittsburgh Courier charities, 158
"Played With Immense Success," 76
Ponce's saloon, Henry, 128
"Postman's Lament, The," 148
Poston, Ted, 49
Preservation Hall, 23, 50, 51, 52, 70, 172, 228, 229, 232, 237, 239, 241, 242
Preservation Hall Jazz Band, 155, 233, 236
Price, Kerry, 39
Price, Sammy, 93, 94, 114, 189, 223, 231
Prima, Louis, xiii, 23, 52–54, 66, 223
Primus, Pearl, 50
Prince Conti Motor Inn (New Orleans), 102, 103
Prince of Wales, 227
Purnell, Alton, 116
"Purple Rose of Cairo," 109

Quinn, Edward Macintosh "Snoozer," 148, 241

Rabanat, Claude, 160
Ragas, Henry, 107
Ramsey, Fred, 114, 125, 136
Rankins, Sam, 242
Razaf, Andy, 158
Razzberry Ragtimers, 85
"Really the Blues," 17
Record Changer, 173
Red and Miff's Stompers, 210
Red Caps, 63
Redelsheimer, Betty "Washboard," 139
Red Hot Peppers, 126, 180
Reinhardt, Bill, 235
Reinhardt, Django, 57, 80
Reinhardt, Reneé, 236
"Relaxin' at the Touro," 78
Reliance Band, 13, 14
Rena, Henry "Kid," 221
Rhythm Club (Harlem), 3
Rich, Buddy, 145, 224
Riddick, Jeff, 96, 148
Ritz-Carlton Hotel (Philadelphia), 74
Riverboat Dandies, 226
Robbins, Freddie, 158
Roberts, David Thomas, 167–70, 200
Roberts, Luckey, 47, 68, 158
Robichaux, Joe, 183, 218, 222, 233
Robinson, J. Russel, 107
Robinson, Jim, 108, 116, 222
Robinson's Floating Opera House, 15
Rockefeller, Nelson, 217
Rockefeller, Mrs. Winthrop, 233, 234
Rodney, Red, 135
Rollini, Adrian, 54–57
Rollo, "Preacher," 44
Rongetti, Nick, 209
Roosevelt Hotel (New Orleans), 21, 64, 65, 66, 98, 181
Roppolo, Leon, 95, 172, 216, 241
Rose, Diana, 39, 52, 71, 76, 105, 138, 140, 160, 161, 162, 164, 170, 185, 191
Rose, Rex, 38
Rosenwald, Lessing, 217
Roth, Jack, 210
Rowe, "Schoolboy," 53, 54
"Royal Garden Blues," 158

Royal Orleans Hotel, 14, 77, 129, 130, 148, 153, 185
Royal Sonesta Hotel, 38
Rummel, John, 170
Rumsey, Howard, 244
Runyon, Damon, 102
Russell, Luis, 126
Russell, "Pee Wee," 19, 20, 69, 99, 177, 196, 209, 210
Russell, William, 16, 17, 21, 38, 52, 91, 114, 116, 125, 136, 229, 230
Ryan's, Jimmy (New York), 45

Saam, Byrum, 54
Sage, Russell, 217
St. Cyr, Johnny, 96, 97, 140, 178, 180, 238
St. John the Divine Cathedral (New York), 47
St. Joseph's Academy (Covington, La.), 220
St. Louis Blues, 166
St. Louis Ragtime Festival, 88
Salinger, Pierre, 76
"Sandstorm," 226
Santiago, Lester "Blackie," 233
Saroyan, William, 10
Saunders, Wardell, 50
Sauter-Finnegan arrangements, 226
Sax, Adolph, 153
Sayles, Emanuel, 226
Sbarbaro, Tony, 107
Scarsdale High School (New York), 220, 221
Schmidt, George, 35
Schroeder, Gene, 231
Schutt, Arthur, 68
Scioneaux, Louis, 67
Scott, Billy, 147
Scott, Hazel, 50
Scott, Zachary, 21
Second Line, 120, 155
Segal, Nat, 206
"Shake, Rattle and Roll," 112
Sharkey's Kings of Dixieland, 170
Shaw, Artie, 101
Shaw, Arvel, 202
"Sheik of Araby, The," 54
"She's Cryin' For Me," 244

Shields, Eddie, 178
Shields Family, 221
Shields, Harry, 14, 41, 46, 64, 77, 81,
    89, 91, 97, 107, 108, 148, 176–78,
    181, 182, 184
Shields, Larry, 107
"Short'nin' Bread," 2
Shoup, John, 76, 151
Shryock Auditorium (Carbondale, Ill.),
    108
Shubert Theater (New York), 105
"Shuffle Along," 103
Signorelli, Frank, 68, 107, 210, 217
Simeon, Omer, 126, 177
Singer, Art, 207
Singleton, Marge, 227, 228
Singleton, Zutty, 127, 227–28
Sino, Louis. See Scioneaux, Louis
Sissle, Noble, 61, 105, 159, 165, 166, 210
"Smilin' Joe." See Pleasant, Joseph
Smith, Bessie, 10, 211, 213
Smith, Jabbo, 236
Smith, Pinetop, 47
Smith, Willie "The Lion," 47, 68
Smithsonian Institution, 76
Snowden, Elmer, 40, 228
Sonnanstine, Charlie, 136, 214
Souchon, Edmond, 13, 45, 78, 79, 88,
    97, 110, 117–20, 140, 144, 218, 228
Southland Records, 65, 96, 170
"South Rampart Street Parade," 219
Spangenberg, Claire, 87.
Spanier, Muggsy, 61, 62, 77–79, 99, 118,
    218, 257
Spargo, Tony. See Sbarbaro, Tony
Spitlera, "Pee Wee," 120–22
S.S. Capitol, 238
S.S. Goldenrod, 88, 119
S.S. President, 218
Stacy, Jess, 231
Starr, Fred, 240
Steele, Al, 142
Steele, Porter, 20
Steifel, Sam, 1
Steinway Hall (New York), 92, 125
Stephens, Ragbaby, 198
Still, William Grant, 165
Stokowski, Leopold, 217
Story, Sidney, 84, 85, 148

Storyville, 85, 128, 148, 227
Storyville, New Orleans, 119, 161
Stuyvesant Casino (New York), 114, 173
"Sugar Blues, The," 213
Sullivan, Joe, 25, 61, 62, 183, 206, 231,
    233
"Summertime," 62
"Swingin' Down the Lane," 241
"Symphony Sid," 158

Taft Hotel (New York), 74
Teagarden, Jack, 101, 102, 103, 142
Tervalon, Clement, 222
Theresa Hotel, 18, 47, 165
"They Raided the Joint," 49
"This Cat Can Play Anything," 39, 229
"This Is Your Life," 118
Thomas, Joseph "Brother Cornbread,"
    220
Tichenor, Trebor Jay, 168, 222, 243
Time-Life Records, 163
"Tin Roof Blues, The," 41, 217
Tio, Lorenzo, Jr., 109, 111
"Tishomingo Blues," 37
Toller, Ernst, 78
Torregano, Joe, 84
Totts, Kid, 108
Tough, Dave, 146
Town Hall (Philadelphia), 40, 201
Tranchina's Restaurant (New Orleans),
    109, 112
Trappier, Arthur, 41
"Treat It Gentle," 60
Trepagnier, Ernest "Ninesse," 225
Tristano, Lenny, 207
"Trouble in Mind," 131
Truman, Bess, 98, 100
Truman, Harry S., 98, 99, 100, 101
Tujague's Restaurant (New Orleans), 107
Tulane Hot Jazz Classic, 136, 169, 227,
    231, 239
Tulane University Jazz Archive, 21, 178
"Turkey in the Straw," 127
Tuxedo Dance Hall, 232
Twentieth-Century Institute of Music,
    207
"Two Wing Temple In the Sky," 148
Tyler, Marion, 165, 166
Tyler, Willie, 165

"Ultra Canal," 148
"Underneath Hawaiian Skies," 97
Unterseher, Neal, 85
"Up a Lazy River," 243

Valdera, Felix, 207
Valentine, "Kid Thomas," 233, 237, 242
Vallee, Rudy, 56
Vastine, Jack, 136, 214
Vaughan, Sarah, 206
Verret, Harrison, 242
Village Gate (New York), 236

Waldo, Terry, 171, 245
"Walkin' by the River," 49
Waller, Fats, 47
"Wang Wang Blues," 77, 243
Ware, Munn, 25
Watters Orchestra, Lu, 214
Wein, George, 69, 70, 187, 197
Wellstood, Dick, 169, 221, 231
Wetterau, Robin, 136, 214
Wettling, George, 75, 224

"When the Saints Go Marchin' In," 117,
    222, 233
Whitcomb, Ian, 105, 200, 245
Whiteman, Paul, 243
Wiggs, Johnny, 16, 36, 39, 64, 65, 108,
    133, 148–50, 153, 175, 177, 192, 206,
    211, 218, 224, 226
Wilber, Bob, 221
Williams, Alfred, 225
Williams, Clarence, 211–14, 225, 239
Williams, Spencer, 157–59, 198
Wolverines, The, 146

Yancey, Billy, 25
Yancey, Jimmy, 47
"Yellow Dog Rag," 166
Young Tuxedo Brass Band, 7, 9
"You're Lucky To Me," 103
"You've Been a Good Old Wagon," 10

Zardis, Chester, 77, 108, 224
Zimmerman, Dick, 105, 195, 245
Zurke, Bob, 5